THE FAMILY IN
ENGLISH CHILDREN'S
LITERATURE

Children's Literature and Culture
Jack Zipes, *Series Editor*

Children's Literature Comes of Age
Toward a New Aesthetic
by Maria Nikolajeva

Sparing the Child
*Grief and the Unspeakable in Youth
Literature
About Nazism and the Holocaust*
by Hamida Bosmajian

Rediscoveries in Children's Literature
by Suzanne Rahn

Inventing the Child
Culture, Ideology, and the Story of Childhood
by Joseph L. Zornado

Regendering the School Story
Sassy Sissies and Tattling Tomboys
by Beverly Lyon Clark

A Necessary Fantasy?
*The Heroic Figure in Children's Popular
Culture*
edited by Dudley Jones and Tony Watkins

White Supremacy in Children's Literature
*Characterizations of African Americans,
1830–1900*
by Donnarae MacCann

Ways of Being Male
*Representing Masculinities in Children's
Literature and Film*
by John Stephens

Retelling Stories, Framing Culture
*Traditional Story and Metanarratives in
Children's Literature*
by John Stephens and Robyn McCallum

Pinocchio Goes Postmodern
Perils of a Puppet in the United States
by Richard Wunderlich and
Thomas J. Morrissey

Little Women and the Feminist Imagination
Criticism, Controversy, Personal Essays
edited by Janice M. Alberghene and
Beverly Lyon Clark

The Presence of the Past
*Memory, Heritage, and Childhood in
Postwar Britain*
by Valerie Krips

The Case of Peter Rabbit
*Changing Conditions of Literature
for Children*
by Margaret Mackey

The Feminine Subject in Children's
Literature
by Christine Wilkie-Stibbs

Ideologies of Identity in Adolescent Fiction
by Robyn McCallum

Recycling Red Riding Hood
by Sandra Beckett

The Poetics of Childhood
by Roni Natov

Voices of the Other
*Children's Literature and the Postcolonial
Context*
edited by Roderick McGillis

Narrating Africa
George Henty and the Fiction of Empire
by Mawuena Kossi Logan

Reimagining Shakespeare for Children and
Young Adults
edited by Naomi J. Miller

Representing the Holocaust in Youth
Literature
by Lydia Kokkola

Translating for Children
by Riitta Oittinen

Beatrix Potter
Writing in Code
by M. Daphne Kutzer

Children's Films
History, Ideology, Pedagogy, Theory
by Ian Wojcik-Andrews

Utopian and Dystopian Writing for
Children and Young Adults
edited by Carrie Hintz and Elaine Ostry

Transcending Boundaries
*Writing for a Dual Audience of Children
and Adults*
edited by Sandra L. Beckett

The Making of the Modern Child
*Children's Literature and Childhood in the
Late Eighteenth Century*
by Andrew O'Malley

How Picturebooks Work
by Maria Nikolajeva and Carole Scott

Brown Gold
*Milestones of African American Children's
Picture Books, 1845–2002*
by Michelle H. Martin

Russell Hoban/Forty Years
Essays on His Writing for Children
by Alida Allison

Apartheid and Racism in South African
Children's Literature
by Donnarae MacCann and
Amadu Maddy

Empire's Children
*Empire and Imperialism in Classic British
Children's Books*
by M. Daphne Kutzer

Constructing the Canon of Children's
Literature
Beyond Library Walls and Ivory Towers
by Anne Lundin

Youth of Darkest England
*Working Class Children at the Heart of
Victorian Empire*
by Troy Boone

Ursula K. Le Guin Beyond Genre
Literature for Children and Adults
by Mike Cadden

Twice-Told Children's Tales
edited by Betty Greenway

Diana Wynne Jones
*The Fantastic Tradition and Children's
Literature*
by Farah Mendlesohn

Childhood and Children's Books in Early
Modern Europe, 1550–1800
edited by Andrea Immel and Michael
Witmore

Voracious Children
Who Eats Whom in Children's Literature
by Carolyn Daniel

National Character in South African
Children's Literature
by Elwyn Jenkins

Myth, Symbol, and Meaning in
Mary Poppins
The Governess as Provocateur
by Georgia Grilli

A Critical History of French Children's
Literature
by Penny Brown

The Gothic in Children's Literature
Haunting the Borders
edited by Anna Jackson, Karen Coats, and
Roderick McGillis

Reading Victorian Schoolrooms
*Childhood and Education in
Nineteenth-Century Fiction*
by Elizabeth Gargano

Soon Come Home to This Island
West Indians in British Children's Literature
by Karen Sands-O'Connor

Boys in Children's Literature and Popular
Culture
*Masculinity, Abjection, and the Fictional
Child*
by Annette Wannamaker

Into the Closet
*Cross-dressing and the Gendered Body in
Children's Literature*
by Victoria Flanagan

Russian Children's Literature and Culture
edited by Marina Balina and
Larissa Rudova

The Outside Child In and Out of the Book
by Christine Wilkie-Stibbs

Representing Africa in Children's Literature
Old and New Ways of Seeing
by Vivian Yenika-Agbaw

The Fantasy of Family
*Nineteenth-Century Children's Literature
and the Myth of the Domestic Ideal*
by Liz Thiel

From Nursery Rhymes to Nationhood
*Children's Literature and the Construction of
Canadian Identity*
by Elizabeth A. Galway

The Family in English Children's
Literature
by Ann Alston

THE FAMILY IN ENGLISH CHILDREN'S LITERATURE

ANN ALSTON

Routledge
Taylor & Francis Group

NEW YORK AND LONDON

First published 2008
by Routledge
270 Madison Ave, New York, NY 10016

Simultaneously published in the UK
by Routledge
2 Park Square, Milton Park, Abingdon, Oxon OX14 4RN

Routledge is an imprint of the Taylor & Francis Group, an informa business

© 2008 Taylor & Francis

Typeset in Minion
by Swales & Willis Ltd, Exeter, Devon

Printed and bound in the United States of America on acid-free paper
by Walsworth Publishing Company, Marceline, MO

Library of Congress Cataloging in Publication Data
Alston, Ann, 1978–
The family in English children's literature / by Ann Alston.
p. cm. – (Children's literature and culture ; 53)
Includes bibliographical references and index.
1. Children's stories, English–History and criticism. 2. Family in
literature. 3. Home in literature. I. Title.
PR830.C513A67 2008
820.9′355–dc22
2007040837

ISBN10: 0–415–98885–3 (hbk)
ISBN10: 0–203–92875–X (ebk)

ISBN13: 978–0–415–98885–8 (hbk)
ISBN13: 978–0–203–92875–2 (ebk)

For the memory of my mother, Joan Margaret Alston,
and for the future of her grandsons, Sam, Joshua, James,
Thomas and Vasilis.

Contents

Series Editor's Foreword

Dedicated to furthering original research in children's literature and culture, the Children's Literature and Culture series includes monographs on individual authors and illustrators, historical examinations of different periods, literary analyses of genres, and comparative studies on literature and the mass media. The series is international in scope and is intended to encourage innovative research in children's literature with a focus on interdisciplinary methodology.

Children's literature and culture are understood in the broadest sense of the term children to encompass the period of childhood up through adolescence. Owing to the fact that the notion of childhood has changed so much since the origination of children's literature, this Routledge series is particularly concerned with transformations in children's culture and how they have affected the representation and socialisation of children. While the emphasis of the series is on children's literature, all types of studies that deal with children's radio, film, television, and art are included in an endeavour to grasp the aesthetics and values of children's culture. Not only have there been momentous changes in children's culture in the last fifty years, but there have been radical shifts in the scholarship that deals with these changes. In this regard, the goal of the Children's Literature and Culture series is to enhance research in this field and, at the same time, point to new directions that bring together the best scholarly work throughout the world.

Jack Zipes

Acknowledgments

I have received help and support from a number of sources. In many ways it is impossible to acknowledge everyone who has contributed whether in the form of useful conversations, debates or the all-important providers of coffees and cakes. I would like to express my gratitude to my colleagues at both Cardiff University and The University of the West of England, Bristol, with special thanks to Martin Coyle and Stephen Knight who have given valuable support and encouragement. Heather Worthington, Louise Harrington and Roberta Magnani have given great insight and assistance in terms of this project but have also provided a constant stream of support, enthusiasm and most importantly, friendship. A special acknowledgement must also go to Peter Hunt for it was Peter's lectures that first awoke my enthusiasm for children's literature. I am grateful not only for his guidance and inspiration but also for his continued encouragement, interest and warmth. Writing a book has seemed to take up several years and I would like to thank Nicki, Charlotte, Emma, Sophie A, Sophie D, Gareth, Will, Clare, Lowri and Chris for sticking it out and still being such good friends at the end. For a book that is all about the family I have a few family members of my own who I would like to acknowledge so thanks go to Helen, Julian, Robin, Anne, Richard, Robert, Jeff and Jan. However, special thanks must go to my parents. I am grateful for my father's understanding, support and faith in my abilities – the type of belief only a devoted dad can have. But for my interest in family I have my mother to thank. Joan Alston died nine years ago but her influence and love with all things to do with the family cannot escape this work. Finally, I would like to thank Dave for his love, ability to tell me when to stop (and start) and enforcement of walks in the mountains: without him this would never have got started, reached a middle and would certainly never have reached an end.

Introduction

If people could only know what is the best happiness of this life, it certainly depends on being loved by those we belong to: for nothing can be called peace on Earth which does not consist of family affections.

(**Catherine Sinclair**, *Holiday House* 1839)

In the end Charlie Bucket won a chocolate factory but Willy Wonka had something even better – a family. And one thing was absolutely certain; life had never been sweeter.

(**Tim Burton, dir.** *Charlie and the Chocolate Factory* 2005)

Catherine Sinclair's *Holiday House* (1839) and John August's screenplay for Tim Burton's film adaptation of *Charlie and the Chocolate Factory* (2005), texts separated by 166 years, reflect the centring of children's literature on family. Family is the ideal, the epic end-point of the Odyssean journey of the fiction, at which home and family are recovered. These texts demonstrate an undiminished desire to centre children's fiction on the ideal that is family. In such fundamentally dissimilar texts it is both curious and surprising that a similar rhetoric of family appears at the heart of the text: true happiness it seems is impossible without the love and support of a dedicated family.

Yet this raises a fundamental problem at the heart of this exploration. We have, we are often told, over the last two centuries and especially over the last five decades, experienced a revolution in family life. The family as a living reality has altered; divorce rates have soared; blended families are commonplace;[1] often both parents work outside the home; children have become more central to family life as is often evident in parental battles for custody; there has been a decline in religious faith: the list of changes, it seems, is endless.

Yet, in spite of this oft-quoted revolution, the depiction of the family in children's literature is, at heart, deeply conservative. Although there are changes in the way in which families are depicted as Philippe Ariès argues in his history of childhood: 'it is not so much the family as reality that is our subject here as the family as an ideal' (7) and the ideal of family remains surprisingly fixed. In

1

the analyses which follow, what is so striking is not the subtle and not so subtle changes in the representation of the family, but the many similarities that exist between the fictional families of the nineteenth and twentieth centuries. Texts that are superficially dissimilar promote typical and inherently similar notions of family from Mary Martha Sherwood's puritanical, and to modern eyes repressive, *The History of the Fairchild Family* (1818) to Jacqueline Wilson's social-reality novel *Tracy Beaker* (1991). Family is inherent in and central to most children's literature. Even if the family is largely absent or parents are pushed to the margins, it lurks in the text, its ideology informing the attitudes of the characters and the development of the plot. Characters are frequently dependent on some aspect of family whether presented as siblings, parents, aunts, uncles or grandparents, and these family members can be good or bad role models. The 'Harry Potter' series, for example, contrasts the Weasleys with the Dursleys to exemplify how and how not to conduct family life, and this comparison is a well-established trope of children's fiction. Yet children's literature rarely asks the fundamental question of what constitutes family, and what, if anything is ideal. Although there is an increasing recognition in contemporary children's fiction that texts must be relevant to the child who does not experience the classic, idealised nuclear family, and there are many texts that address divorce, abuse, homelessness, and other socially-aware themes that contrast with the cosy nuclear family ideal, that ideal remains fundamentally intact. Equally, nineteenth-century texts often dealt with parental absence, usually owing to untimely death. The fact that the family is 'fractured' may drive plots, but it is not used to question the received ideals of family or to establish different social models in which children could be socialised and protected. Even where there is no family, a surrogate family is created. In spite of all the pressures on the nuclear family, it is culturally still promoted as an ideal and the norm in children's literature and in other texts aimed at a juvenile audience. Children's literature promotes a specific ideology; it attempts to instil in its readers certain values which dictate how families should be: loving, respectful, preferably with two parents, contained in domestic harmony and sharing wholesome home-cooked family meals. Yet the relevance, function and significance of family are never brought under scrutiny.

In order to chart the depiction of family in children's literature over the extended period 1818–2003, I treat a wide range of texts, beginning with *The History of the Fairchild Family* (1818) and concluding with J.K. Rowling's *Harry Potter and the Order of the Phoenix* (2003). The texts that I have chosen tend to be very popular, are mostly still in print and have either excited critical debate or have been widely read by children, and, in some cases, both. As this is a broad study, I have included books for most ages, from picture books to those that may be loosely classified as teenage fiction. To exclude books simply because they did not fit a specific age category would detract from my argument. The ideology promoted in children's literature moves across age groups, and my argument depends on this continuity. For similar reasons, I have studied texts in different genres. As Foucault argues in *The Archaeology of Knowledge* discourses cross the artificial boundaries of genre and authorial corpora. Thus, while the majority of texts in this book could be classed as domestic or realist fiction, I have included texts that can be categorised as fantasy, fairy tale or adventure stories. Although the texts used here are mainly British, the inclusion of some American and Canadian children's literature seemed appropriate: it would be an incomplete study of the family that failed to include Louisa May Alcott's *Little Women* (1868) or L.M. Montgomery's *Anne of Green Gables* (1908), as these texts have influenced countless other domestic stories, past and present, on both sides of the Atlantic. They have become part of an Anglo-American culture and they share many cultural concerns with their British counterparts. The focus of this study is on children's literature that is written in English for while there remains a space in which to discuss the depiction of the family in international children's literature, what I concentrate on is the emergence of ideological concerns about family over the last two centuries in Western culture.

There is a certain inevitability in that the families dealt with here are seemingly of a similar kind and class, yet there is a diversity in the range of families as children's literature often includes single-parent families, extended families (who often care for the child protagonists in nineteenth-century literature) and families from working-class backgrounds. However, while the majority of families addressed could be considered as middle-class, the book deals with the upper class in the depiction of the Fairchild family and with the working classes through the analysis of Margaret Sidney's *Five Little Peppers and How They Grew* (1881), Eve Garnett's Ruggles family from *The Family From One End Street* (1937), John Rowe Townsend's *Gumble's Yard* (1961), Roald Dahl's *Charlie and the Chocolate Factory* (1964) and *Matilda* (1988) and finally Jacqueline Wilson's *The Bed and Breakfast Star* (1994). It seems to me, though, that in children's literature the issue of class pales into insignificance when faced with the impact of the ideological emphasis on the family. Often the reader barely notices the class of the protagonist and this is due to the overarching middle-class nature of children's literature. While a family in children's literature might be working-class it is often represented through and seen from a middle-class perspective, for children's literature emerged from and was initially intended for the middle-classes. As Andrew O'Malley argues in his analysis of childhood in the eighteenth century, 'children's literature became one of the most crucial mechanisms for disseminating and consolidating middle-class ideology' (11). It was the middle classes who both initiated and read children's literature in the eighteenth century and from here children's literature emerged as a way in which to educate its readers about their ideological positions with regard to other classes, religion, education and essentially, family (O'Malley 1–4). While such pedagogical literature has perhaps become more muted over the last 200 years a reliance on middle-class perspectives of how families should live remains. With this in mind, Garnett's Ruggles family can be compared with Sherwood's Fairchild family; the distance between them in terms of history and class is minimised because both have been shaped by similar ideologies that promote how families should behave and interact. In the light of this, the remit of this book is not to consider the middle or working-classes separately but to focus on how the promotion of family ideals impacts upon a broad spectrum of the children's literature of the last two centuries. Inevitably, there will be omissions, but the texts here must stand for thousands of others including those that are forgotten or out of print. The selected texts are largely canonical and are the most influential in terms of the construction of the ideological fictional family.

This book is organised in two parts: one is chronological and the other is thematic. Because of the time period dealt with and consequently the high volume of texts, I have contextualised them historically and charted their chronology. Part 1 establishes the chronological and historical context of the texts. This historical overview and my organisation of children's literature specifically in relation to family provides a detailed chronological analysis of portrayals of family and its place in the texts. What this section demonstrates is not so much the contrasts that exist between periods but startling similarities of the ideological subtexts of family intrinsic to children's literature. More specifically, Chapter 1 gives a historical account of the family over the nineteenth and twentieth centuries while the following two chapters focus on the representations of family in children's literature. As the study concentrates on the depiction of the family in children's fiction in terms of ideology and nostalgia it is crucial to consider how this compares to changes that affect the family in reality. In its chronological analysis of family in children's literature over the nineteenth and early twentieth centuries, Chapter 2 investigates the increasing complexities of family in children's literature from *The History of the Fairchild family* to *Peter Pan* and sets this in conjunction with particular tropes that epitomise the texts. Following on from this, Chapter 3 considers the twentieth-century depictions of family across a range of texts, reflecting the ever-expanding world of children's literature.

The first section considers the chronology of family, the families in reality, in ideal terms, and examines the relationship between the two in children's fiction. The debate moves on in the second section to concentrate on smaller but important themes. In this second section, the book looks at the internal workings of the family analysing the representation of homes, domestic spaces and food in a range of texts. The argument moves from the perspective of the outward observer to the privileged insight into the insular, private workings of family. The reader is taken from outside to inside, from external to internal; from the concept of home via the spaces which construct the home and, by way of the food the family consumes, into the very body of the individual family member. As the book develops, its examination of family becomes more intimate moving from the social structuring of family and concluding with a focus on the individual.

The emphasis in the second part of the book is on the family as a unit. Having considered the family in terms of chronology and social change this section builds on this foundation as it delves into the sites and functions of the family in children's literature, allowing direct comparison of nineteenth- and twentieth-century fictional families. Central to the analysis is the concept of home and its relevance to family and family life; the ways in which the home is divided into family-specific spaces; and finally, the function of food in the family – where it is eaten, its importance, its constituents and its effects. I have concentrated on these themes because, in terms of family, I contend that these factors most clearly delineate the ideal family in ideology, and it is in these aspects in which family well-being or conflict is most apparent. And of course, the representation of home, space and food in children's literature must, by implication and of necessity, incorporate the relationships between children, parents and siblings.

Through the analysis of these various aspects of the depiction of family life in children's literature over nearly two centuries, it is possible to trace changes in the presentation of families. Previously, historians of children's literature have tracked changes in the treatment of the family but have often focused on other aspects of children's literature.[2] The traditional reading has been that the fictional families of children's literature respond to the changes from the nineteenth-century patriarchal familial system to the alleged post-1960s collapse of the family. Yet, in marked contrast, here I show that the ideology of the nuclear family still remains central to children's literature but is a largely unexamined ideological presentation of a normative family life. In adhering to these social norms, which do not reflect the diversity of family life in the modern Western world, children's literature offers what Foucault calls a 'disciplinary discourse' which serves to create subjects who will in turn desire, and so replicate, the ideal family. In spite of the decline of patriarchy, the rise of feminism and all the economic, cultural and social changes that have bombarded the family in the last two centuries, the ideal of family is still cherished. Children's literature is not on the brink of revolution in its depiction of the family, nor can we argue that it has undergone the transformation that the social changes of the last 200 years may have led us to expect. Fictional families may have changed, but the all-important, two heterosexual parent ideal is still in the ideological foundation of twenty-first-century children's literature. Yet, even as the text re-presents the world to itself, it also shapes that world. In so doing, children's literature both runs the risk of wallowing in a nostalgic and perhaps ahistorical vision of ideal nuclear families, but also, and perhaps more seriously, of creating a vision of family life and its values which does not match the lived experience of its audience. Children's literature is where we can see most clearly our nostalgia for the past, but equally, it is crucial in determining attitudes towards the future.

Chapter One
History of Family: The Growth of a Cherished Institution

It is no doubt true that since the beginning of the human race men have built homes and begot children, and it can be argued that within the great family types, monogamous and polygamous, historical differences are of little importance in comparison with the huge mass of what remains unchanged.

(Ariès 7)

Families are complex social constructions, and as Lissa Paul reminds us, 'history is messy' (25). When it comes to mixing families and histories the contradictions and complexities are immense and for this reason it becomes increasingly difficult, if not impossible, to begin to categorise, define, or map the changes in families over time without making generalisations and eliminating some of the diversity that no doubt existed/exists. The definition of family cannot be a fixed one, for families are fluid; they vary considerably in their make-up and in their traditions, and they are always culturally specific. There are, of course, many different types of family, and while I recognise this diversity, this study focuses on the middle-class family that is presented, often to the detriment of others, in children's fiction. The definition of middle-class is in itself fraught with difficulty and contradiction, but it is my contention here that families in children's literature are often middle-class and even those who cannot be so easily labelled tend to be described in terms of an ideology that is associated with the middle classes. As a consequence of its rise as written popular fiction from the eighteenth century onwards children's literature has been used as a pedagogical device in order to instil a certain set of beliefs that promote middle-class values and ideals.[1]

To further complicate such definitions of family, each one of us comes from some kind of family environment and therefore we cannot easily discard the cultural baggage we inevitably carry: family is always personal and every individual has a story to tell. But while the recognition of diversity and fluidity of meanings is imperative it is also important to acknowledge and account for basic patterns and changes. This chapter will first consider the significance of the culturally constructed concept of family, particularly the nuclear family, will then offer a brief analysis concerning the pre-modern family, and will conclude by examining changes that have occurred, mainly across the nineteenth and twentieth centuries. This chapter does not attempt a comprehensive history of family, but offers a basic outline: a set of ideas, ideals and a deconstruction of assumptions which is helpful in situating my central concern, that is, the significance of family in children's literature.

Concepts of Family

The concept of family is genetically programmed: procreation requires pair bonding to ensure the survival of the species. In conjunction with this, the creation of communities and larger families also affords a method of survival since the group can defend itself better than the individual and the gene pool is widened. The grouping of humans for safety and survival is a basic Darwinian concept; beyond this most other familial structures, traditions and customs are culturally constructed and are influenced by the times, environments and conditions in which people live. While the family is socially variable in its structure, the concept of family in its various forms affects all humans, and, despite cultural changes, this concept of family remains central to human ideology. Indeed, by the twenty-first century, with the rise of the self-sufficient individual, one could be excused for wondering why the family structure continues to be intrinsic to human life, and perhaps this is to do with a basic animalistic survivalist instinct that remains in our psyche.

Equally, the constant promotion of the ideology of the family within society also ensures the continued idealisation of, devotion to and reliance on the family unit. One of the ways this ideology is promulgated is in literature, but while adult literature tends to celebrate the individual, children's literature is steeped in family matters. As the child learns from his/her parental role models, and competes against and works with siblings, he/she learns to co-exist with others. Literature for children, it seems, is the perfect space in which to foster both the Darwinian and cultural concepts of family, to introduce children to and immerse them in a set of adult constructs and ideals.

In our everyday lives we are constantly reminded of the significance of family. It remains, as Catherine Belsey proposes, 'our culture's most cherished institution' (*Shakespeare* xiv). Tony Blair implied the synonymity of family and state when he argued that '[w]e cannot say we want a strong and secure society when we ignore its very foundations: family life'. The placing of traditional family values on a moral pedestal is a fairly common way in which to gain the favour of the public. The Royal Family and its behaviour, constantly charted and monitored in the media, is an example of the significance of maintaining and asserting 'proper' family conduct. This particular family is a public institution, and was perhaps at the peak of its popularity when Queen Victoria and Prince Albert metaphorically established themselves as mother and father of the nation, thus linking family and state. The Victorian period was one in which the ideology of the family was at a height and therefore it is difficult to say whether the intense interest in the Royal Family was a product of, or a response to, the time. In terms of class, similar notions of family were beginning to emerge between the royals as aristocracy and the middle-classes. Whereas in the eighteenth century the aristocracy had often been portrayed as wasteful and idle, here the Royal Family set an example of perfect family values thus emphasising the powerful ideological status of the family in the nineteenth century.

Public interest in the family affairs of the Royals has not always been beneficial, as the Royal Family has often suffered unpopularity resulting from a breakdown in traditional family relationships: the Queen Caroline affair caused much controversy in 1820 when George IV tried to divorce his Queen;[2] Edward VIII decided to abdicate because he wanted to marry the twice-divorced Mrs Simpson in 1936, and the Prince Charles-Princess Diana-Camilla triangle excited the tabloid press on a fairly regular basis with concerns about family relationships, divorces and affairs.[3] Family, and how people conduct their family lives, it seems, matters. The myth of the loving nuclear family is a powerful one, and as a myth it has inevitably become naturalised, for as Belsey argues '[w]hatever is customary comes in due course to seem natural' (*Shakespeare* xiv). In naturalising and promoting the loving family other types of family tend to be at best marginalised and at worst demonised; essentially, they become other.

The ideal of the family is not simply an innocent idealistic fantasy but an ideological system in which issues of power and control are embedded. This is evident in Michel Foucault's work on the study of power. The distinction that Foucault makes between disciplinary and sovereign power is useful in explaining why we persist – and are encouraged to persist – with the ideal family. In premodern society, sovereign power, as the name suggests, invested all power with an influential, usually male, figure, for example, the king, priest or father. Power in this system was ordained by, for example, God, and this system of control was apparent both in the running of the nation and in smaller institutions, such as the family. In a white, Western patriarchal society, each household was a microcosm of the macrocosmic kingdom and this is crucial in controlling the populace, as Lawrence Stone makes clear: 'For the state, Passive Obedience to the husband and father in the home was the model for and guarantee of Passive Obedience to the king in the nation' (*The Family, Sex and Marriage* 654).

To kill the king was high treason and the king is head of state and the father is head of the home. The parallels are clear in that husband murder was called 'petty treason' and women were burnt for this until the eighteenth century, and to kill the king was 'grand treason'. Yet while the father's position obviously embodies power on a much smaller scale than that of the king, the mechanisms of power and control on which they rely are remarkably similar. This process of control is still, to a certain extent, evident in the family that we will see in Mary

Martha Sherwood's *The History of the Fairchild Family* (1818). The mechanisms of sovereign power were not adequate to deal with the very large urban populations that developed in the nineteenth and twentieth centuries and therefore a new system of control emerged which Foucault terms disciplinary power.

Disciplinary power, according to Foucault, works on the individual to produce an obedient subject. Disciplinary power functions through ideology: concepts, values, rules, morals, all the mechanisms which permit the peaceful co-existence of masses of individuals, come to seem 'normal' and 'natural' because the individual internalises the ideology which produces them. But the ideologies which circulate in society have a controlling effect – they are part of a system of power that infiltrates the whole of society. As Simon During observes:

> Disciplinary power works in quite strictly deliminated spaces, though its pathways and mazes spread across social totality, unlike sovereign power which is centralized and evaporates at the margins. It is deritualized and privatized, working on individuals as individuals rather than either as members of castes or as markers of a wider cosmic or social order. Its object is behaviour and the individual body; its tools are surveillance, examinations, training and its sites, factories, prisons, schools, hospitals. (151)

I contend that the family can also be read as a site of discipline; it is a site of surveillance. Within the family children are constantly under observation by parents and are therefore under constant parental guidance and control. Family is where the child is first immersed in ideology. Equally, the family unit is a disciplinary institution which conforms to state-promulgated ideologies. These ideologies dictate patterns of behaviour which insist on conforming to culturally constructed conventions of family.

Within the family, disciplinary power works on the individual: in Foucauldian terms the emergence of disciplinary power responds to the rise of the individual in the nineteenth and twentieth centuries and also functions to construct that individual. Disciplinary power relies on the self-policing that results from the internalisation of ideology, and such self-policing is intrinsic to an understanding of the family and its role in society and in literature. The family in children's literature especially, I suggest, has a strongly ideological and disciplinary function. Family values are embedded in our culture and we feel ourselves constantly monitored and observed with regard to our families, for the ideology of family is itself a disciplinary system and one that is largely self-imposed. The family remains a central locus of power and we judge by family values and continue our family rituals as if being constantly observed, comparing our families to others, both real and imagined.

Therefore the home, in a sense, is as much a site of surveillance as the hospitals and prisons, and as we police ourselves and care for our own children in a family environment, the state need not concern itself directly with issues of family. In families, a system of order and discipline is established that inculcates in the young, and the adults, a degree of compliance to systems of power. It comes as no surprise then, that when journalists and moralists publicise concerns about the demise of the family the government begins to intervene, for the family across class divides is crucial in maintaining the order of the nation. Tony Blair's speech was not only intended to rouse emotive feelings but was also a reminder that many issues of state power are reliant on the discipline of the family.

It seems that a paradoxical situation attaches itself to issues of family; on the one hand we adhere to the myth of the ideal nuclear family and on the other there is recognition that this nuclear family is no longer entirely workable. The state, though, has a vested interest in the maintenance of the institution of the family and consequently interferes in an attempt to promulgate the 'basic values' of family life. In interfering in family life the government must tread carefully, for the imaginary ideological family is also invested with a deep sense of privacy, and interference is unwelcome, resulting in the government coming under fire for inculcating a 'nanny state'. Most recently the parliamentary bill on the physical punishment of children has raised fears about state interference with personal choice.[4] Similarly, some parents have, controversially, been imprisoned because their child has played truant from school, and increasingly there are media reports that suggest parents can no longer control their children.

This lack of parental control may indicate a shift in the position of the child in the family. As Christina Hardyment has suggested in her book *The Future of the Family*, the child has become, in our twenty-first-century capitalist society, a consumer as opposed to a contributor; rather than contributing to the family finances the child consumes products manufactured outside the home with his/her parents' money. Perhaps then, if there is really a loss of parental authority in contemporary society, then it is in literature for children that we find the best location to impose family ideology on children, to indoctrinate them with role models and to promulgate the family values which allow society to function in a specific way, in so far as we can in the present context. Thus perhaps we have not become so detached from the early nineteenth-century writers of children's literature who are often regarded as being overly didactic in their teachings.

Family is essential to society and, although it is subject to historical change, the importance of the family as the central locus of power and control remains inherent in human lives. Family is biologically useful, and yet the nuclear family, no matter how much it becomes naturalised by myth, is always a social and cultural construct. This construct has important political implications. Even those families that break down and no longer fit into a conventional pattern are still controlled by state and self-discipline for they are engulfed by the myth of the ideal nuclear family that is promoted by the media, politicians, and individuals. As Belsey points out there are very few happy marriages in Jane Austen's works and yet weddings still form the basis of the happy endings in her texts (*Shakespeare* 121). Individuals even now tend to form relationships and have families regardless of the happiness or otherwise of their parents' marriages; we live in hope that the happy endings and romantic comedies of fiction and film might come true and yet we remain aware of the difficulties facing the family, of the impossibility of the Hollywood dream that is exemplified in *The Waltons* (1972–81) or comedies such as *Sleepless in Seattle* (1993). Despite ongoing anxieties concerning families the myth of the ideal family remains strong; encouraged by all mechanisms of power it remains essential to the way in which our society works. While great changes have occurred in the constitution of family, ideals and dreams seem to have remained fairly consistent for the 200 years on which I focus, and probably for some time prior to that; we are, and perhaps always have been, almost obsessed with the family that, ideally, *should* exist.

The Pre-Modern Family

While the majority of material considered here will be drawn from the period 1818–2000, it is also necessary to look at how this 'modern' family evolved in order to understand it fully. In *The Origin of the Family, Private Property and State* Friedrich Engels investigated the role of family in early human life and insisted that as the means of production were communal, families did not exist; instead, there were communities that worked together. Engels argued that as time moved on more restrictions were placed upon this communal society and eventually, as individuals began to own property, the nuclear family began to emerge. This was because monogamous marriage was encouraged in order to ensure that the father would pass on property to his rightful heir.

Similarly, Lawrence Stone argues that before the seventeenth century, relations tended to be community-based rather than family-based as families did not necessarily have any more emotional attachment to their wives and children than to their neighbours:

> In the sixteenth century, and almost certainly for at least a millennium before it, the characteristic type, especially among the social elite, was what I have chosen, for lack of a better term, to call the Open Lineage Family, since its two most striking features were its permeability by outside influences, and its members' sense of loyalty to ancestors and to living kin. The principal boundary circumscribed the kin, not its sub-unit, the nuclear family. (*Family, Sex and Marriage* 4)

In addition, Stone points out that children would leave home between the ages of seven and fourteen, and both Stone and Philippe Ariès argue that as a result of child mortality rates – Stone puts the figure of child mortality before the late eighteenth century at between 30 and 50 per cent – parents did not form the same emotional attachment to their children (*Family, Sex and Marriage* 651; Ariès 37).

These arguments have been criticised by Linda Pollock, who gives many examples and accounts of loving relationships between parents in *Forgotten Children: Parent-Child Relations From 1500–1900*. Davidoff *et al.* are quick to emphasise that both sides of the argument have been criticised; Ariès and Stone for making generalisations from their sources, and Pollock for not giving sufficient social context for her work (Leonore Davidoff *et al.* 40).

It is inevitable that these conflicts appear in debates concerning the family, for if the fluidity of family is taken into account then it becomes clear that the historian is bound to be able to find some examples to back either case. Further, as we can never really know what went on in the minds or homes of the generations before us, family histories can never be entirely accurate or comprehensive. It is not unlikely that some parents loved their children, and yet parents were also more accustomed to losing their children than we are today, and it is possible that they had different grieving or coping strategies. While careful not to limit by date, Stone locates the next stage of family after the open lineage family to be the 'restricted patriarchal nuclear family'. This family type, according to Stone, emerged from about 1530 onwards and peaked between 1580 and 1640, before fading out gradually in different areas and classes. The early proto-nuclear family saw loyalty to lineage, kin and community replaced by greater loyalty to the state or Church and Stone argues '"boundary awareness" became more exclusively confined to the nuclear family, which consequently became more closed off from external influences, either of the kin or of the community'(*Family, Sex and Marriage* 7).

As a result of the exclusivity of the nuclear family, the father became more powerful as head of the household and the Church began to gain more control of family life as is partly reflected by the fact that in the sixteenth century births, marriages and deaths were recorded by the parish. Indeed, the Church itself is bound in the hierarchy of the family with God the Father, Mary the Holy Mother and of course the Son. Belsey points out that the Reformation transformed the place of marriage: while in medieval times celibacy was regarded as a way of perfection, by the sixteenth century marriage had replaced monasticism as 'a terrestrial paradise' in which 'the love between husband and wife [was] an analogue for the love of God'(*Shakespeare* 19–21). The family, then, was beginning to change, broadly speaking, from an all-encompassing community to a smaller, more inward-looking group, one in which both the Church and the father had an increasing influence, and one that was generally founded on an ideal of romantic love. For Stone the final stage of family is the 'closed domesticated nuclear family, [which] came into being sometime after the 1640s and predominated in the eighteenth century. This family, Stone argues, 'was the product of the rise of Affective Individualism. It was a family organised around the principle of personal autonomy, and bound together by strong affective ties' (*Family, Sex and Marriage* 7).

Thus, the modern family, which we generally recognise today as being nuclear, began, though very slowly, to emerge in the eighteenth century, and this family model was later almost sanctified, placed as it was on an ideological pedestal in the nineteenth century. Of course, Stone can be criticised for drawing speculative time lines and imposing broad definitions on certain types of families in certain periods, and yet he qualifies this by stating that most of his sources originate from those people who visited London frequently or lived in the capital, and recognises that the plurality of family does not lend itself easily to categorisation (*Family, Sex and Marriage* 10). Indeed, Stone goes on to suggest that the only steady linear change has been an increasing concern for children, and he is also careful to emphasise that the three types of family discussed overlapped each other and have never fully vanished (*Family, Sex and Marriage* 10, 683). The foundations of the nuclear family were perhaps set as early as the sixteenth or seventeenth century, but the growth was gradual, and encompassed several varieties of families and different rates of change. The term 'family', for instance, still included servants up until the seventeenth century, and for some families probably well after that. The ideology of the family began to be imposed upon and gradually internalised by the individual, so that by the time Rousseau wrote *Émile* in 1762, with his argument that families are the only basis for a healthy society, a distinct system of ideals concerning the family had been established, regardless of how individuals were actually conducting their family lives.

The Modern Family – Nineteenth Century

Historians and sociologists cannot agree when the modern family came into existence, and in many ways this disagreement is an obvious one, for to give a date or period would be too simplistic. Changes in families vary from upper class to lower class, from the urban to the rural, and from family to family. Deborah Chambers argues that the period between the 1780s and 1840s was a key area of change from which the modern era of family emerged while Ariès and Stone argue that the change took place between 1500 and 1800 (D. Chambers 36). As Davidoff *et al.* point out, 'the search for a precise turning point is necessarily an elusive one, whether for the end of an idyllic past and the start of the modern nightmare, or for the beginning of progress from backward poverty to modern affluence' (20).

Yet, as suggested earlier, every study has to start somewhere and Davidoff *et al.* begin their history of family in the 1830s, having argued, in line with Chambers, that the starting point for the emergence of the modern family is traditionally recognised as being somewhere between the 1780s and 1840s. I suggest that it is no coincidence that the emergence of the modern concept of the family responded at some level to the increasing emphasis on the innocence of the child that is evident in the works of Romantic writers such as Rousseau and Wordsworth, and that the development of this concept of the family in part coincides at some level with the production of children's literature. As the child becomes more important to society in the eighteenth and nineteenth centuries, it follows that parents invest more time and emotion in him/her and that in an increasingly literate and literature-aware society, literature that is different from literature for adults begins to emerge. Indeed, as O'Malley points out children's reading in the late eighteenth century '[. . .] took on a greater urgency [. . .] as parents, writers and pedagogues saw the conditioning of the rising generation as essential to creating [. . .] a new class order with the middle-classes at its moral and productive centre' (124). The emergence of literature written for children then helped to establish middle-class values concerning the family and the child's status within it. The child is no longer simply considered to be a smaller version of the adult but is defined through his/her difference from the adult and it follows then that adult and child become distinct within ideology.

Sara Thornton argues that the appearance of the innocent child results in new classifications being made regarding the definition of child as opposed to adult:

> Whereas earlier cultures divided childhood from adulthood by means of social situation and dependence, the Victorians used biological factors such as menstruation and ejaculation. Thus we see a sexual construction at work and the need to see the child as non-sexual or latent. (129)

Sexuality becomes the province of the adult and consequently the child is seen as a body in need of protection; virginity and innocence become synonymous, hence the frequent images of Victorian fathers cradling their infant girls – in a sense protecting their virginities (Tosh, *Masculinity and the Middle-Class Home* 85). This new distinction between adult and child is important in the rise of the modern nuclear family, for it places the child at the centre (ideologically at least) of the family. Families are now run, partly, to care for the children, whereas previously they had been run for adults with children playing an important role as contributors to the economic unit (Flanders 41). Paradoxically while the child is given a more central role, idealistically speaking, in the family, the child and adult move physically further and further apart since spaces within houses become more segregated; while in early modern times a couple's privacy, depending on their wealth, may just have been a curtain around the bed, by the nineteenth century middle-class parents and children are sometimes divided by whole floors, and this is partly in response to the nineteenth-century separation of children and sexuality.

Definitions, classifications and legislation characterised the nineteenth century, and the separation of the 'pure' child and 'sexual' adult resulted in an elimination of any connections between the child and sexuality in the middle-class home; sexual acts were secret, and thus became viewed as sinful unless committed within a monogamous marriage in the privacy of the home. Even pregnancy was regarded as something that should be concealed as far as possible, and the sexual was very much pushed to the margins of the middle- and upper-class home (Flanders 15–17). The nineteenth-century nuclear family, with its private house and inward attitude, established a wealth of barriers and secrets between adults and children, private and public, that had probably not existed on the same scale when families were more community-based. Divisions between children and adults seem to have been prominent; Tosh, for example, emphasises that while the theories of Rousseauian Romantics and the Evangelical movement were antithetical, what they had in common was their concern with the seclusion of the child:

> Protective seclusion was vital to both: to the Romantics because children needed a playground beyond the reach of the adult world; to the Evangelicals because children's delicate spiritual state was so vulnerable to corruption. (*Masculinity and The Middle-Class Home* 42)

The nursery, a relatively new concept in the nineteenth century, can be considered to be a result of these beliefs, but while it served to give children their own space it also often added to their alienation from their parents (Flanders 28). Many children from Victorian middle- and upper-class families barely saw their parents and when they did it was at a specific time and they dressed and behaved well for the meeting. This can still be seen in Edwardian children's literature when Mary Lennox is dressed up to meet her uncle in *The Secret Garden* (1911). As Kimberley Reynolds points out, this resulted in a somewhat skewed perception of both adulthood and childhood:

> [I]f Victorian children were encouraged to regard their parents as omnipotent and ideal, bourgeois households elevated childhood to unprecedented heights. Just as the pattern of distance-parenting was capable of concealing parents' foibles and failings, so it tended to present only the pretty and angelic face of childhood to parents, leaving the tantrums and tedium to their full-time carers. (*Children's Literature* 3)

The Victorian ideal of the family all together can be deconstructed here, for while contemporary paintings might have represented them in this way and no doubt some families practised this close living for others, children and parents were emotionally and physically further apart than ever before.

Children were seen as ideologically central to family life, and yet were often moved to its margins. The child was seen as the saviour of the man, as is evident in fiction such as Frances Hodgson Burnett's *Little Lord Fauntleroy* (1886), but the cult of childhood was an adult construction that served the adult: the adult could look back towards childhood as a time of innocence, again emphasising the divide between adult and child. The physical separation of adult and child on a day-to-day basis could only serve to increase the over-romanticising of the child, as the infant's misbehaviour was left for the servants to deal with, thus preserving parental ideals. It can also be argued that this separation of adult and child culminated in fiction at the beginning of the twentieth century in J.M.

Barrie's *Peter Pan* (1911), in which childhood was situated on its own island, well away from the parental world.

Alongside the paradox of the child becoming at once more central to the family and at the same time more distanced from it, the role of the nineteenth-century father is also a rather confused one; the father was both the head of the family who invested time and love in his children, and the authoritarian figure who stood distanced from the emotional needs of family. This paradox is represented in nineteenth-century children's literature, for while Mr Fairchild is a father who is amused with 'anything that entertains my family'(Sherwood 173), in contrast the fathers in Catherine Sinclair's *Holiday House* (1839) and later in Frances Hodgson Burnett's *The Secret Garden* both leave their children to travel in Europe after the death of their wives. In principle, it was the father who took on responsibility for the protection of the children; he worked to ensure they had a secure home and, as head of that home, was expected to shield them from threatening or disturbing knowledge (Tosh, *Masculinity and the Middle-Class Home* 85). This, of course, was the idealised image of family and especially of paternal relations. As Tosh makes clear, the home was held to be a man's place and not just because it was his material possession but because it was the place where his emotional needs could be met. Nineteenth-century fathers were 'expected to be dutiful husbands and attentive fathers, devotees of hearth and family' (Tosh, *Masculinity and the Middle-Class Home* 1). The ideology of the 'proper' family was strong in the nineteenth century. Family was presented as a refuge from the world, as 'more than a social institution, it was a creed and it was held as a dogma carrying all the force of tradition that family life distinguished England from less stable and moral societies' (Wohl 10).

Clearly, this ideal did not work in practice for all families. Wohl, in his study of different Victorian fathers' memoirs, emphasises that for some fathers the sending of boys to boarding school came as a relief since many fathers found their children noisy, bothersome and irrational, but Wohl then goes on to argue, somewhat logically, that while '[s]overeignty and remoteness' were predominant in fathers they were by no means universal traits (60–1). While the good, ideal father would enjoy his time at home with his family away from the world of work, an increasing number of men felt the need to escape from the throes of domesticity, illustrating an alternative side to the Victorian family. Men could temporarily evade the family by becoming members of any of the male-only clubs that existed in eighteenth- and nineteenth-century England, and they could also escape domesticity entirely by fleeing to the colonies: 'The appeal of the empire as the place for a strenuous men-only life at this time was clearly in tune with a broader tendency to shun domesticity in Britain itself' (Tosh, 'Imperial Masculinity' 80). The enclosed idyllic, idealised family had its deserters and while the Victorians liked to be perceived as a society concerned entirely with family values, there were always those who defied this and by their very deviancy defined those values.

The position of the father changed during the nineteenth century for, while on the one hand the father was often seen as the god-like head and protector of the home, on the other his authoritarian fatherly rights were slowly being brought into question (Davidoff *et al.* 109; Tosh *Masculinity and the Middle-Class Home* 90). For a good part of the century the children, like wives, were considered in law to be the father's property. The Caroline Norton affair illustrates the fact that the system was highly patriarchal, with the courts often being reluctant to interfere with the rights of fathers. Caroline Norton was physically abused by her husband, who then in 1836 accused her of committing adultery with Lord Melbourne. But having lost his case, he was unable to divorce his wife, as Caroline had been found not guilty of adultery, which was the only ground for divorce at the time. Once the couple separated, George Norton had legal ownership of the children, house and even Caroline's earnings, and consequently, Caroline launched a campaign regarding women's rights and infant custody.[5]

As a result, the Infant Custody Act (1839) was passed by Parliament, giving the mother the right to petition the Lord Chancellor for a hearing regarding her access to her children, but the mother had to prove that her character was unblemished while the father only had to justify his denial of access. For the majority of separated mothers this was an impossible 'right', and even in the case of Caroline Norton, a woman with impressive contacts, her husband escaped this legislation by moving to Scotland with their children. Further legislation regarding divorce was passed in 1857 which allowed the injured party in a marriage, regardless of their gender, to petition for divorce, and also resulted in custody of the children normally being given to the innocent partner. As Davidoff *et al.* point out, 'for the first time, a father's behaviour as a husband began to affect his rights as a father' (142).

While it was feared that many wives would leave their husbands as a result of this Act, the effects, in reality, were minimal; women were still largely controlled by the husbands and fathers who remained in charge of family's material resources. Equally, wages for women were poor and until the Married Women's Property Act (1870) married women had no right to own property – all belonged to the father/husband (Davidoff *et al.* 142–3). Stone contends that the Matrimonial Causes Act (1857) was in fact a conservative piece of legislation which aimed to reduce adultery, improve the legal position of wives, and perhaps most importantly, help secure the institution of the family. While Stone argues that the Act brought about few practical changes in family life for the majority, he goes on to suggest that the Act was successful in dissolving the Church's control over marriage in favour of state control, recognising that women should be given some rights, and he also insists that the debates preceding the Act channelled the way for further reforms that shaped divorce laws until the 1960s (Stone *Road to Divorce* 383–9).

As is evident with legislation regarding divorce and child custody, while the family was encouraged as a private haven, state interference was, somewhat paradoxically, also increasing. The state register of births, deaths and marriages was established in 1837; increasing numbers of health officials were employed by the state in order to monitor families; in 1853 compulsory vaccination against smallpox was introduced for all new babies, and in 1876 elementary education was made compulsory for children between the ages of five and ten.[6] Families, in all forms, were increasingly being disciplined and policed. Compulsory education represented the greatest interference as it resulted in children going to school rather than contributing economically to the household and in addition it allowed further state interference through the creation of truancy officers, school medical services and sanitary officers who could call into question a parent's, generally the mother's, upbringing of the children (Davidoff et al. 123).

These infringements on the sanctity of the family are also attacked in some of the children's literature of the period. In Catherine Sinclair's *Holiday House* (1839), for example, the narrator complains of young children being 'thrust into preparatory school', of older boys being sent away to 'distant academies' and remarks that the happy circle of family is 'all at an end in the present system' (243–4). *Holiday House* demonstrates an increasing anxiety with regard to interference in the domain of family and the anxieties that were felt across the social spectrum, from the working class to the upper-middle classes. Nor is this of purely historical interest; concerns regarding state interference in family and also the demise of the happy family are as common in the twenty-first as in the nineteenth century.

Alongside governmental reforms and checks, much literature was produced that also concerned itself with the home and childcare: J.C. Loudon produced manuals on how rooms should be equipped and designed while Jane Loudon sold many copies of her handbook on flower gardening (1841); *The Magazine of Domestic Economy* was first published in 1835 and was aimed at the middle classes with its guidelines on household management (Davidoff and Hall 187–9); Wohl lists several family journals that were produced including *The Home Circle, Family Economist,* and the *Family Treasure,* and of course Mrs Beeton's influential publication *Book of Household Management* was published in 1869 (9). The literature and legislation illustrate the importance the nineteenth-century populace placed on the family. The family had to be run in a set way, and acted as an analogy for the health and strength of the nation. Constant reforms, legislation and the publication of advice books ensured that society was well aware of the dominant ideology of family, and also served to normalise specific ways of managing a family. The individual could police not only his/her own family but also, by example, all the other families within the district, thus exerting an invisible and efficient discipline.

While families operated differently depending on class or period, the ideals were always evident. Tosh argues that domesticity was largely a nineteenth-century invention and the impact of this can be seen in the way their ideals still, in many ways, shape our present expectations of families (*Masculinity and the*

Middle-Class Home 4). In parallel with a greater ideological emphasis on the family and state interference in social matters, especially health and sexuality, mortality rates dropped considerably over the course of the nineteenth century. Infectious diseases and malnutrition became less common as, on the whole, standards of living improved and parents and siblings lived longer (Flanders 41; Davidoff *et al.* 133).

The modern ideal of family began to emerge and take hold of the imagination in the nineteenth century: the Romantics put their emphasis on the child; the Evangelicals promoted the morality of monogamous marriage and family life, and the state of the nation was linked metaphorically to the family. The obsession with family is paralleled by the opening of several institutions in which to house (put away) those individuals who did not fit into the ideal of family and therefore society. These institutions were workhouses for the poor, orphanages for the parentless, prisons for correction, and mental institutions for the socially deviant. Domesticity, it seems, was not for all. Many men shunned it. Children were in fact often separated from their parents, and legislation was introduced that did, in theory if not in practice, make petitioning for divorce possible for women as well as men. What is important is the promotion of the ideal, for it is the nineteenth century that shaped our current beliefs of what families should be and how they should operate. We remember Louisa Alcott's *Little Women*, Queen Victoria and Prince Albert, and Mrs Beeton's advice books with a sense of nostalgia for the lost family and whether it is really the lost family that never was does not seem to matter, for we rarely look in any detail at the intricacies of the families because it is the ideal that concerns us. Then, as now, it seems, there were slips and complications, but there always existed a firm concept of what the good family should be. By the end of the century ideologies concerning the family had been internalised to such an extent that the nuclear family was apparently the only satisfactory model of household management.

The Modern Family – Twentieth Century

The family remains, at the end of the twentieth century, a subject of contention, complexity and passionate debate. In an article in *The Times*, in 1998, cliché-ridden fears concerning the family are voiced:

> The story of the modern British family is a saga of terror, greed and stupidity spanning at least three decades. We're now approaching the climax, which, if we can't fix the ending fast, will be the Armageddon of our basic instincts. (Brayfield 19)

The emotional investment in the institution of the family is immense, and while I recognise that the comment is taken from a somewhat conservative broadsheet its hyperbolic tone serves to illustrate the cultural significance that is placed on the family. The quotation naturalises a certain type of family and suggests that families which do not adhere to this can be and, more didactically, need to be repaired; in an oddly domestic analogy, the family is alluded to as if it is an unravelling tapestry whose loose ends require stitching back into shape to avoid social catastrophe. The quotation illustrates Foucauldian theory perfectly. In suggesting that families are 'getting it wrong' the article emphasises the power of an internalised ideology; it reveals a certain amount of fear regarding families which move away from the normalised ideal and calls for a return to an organised system of family in order to see the continuance of society thus leaving no room for diversity within family types.

The quotation also serves to remind us that the twentieth century saw unprecedented changes regarding the family unit: the number of children in the family has been reduced considerably as contraception is widely available and infant mortality is now a rarity rather than a factor of everyday life; divorce is relatively easily obtainable; many children remain in education for longer and are often parentally supported well into early adulthood; adults often choose to remain childless; blended families are common as parents re-marry and gay families are increasingly becoming accepted. Materially, the changes are immense, and yet culturally there remains a tendency to yearn for a lost golden age of nuclear family values, to promote the family that eats and plays together with a father, a mother and their children. This powerful image is part of the ideology that we unconsciously internalise; such a family is a cultural construct and its representation is reiterated daily in television programmes, films, and literature, especially literature for children. The family, of course, as in the nineteenth century and well before that, remains a slippery construct, and during the late twentieth century the term became more open to a variety of meanings and definitions.

The central position of the child in the family remained important, and even increased in importance, during the course of the twentieth century. Children's literature has exploded, with thousands of titles being published and millions of copies being bought every year; advertisements are now aimed at children; even foods such as yoghurt and pasta shapes are marketed with children in mind. Items are bought especially for children, suggesting a distinct role reversal from the beginning of the nineteenth century as adults are now concerned with satisfying the consumerist demands of their children. It is not only in terms of consumerism that the child holds a newfound power but the child has also become emotionally central to the family. Emotionally entrapped parents often say that they will stay together 'for the sake of the children', demonstrating the effect of the myth of the nuclear family, but also illustrating the centrality of the welfare of the child to the modern family.

This change has been gradual over the century since a number of laws improving children's rights have corresponded to and complemented the cult of the child. As a result of these legislative changes, alterations in attitudes towards the child also became evident; instead of being seen as a working individual the child was increasingly seen as vulnerable, and further protection was found accordingly. In 1901 under the Factory and Workshops Act the minimum working age was increased to twelve and the importance of nation-wide education was promoted. This was followed by The Children's Act (1908) which established juvenile courts for children, made sexual abuse within the family a matter for the state to deal with rather than the Church and consequently demonstrates the limitation of Church powers in favour of the secular. Further powers were given to the local authorities under The Children's Act (1948), which ensured that each authority had a children's officer and emphasised local authorities' duty to ensure that children who were at risk were taken into care and, towards the end of the century in 1989, the Children Act legislated for the child to be involved in decisions that concerned him/herself. Of course, this is a simplified list and the Acts have all been the subject of much debate too detailed to embark on here, but what the list shows is an increasing acknowledgement of the child as an individual who is entitled to rights and to protection from adults. The child has become the key figure of the family, for as adults, we like to look back towards childhood, to indulge ourselves in its presumed innocence, and also to think that we have the power to protect those whom we assume to be more vulnerable than ourselves.

In parallel with the increase in awareness of and state regulations concerning the child, the status of the mother was also heightened during the twentieth century. All women over thirty were given the right to vote in 1918, and in 1928 all women over the age of twenty-one were enfranchised thus giving them the same voting rights as men. Various women's pressure groups forced the state to recognise the position of women in society and gradually women's status began to change. The effect of this on the middle-class family was perhaps felt more directly in the latter half of the century when more and more mothers went out to work (mothers from the working classes had usually worked due to necessity).[7] While legislation decreed more equality for women, the pressure to conform to the stereotype of the ideal mother was perhaps no less than it had been during the nineteenth century. Those who did not conform were often pushed to the margins of society; in the first half of the twentieth century, single mothers, for example, were often forced to hide their pregnancies as they were sent away from the confines of the family to have the child and then encouraged to put the child up for adoption.[8] Further, infant mortality during the inter-war years was regarded as a failure on the part of mothers rather than as a reflection of the poverty in which some families lived, and state interference was again evident in the establishment of schools for mothers in the early 1900s (Davidoff et al. 208).

Advice literature was widespread and it tended towards the training of children to behave in a proper socialised manner and to respect their elders. There were many examples of this didactic literature, and the manuals were popular with mothers, who followed them faithfully rather than listening to the experience of their own parents and grandparents. In Dr Truby King's strict childcare routine, parents were warned not to spoil children and were advised to rely on clock-based feeding and strict sleeping routines. All these practices were emphasised in *The Mothercraft Manual* which was published in Britain from 1922 to 1954. In 1946 Dr Spock's famous *Baby and Child Care* gave an alternative approach to childcare, as it stressed the need for parent-child affection and played down worries about spoiling children, thus stressing a more child-centred view of parenting (Reynolds *Sociology, Politics, the Family* 25). Indeed, baby manuals still take up several shelves in our bookshops today, with self-help author Gina Ford insisting that children should be managed in a specific way. Alongside such books countless television programmes are dedicated to teaching us how to look after and discipline children. The ideal mother took pleasure in parenting and saw motherhood as a vocation and, in part as a result of this, the role of the nanny diminished from the Second World War onwards, making her last claim to fame in P.L. Travers' *Mary Poppins* in 1934 (Reynolds *Sociology, Politics, the Family* 32). The relationship between mother and child was seen as intrinsic to the bringing up of a generation of good citizens and the trend towards having smaller families increased the amount of quality time parents could spend with each child.

The availability of the contraceptive pill from 1960 onwards was significant in giving women the power to choose the number of children they had and also gave them more sexual freedom to have different partners without a fear of pregnancy. In conjunction with the greater sexual freedom of the 1960s women also increasingly began to have their own careers and gradually there developed a greater variety of families: those in which both parents worked; families run by single mothers after divorce or separation rather than widowhood; and families with step-siblings and step-parents. These trends were reflected in children's literature with the publication of John Rowe Townsend's *Gumble's Yard* (1961) and Judy Blume's *Forever* (1975), amongst others. But the ideal of the nuclear family and the mother at home remained, in both reality and literature (and perhaps in some circles still remains) part of cultural ideology, and certainly up until the 1980s, if not later, mothers were often criticised for returning to work when their children still needed daytime care – the ideology demanded that they invested all their time and emotion in their families. As Deborah Chambers points out, while the term 'family man' is regularly used, 'family woman' sounds strange, for the woman in our imagination is intrinsic to family; essentially, she *is* family (102). While conservative voices still come out in protest as is evident in Brayfield's *Times* article, there has been a gradual cultural acceptance of the fluidity of the family from the 1960s onwards. The legal rights of women have been changed accordingly throughout the century, though it is worth remembering that cultural patriarchal expectations of women have been somewhat slower in acknowledging and responding to those changes.

Women's rights have altered beyond recognition since Caroline Norton's experience in the 1800s. Custody is now normally given to the mother in the case of divorce and it is fathers' pressure groups that are left to campaign for greater access to their children. Reforms to divorce legislation have been ongoing through the century and have gradually made divorce accessible to both sexes and to rich and poor alike. In 1923 reforms were made that made it possible to obtain divorce if the innocent party could prove one matrimonial offence (prior to this it had been two). This, as Stone points out, resulted in 'hotel bill' divorce as the husband could provide his wife with a hotel bill as evidence of his adultery and the two, in effect, divorced by mutual consent (*Road to Divorce* 397). In such a context, divorce remained the privilege of the more wealthy sectors of the population.

In 1937 further reforms were made which made it possible to petition for divorce not only due to adultery but due to desertion, cruelty, habitual drunkenness and incurable insanity, though divorce was not an option until the couple had been married for five years. There was an increasing recognition that divorce was a necessary part of many peoples' lives and in 1948 financial support was given to couples from poorer backgrounds to help them obtain a divorce. The major change with regard to divorce law took place in 1969 when it became possible to file for no fault divorce (Stone *Road to Divorce* 392–410). In accordance with these reforms the divorce rates steadily increased between 1900 and 1969 and soared from 1969 onwards: in 1901 there were 0.08 divorces per 1,000 couples; in 1950 this had risen to 2.8, and by 1987 the figure stood at 12.6 (Stone *Road to Divorce* 435–6).[9] There are many possible reasons for the increase in divorce rates other than the legal reforms; the rise of the self-sufficient individual has resulted in men and women seeking personal pleasure and satisfaction rather than devoting their lives entirely to family or groups; life expectancy has increased and so couples are expected to live together for longer than ever before; and divorce has become so common that it has lost the social stigma that was placed on it at the beginning of the century. That divorce is now commonplace is reflected in children's literature's frequent representation of divorce in texts by, amongst others, Anne Fine and Jacqueline Wilson; if we portray divorce to those whom we assume to be most vulnerable then it is usually a sign that it has lost its stigma.

Figures also suggest a rise in divorce rates after each of the two world wars and again there are several possible causes: women who had been left to care for their children and whose labour had been essential on the home front experienced a greater independence than ever before and many found that their lives had changed to such an extent that they did not want to return to the pre-war years of submission to their husbands – a theme emphasised in Michelle Magorian's *Back Home* (1985). In addition, many soldiers returned so psychologically damaged that they could no longer cope with a marriage, and equally, many women had formed new relationships during their husband's absence. The Second World War also served to separate the family more dramatically than ever before as the evacuation of children, as depicted in Nina Bawden's *Carrie's War* (1973), from the major cities to live with strangers in rural areas contradicted all the legislation, literature and ideology that aimed to promote the nuclear family. The family, then, has seen dramatic changes in its make-up during the twentieth century with divorce becoming a part of everyday life, yet the legislation in 1969 which made divorce more obtainable was, paradoxically, intended to legitimise new relationships and promote the family, for it allowed unhappy couples to divorce and establish or legitimise new relationships, and create a traditional family for any children who were products of new relationships.

The move towards smaller families – as illustrated by the fact that the neighbours pitied the unusual Ruggles family for being so large in Eve Garnett's *The Family From One End Street* (1937) – has often been seen as the greatest change in the family over the century (Davidoff *et al.* 187). But, it can also be argued that families have begun to increase in numbers again, with step-siblings and step-parents making up what are often termed 'blended' families. Contemporary children's literature reflects this changing pattern with its concern regarding the relationships between children and step-parents, half-siblings and so on, as evident in Anne Fine's *Goggle Eyes* (1989), Gillian Cross's *Wolf* (1990), Jacqueline Wilson's *The Suitcase Kid* (1992) and many more. And yet there remains always a hope in much children's fiction that family life will adhere again to an ideal, one in which all relatives communicate effectively, and largely one which has two heterosexual parents; there is a constant harking back to an ideal of the nuclear family which appears to lie deep in our psyche both in the literature that we give to our children and in our everyday lives.

While the concept of the nuclear family remains strong, there is in reality an increasing acceptance of alternative families, and some critics have also pointed out the return to the growing importance of the extended family. With the majority of mothers now returning to work while their children still require childcare, grandparents are often called upon to look after the offspring; indeed, social services also often call on grandparents to take custody of the children if the children are deemed to be at risk from their own parents (Hardyment *The Nuclear Family is Dead* 7). Further, it is no longer unheard of for the father to provide full-time childcare, and fathers are now expected to embrace fatherhood and the accompanying household and parenting chores. Specific roles within the family have, as we have seen, become more blurred in recent years, and while we still depend ideologically on the myth of family we have also begun to recognise its diversity. Strange then, with these extensive material developments, that the nuclear family with all its ideals and specifications should maintain such a cultural hold over our imaginations, for there is no reason why the nuclear family is any more likely to exist for eternity than any other family type that existed before it and no reason why it is better or worse than any other way of organising our society into groups. We are left, then, with an age-old paradox: the family has both changed beyond recognition over the last 200 years and yet in many ways our approach and attitude towards the family has hardly changed at all.

Much the same is true of the representation of the family in children's fiction and the following two chapters emphasise this dichotomy. While the chapters chart the material changes, they focus on the dominant static ideology of the family implicit in children's fiction. Foucauldian principles of discipline are evident in the constant promotion of a particular type of family, while those families that deviate from this ideal are depicted as other. Even in the more modern texts the traditional family is depicted as desirable as it provides a foundational ideology to even the most unconventional of fictional families. The families in children's literature have by no means always been perfect, and tensions are evident in the most seemingly tranquil families, but what the following chapters show through their chronological approach is that the influence of the ideal, of the myth, is more significant than the reality. The conclusions reached in this chapter and those reached in the following two are in fact remarkably similar; we remain obsessed with the type of family to which we all aspire, the type of family we should promote to our children. Adults cling to the notion of the perfect family promulgated by society and there seems to be little chance that adults will present their children with anything that contradicts this illusion. Children's literature, despite its potential to be revolutionary, is, in terms of family, chronically conventional.

Chapter Two
1818–1914 Depictions of the Nineteenth and Turn of the Century Family: From a Good Beating to the Flight to Neverland

The family is central to children's literature. The sanctity of the family home, the warmth and domesticity implicit in the very word itself, the continuity and security inherent in the cultural – and literary – construction of family, are often contrasted with the insecurity and unpleasantness of the wider world. Catherine Sinclair's *Holiday House* (1839) informs its readers that, in idealised form, good families are 'a little world in themselves' (242), and it is this microcosmic concept of the family as a perfectible version of an imperfect world that has shaped children's literature for nearly two centuries.

This chapter charts the changes in the representation of the family from 1818–1914, focusing firstly on the move from texts that concentrate on adults to those that privilege the child, a literary shift that paralleled the changing position of the child in real life. The majority of the families in this chapter could be classified as middle or upper class and this is in many ways fitting in terms of the audience that nineteenth-century children's literature was designed to address. Margaret Sidney's *Five Little Peppers and How They Grew* (1881) is concerned with the poverty stricken Pepper family and yet it is discovered that the family have blood connections with the wealthy and fittingly named Kings and thus the conclusion of the text sees the end of the Peppers' financial anxieties. British texts that deal with the poor tend to do so with a somewhat patronising need to save them. In Hesba Stretton's *Jessica's First Prayer* (1867) Jessica is saved from her illness and drunken mother by Daniel and the Minister at the Church. The poor are acknowledged but Jessica's mother is demonised for her neglect of her daughter who has grown up without religious instruction. Jessica herself adheres to the middle-class notion of the child as the saviour of the man as she redeems Daniel and thus the story becomes as much about the middle-class man's redemption as the poor child's move to the more comfortable middle classes. Charles Kingsley's *The Water Babies* also deals with the poor orphan Tom who has been exploited as a chimney sweep by the evil, aptly named, Mr Grimes; again here the narrative slips in to didacticism, and while it serves to address concerns about child labour and neglect in the nineteenth century, it also posits the possibility of Tom's redemption though education and middle-class values. While there are representations of the working classes in nineteenth-century children's literature they are generally written from a middle-class perspective as working-class children are encouraged to forget their past heritage and emulate the values of their new middle-class protectors. As Jessica 'saved' Daniel and thus the two established their own family as Daniel became Jessica's guardian, there is an increasing presence within nineteenth-century family stories of the theme of the child as saviour of the adult. Alongside this there is a sense that the family is becoming ever-more complex as we see a change from the conventional familial roles depicted in Mary Martha Sherwood's *The History of the Fairchild Family* (1818) to the emotional complexities that shape Charlotte M. Yonge's *The Daisy Chain* (1856) and the ambiguous role of the father in J.M. Barrie's *Peter Pan* (1911). But these changes are set against firmly established patterns and ideals that remain, I contend, unchanged in this period: the devotion to family; the need on the part of the child character to satisfy and gratify parental figures; the venture out into the world and the idealised return to the bosom of family; the sibling 'pecking order' so redolent of Foucauldian theories of discipline; and the constant promotion of a specific ideological and idealised family unit.

1818–1839 the Early to Mid-Nineteenth Century

Sherwood's *The History of the Fairchild Family* (1818), Catherine Sedgwick's *Home* (1835), and Sinclair's *Holiday House* (1839) are all very insular texts which concentrate on the family; the action usually takes place within the family and is the concern of the family members. While the texts have the centrality of the family in common, certain changes and developments are also evident as we read through them chronologically. The Evangelical stance in *The History of the Fairchild Family*, which represents children as having 'wicked ambition' and encourages them to be strictly managed and well-behaved, is gradually replaced with a greater acceptance of children's tendency towards mischief. By the time we reach *Holiday House* the influence of Jean-Jacques Rousseau's thinking on childhood is evident as the text emphasises the children's need to examine and acknowledge their own virtues and vices and makes clear the importance of childhood in its own right. The child characters in both *Home* and *Holiday House* are beginning to be allowed to ask questions and are at times portrayed as better natured than some of the adults who surround them, thus reflecting the concerns of Rousseau and Locke with the child as a figure of adult redemption. Further, the conventional nuclear family evident in the two earlier texts has vanished in *Holiday House* as the children are brought up by a rather eccentric uncle and their grandmother after their mother's death and during their father's absence.

There remain, though, several constants in the three texts. Hard work, frugality and honesty are all portrayed as essential to the sanctity of family – as they are in several contemporary texts – and a theme of instruction runs through all the texts, for all are posited as manuals intended to influence and benefit their readers' families. The texts have in common a desire for order, as everyone has their place in the strict power structures that shape the family. These power structures reflect both the Foucauldian concerns discussed in the previous chapter and Christian dogma: there is a ruler (God/Father) and the children are taught within the family to adhere to his rules. The family remains the perfect place in which to ensure that children become obedient subjects. As John Rowe Townsend points out:

> the moral stories which dominated "official" children's fiction until well into the nineteenth century were rooted in some or all of the same attitudes. Children must obey and take instruction from their parents; the aim of such instruction was to instil religion and morality and indeed, for many writers, to save souls from hell. (78–9)

While *Holiday House* may seem radical in comparison to *The History of the Fairchild Family* the changes are not all-encompassing, for the divide between adult and child, while slightly more flexible, remains intact. Certainly, adults are still empowered in the texts: both Mr Fairchild and, in *Holiday House,* Grandmamma take care to emphasise to the children that parents are representative of God within the family. Whatever differences there may be in tone and attitude between the texts, essentially divine authority and order must be maintained.

The History of the Fairchild Family establishes a definite order of precedence within the narrative, as the parents are named before the children and the children are then introduced in order of age – a trait that is common even in recent children's literature. A certain type of idealised family is promoted, and, while religion is central to the text in a way that no longer usually applies to current children's fiction, it serves to teach certain morals and behaviour patterns that are still encouraged today. For example, the Fairchild children may be described as naughty, but they remain, on the whole, respectful and considerate. Subsequent fathers in children's literature have always had difficulty emulating Mr Fairchild and his god-like status: he is strict, and yet also warm and attentive, never unfair, and almost always in control of his emotions. There are few later fathers who are given this godly position in children's literature and it can be argued that fatherhood, though always important, is not celebrated in this unquestioning manner again until we meet Arthur Ransome's father-figure Commander Walker in the 'Swallows and Amazons' series of the 1930s and 1940s.

The History of the Fairchild Family presents itself as a 'practical moral guide to family'(Tucker and Gamble 8). Its position as moral educator as well as a good story is evident from the opening paragraph:

> Mr and Mrs Fairchild had three children: Lucy, who was about nine years old when these stories began; Emily who was next in age; and Henry, who was between six and seven [. . .] They did not wish their dear little children to be handsome, or rich, or powerful in the world; all that they desired for them was, the blessing of God; without which all this world can give is nothing worth. (1)

David Grylls explains the idea of rank inherent in Victorian society thus:

> In nature, man ruled over animals, and God ruled over man; in society, kings and governors ruled over their subjects, husbands over their wives, parents over children. To flout or confound the system of order was to violate God's decree. Part of Adam's sin was to put Eve over God. (24)

It is certain that neither Mr Fairchild nor the omniscient narrator will make the same mistake as Adam. The father's position is never truly questioned within the text and is only briefly tested by Henry when he refuses to learn his Latin. Henry is exiled from the family circle because his rebellion has incurred the wrath of God/Father and, on apologising, he is reminded that parental power is absolute: '[. . .] and I hope that what you have suffered these two days will be a warning to you never to rebel against your father' (Sherwood 160). Partly, this represents the patriarchal power of the period, but it also responds to certain anxieties concerning the questioning of the status quo. Mrs Fairchild's assertion that each child should remain in his/her God-given place, as 'ambition makes people unhappy, and discontented with what they are and what they have' (Sherwood 61), demonstrates not only the importance of order within the family, but of social order within the wider world.

The History of the Fairchild Family demonstrates by example correct social behaviour, an awareness of social position and social boundaries, and so supports the social status quo. Further, as literature, it acts to produce the obedient subject through ideology; it has a disciplinary function in Foucauldian terms. But there are examples of the breakdown of social and family order in *The History of the Fairchild Family*. To break away from order is to challenge convention and to question authority, something that is usually discouraged in children's fiction. In *The History of the Fairchild Family*, when their parents are away Emily and Lucy neglect to do their chores and consequently are reprimanded as their day ends in trauma (Sherwood 44–50). The literature controls the child reader by example, simultaneously empowering the parent and reinforcing religion and a patriarchal system of government, and it does this by constant reference to the family with an emphasis on how the family should conduct itself and, by implication, how the individual should behave in society.

This emphasis on how families should behave is still apparent in recent children's fiction, for specific systems of behaviour are often encouraged. The privileging of one way of conducting a family over another is a frequent theme in children's literature, from Mary Martha Sherwood's writing to that of Judy Blume. A bad family, by example, simply reasserts notions of the dominant ideology; in deviating away from what is constructed as the norm it becomes other and as a result serves to promote the qualities of the 'good' traditional family. It is in looking at other families that the Fairchilds' pious morality is most evident, for the Burke family, the Nobles, and even Mrs Fairchild's own aunts, are described only to accentuate the worthiness of the Fairchilds. The children are shocked that their mamma's aunts would play cards and go out, that Augusta Noble's parents spoil her, and that breakfast time at the Burkes is a chaotic affair.

This sets a standard for later children's books, as can be seen in the account of the family whose son disgraces them in L.M. Alcott's *Little Women* (1868) or the Moffats in the same text, who try to lead Meg into a world of vanity and loose morals, or, to take more recent examples, Judy Blume's *Superfudge* (1980) in which Fudge's friend's family are frowned upon as they watch television while eating, and in J.K. Rowling's 'Harry Potter' series (1997–2007) where the Dursleys are unfavourably compared to the Weasleys at every turn. Family is a strict affair, and Mary Martha Sherwood emphasises that there is only one kind of family permissible if the children are to be brought up in the correct manner, fearing God and respecting their parents. The constant comparison of families is still used to promote certain ideals in modern children's literature, and while the difference in the tones and styles between nineteenth and twentieth-century texts might disguise this similarity, the didacticism still hovers below the surface of much writing for children.

Children's literature is very rarely only for children and *The History of the Fairchild Family* is no exception. Both parents and children are often preached to in children's texts and while in Sherwood's work this seems obvious to a twenty-first-century critic, that same critic might not recognise it so quickly in Anne Fine's writing. In *The History of the Fairchild Family* parent readers are warned that 'poor children who have not good fathers and mothers to take care of them do very wicked things' (Sherwood 50) and this concept is reinforced when Augusta Noble, who has not been brought up in the fear of God, is burnt to death in a house fire. In contrast, while Miranda's maternal musings in Fine's *Madame Doubtfire* (1987) are less dramatic they still subtly remind adult readers of their duties to their children:

> All too frequently in the last few years, she [Miranda] had been forced to regard herself as an unresponsive and distant parent [. . .] too often too bloody tired, to sit and listen with any pleasure to her children's conversation. (85)

Both sections are aimed at the adult; both concentrate on adult fears, and both dictate certain ideals about how to care for a family. While the Fine passage recognises problems in the main protagonists' family as opposed to *The History of the Fairchild Family* which criticises other families, both serve as exemplars of what to avoid when managing a family. While the Sherwood family could be classed as upper class as the father does not have to work, Fine's Hilliards sit rather differently on the social scale yet both families are encouraged to adhere to similar ideals. Of course, there are stark differences between the texts, but the emphasis on educating parents remains an important part of our literature. *Madame Doubtfire* remains a text primarily aimed at children with the odd nod to parents, but *The History of the Fairchild Family* can be seen as the opposite, an adult's manual on family with the odd nod to children. Although *The History of Fairchild Family* may seem alien to a modern readership, when we look beyond the details to the wider messages and aims behind them we can begin to recognise the same conservative attitudes that are still present in more recent generations of texts for, while religion is now rarely mentioned in children's literature the ideal family, in which individuals cohabit contentedly and with mutual respect, remains key.

Home, separated by seventeen years and the Atlantic Ocean from *The History of the Fairchild Family*, retains some of Mary Martha Sherwood's didacticism; the tone, though, is somewhat warmer. The children are described in a manner more reminiscent of Rousseau's works than the deeply Calvinist theme which is at the forefront of Sherwood's work. Haddy, in *Home*, is, for instance, described as having the 'unperverted mind of a child', in distinct contrast to the innately sinful nature of children emphasised in *The History of the Fairchild Family* (Sedgwick 30). Similarly, while a sense of order is certainly prevalent in *Home*, the children can begin to question the adults:

> "Aunt Betsey," called out little Haddy, who unluckily observed her aunt trespassing against one of the ordinances of the table, "it is not proper to use the butter-knife!" [. . .] "I wonder which is worst," she [Aunt Betsey] replied, "to use my own knife as I was brought up to or for a little saucebox like you to set me right." (Sedgwick 31)

The child, in this case, is better mannered than the adult; Haddy uses the correct title for Aunt Betsey, whereas Aunt Betsey labels her a 'little saucebox'. Haddy has been brought up to comply with the custom of the dinner table whereas Aunt Betsey ignores it. Here, the adult is not always right, and this is a theme picked up in L.M Montgomery's *Anne of Green Gables* (1908) when Mrs Rachel Lynde offends Anne by labelling her 'ugly' (72). Equally, it is common to find children who are more polite than adults in modern children's literature. The well-intentioned child is able to question the bad-tempered adult who does not listen to advice or comply with the orders and customs of the family. The child is becoming more central to the literature, and while, as yet, the child is far from empowered, there remains a sense that he/she is beginning to hold a more prominent position within the family in children's literature.

The major difference between *Home* and *The History of the Fairchild Family* is in *Home's* portrayal of the Romantic child. In addition there also exists a cultural divide in that in *Home* the children are expected to work within the family more than the Fairchild children were, and in *Home* the emphasis is on practical help rather than lessons and religion. This work ethic serves to create a more harmonious environment as Mrs Barclay explains to Aunt Betsey:

> Ah, if all the individuals of the human family would do their part, there would be no wanderers, no outcasts. The chain of mutual dependence would be preserved and unbroken, strong and bright. All would be linked together in the bonds of natural affection and Christian love, – the bonds of unity and peace. (Sedgwick 102)

Again, didacticism is evident as the text addresses the consciences of adults and children. There is something almost elegiac about Mrs Barclay's tract but the tone is somewhat patronising; the Barclays know best, and place themselves in a morally superior position. While the tone is distinctively nineteenth-century, the message is unchanging for it is not so very far from the message at the end of Anne Fine's *The Granny Project* (1983), where the children and parents realise that they should have compromised and worked with each other in order for each member of the family to share in the care of granny.

Catherine Sinclair's *Holiday House* (1839) comes at the end of this section partly because of its publication date, but also because it is a transitional text. The recognisable theme of Godly parents is still evident and the text maintains a theme of instruction, yet the concentration on the nuclear family as seen in Sherwood and Sedgwick's texts has vanished, and the focus has turned towards the individual child in a manner that sets the scene for Nesbit and Burnett later in the century. Despite these changes and the fact that the children are brought up by their uncle and grandmother, *Holiday House* remains very family orientated, and consequently the institution of the family is defended at every turn. The major shift is that the children are not always portrayed in the company of adults and as a result childhood is celebrated in its own right. Dennis Butts points out that the works of Locke and Rousseau were influencing European perspectives on childhood at this time and goes on to argue that Romantic reflections on childhood by Blake and Dickens were a product of this ('Introduction'). Indeed, Charles Dickens' *Nicholas Nickleby* and *Holiday House* were published in the same year and both attach much significance and emotional investment to the figure of the child. The child is becoming central to the family and, as David Rudd suggests, *Holiday House* can be read as an 'exploration of different conceptions of the child and the consequences of these for the rearing of children' ('The Froebellious Child' 54). While *Holiday House* is similar to the previous texts in its interest in how children should be brought up, it differs in its concern for the actual child.

Humphrey Carpenter and Mari Pritchard suggest that *Holiday House* was the first family story in which 'entertainment played as large a part as instruction'(256). It is impossible to forget that instruction remains an essential part of the text as the author's introductory epigraph reminds the reader that 'of all the paper I have blotted, I have written nothing without the intention of some good' (Sinclair 5). *Holiday House*'s didactic tone is firmly directed at the adult rather than the child reader as it reasserts Rousseau's own adult-centred message concerning the break-up of family:[1]

> Very young children are thrust into preparatory school – older boys go to distant academies – youths to college and young men are shipped off abroad, while who among them can say his heart is in his own home? Parents, in the meantime, finding no occupation or amusement in educating their children [. . .] If people could only know what is the best happiness of this life, it certainly depends on being loved by those who we belong to; for nothing can be called peace on Earth which does not consist in family affection, built in a strong foundation of religion and morality. (Sinclair 243)

The initial listing of institutions, which steal the child from the home, suggests a certain inevitability as the order of society intervenes with the order of the family and thus the 'natural' laws of God. The unity of the family, the text suggests, is under constant siege; the positive traits of the families in Sherwood, Sedgwick and Sinclair is their ability to stand strong against, rather than with, the institutions of society. This attitude is also evident in texts like Eve Garnett's *The Family from One End Street* (1937) or John Rowe Townsend's *Gumble's Yard* (1961), where the families avoid state interference, preferring to deal with matters themselves in order to maintain family solidarity.

Holiday House implies that state interference in family is contaminating – it disturbs the 'naturalness' of the family. The same attitude is evident in the portrayal of childhood: too many rules and infringements damage what it constructs as the purity of childhood. The children are allowed to be mischievous, but it is emphasised that they are inherently good. The children in *Holiday House* may start a fire which then burns down part of the house, invite friends round without permission, and cut off their own hair, but Laura would 'rather have died than told a lie' and Harry selflessly saves Laura from the bull when 'many selfish people would have run away alone'(Sinclair 54; 144). Gillian Avery's comment that the children are simply destructive is, in the light of this, a little unfair as emphasis is placed on justice and on treating children with respect ('The Family Story' 339). Here *Holiday House* is similar to *The Granny Project* as it pursues the matter of family learning and co-operation, deconstructing the myth that all nineteenth-century children's texts promote the idea that the children should be seen and not heard. Further, following Rousseau's idea that children should be allowed to 'taste all the innocent pleasures' of their age rather than be forced to study the Bible (374), in *Holiday House* Laura and Harry are free to be naughty in their childhood but by the story's conclusion they have gone through their rites of passage, becoming adults as they watch over the death of their brother Jack.

All three of these nineteenth-century texts tell the tale of the journey of the family. This journey is one of self-realisation in which, with the help of the adults who surround them, the children grow from selfish, perhaps slightly wild children, into mature, Christian adults. The move to adulthood is often marked in nineteenth-century fiction by the loss of a member of the family. Harry and Laura in *Holiday House* begin to mature after the death of their brother who, Rudd suggests, acts as a Christ-like figure sacrificing his life for the good of his siblings (The Froebellious Child 66). This can also be seen in later texts: in *Little Women* Jo becomes 'quite a lady' and Meg becomes engaged after the near-death experience of both their father and sister. Such an experience serves to strengthen the idea of family; the family unit is represented as essential and god-given and as a result all members must do their utmost to preserve it. This notion of almost losing, or actually losing, a family member and thereby reinforcing the importance of the whole family is equally evident in modern children's literature, where death is replaced with divorce or separation. In Fine's *Madame Doubtfire* or Jacqueline Wilson's *The Suitcase Kid* (1992), when family unity is under threat it becomes even more precious, and the characters must learn to work and co-operate with each other. These three early books lay the foundations for the thousands of texts that succeed them, for while some elements become archaic and patterns of change are never smooth, the major concerns with regard to family remain timeless.

1856–1881 the Mid- to Late Nineteenth Century

In 'How Children's Lit Changed' Dennis Butts argues that although the 1860s, with the publication of Charles Kingsley's *The Water Babies* (1863) and Lewis Carroll's *Alice's Adventures in Wonderland* (1865), is often heralded as the start of the first golden age of children's literature, significant developments were actually taking place as early as the 1840s. This decade saw a variety of texts come to the market: Edward Lear's verse; Richard Henry Horne's *Memoirs of a London Doll* (1846); Captain Marryatt's adventure stories, including *The Children of the New Forest* (1847); and, as Butts points out, Barbara Hoffland's domestic stories dealt with bankruptcy and a useless father ('How Children's Lit Changed' 154). Literature for children no longer had to be so serious and full of reason, and it began to emphasise the importance of emotion and feelings. Butts suggests that there was a relaxed didacticism in the 1840s, although I consider it important not to overestimate this; relaxed didacticism is still didacticism, and while the texts discussed in this section are more subtle than *Holiday House* or *The History of the Fairchild Family* they still covertly promote a certain way of life ('How Children's Lit Changed' 160). The promotion of established ideals concerning families in Charlotte M. Yonge's *The Daisy Chain* (1856), Louisa M. Alcott's *Little Women* (1868), and Margaret Sidney's *Five Little Peppers and How They Grew* remains evident but it is also important to acknowledge the growing complexities within these families and an increasing interest in the individual characters and their feelings; an interest which continues to feature in contemporary children's literature.

The Daisy Chain has been somewhat overlooked in modern histories of children's literature. While there are several editions of *Little Women* or Susan Coolidge's famous 'Katy' series in print, *The Daisy Chain* is not offered by any mainstream publisher.[2] The text's significance, however, is paramount as it lays the foundations for both *Little Women* and the 'Katy' series: in both the Carr and May families, in the 'Katy' series and *The Daisy Chain* respectively, the children are brought up by their widowed father – who, in both stories, happens to be a doctor – and the families are run by the eldest sister who lies paralysed in her bed (Avery *Behold The Child* 168). In addition, as Butts and Briggs point out, Alcott's Jo March owes a great deal to Ethel May (134), as Ethel, like Jo, is described as being 'just like one of the boys', has difficulty controlling her eagerness and ambition, enjoys studying, and finds it hard to meet the standards of tidiness and delicacy that is expected of her sex (Yonge 73). We can see in the portrayal of Ethel, who is described on the first page as 'trembling from head to foot with restrained eagerness, as she tried to curb her tone into requisite civility' (Yonge 3), that Peter Hunt's suggestion that Yonge 'reinforced the domestic role of women, as pallid mothers or dutiful daughters' is fitting (Hunt *An Introduction* 52). The similarities are stark and the images of constraint and order remind the readers that while these families may seem more liberal than the Fairchilds, an underlying subtext of control remains.

But *The Daisy Chain* is also striking because of its differences from other nineteenth-century texts; in many ways it is a text that is ahead of its time – as relevant to the twentieth century as to the nineteenth century. The father perhaps, like the father in *Madame Doubtfire*, questions his own ability, and is portrayed in a sensitive fashion as an individual character rather than just a father; he turns to his eldest daughter for consolation when he feels he has treated his children unfairly: 'A fine father I show myself to these poor children – neglect, helplessness, temper – Oh Maggie!'(Yonge 243). In addition, Dr May no longer sits at the head of the dinner table to carve, forgets Norman's birthday, sometimes avoids the family meal as it is too painful after the death of his wife, and yet he is still described as 'a parent who could not fail to be loved and honoured' (Yonge 152). The father has become real and human, a sympathetic figure but one who retains respect – the family story, it seems, has made room for such a figure. *The Daisy Chain* also shows its diversity in the sympathetic manner in which it addresses Norman's depression after the death of his mother. The depression is treated by Dr May in his medical capacity, but the very fact that it is addressed at all is unusual in nineteenth-century children's literature. *The Daisy Chain* acknowledges complications and weaknesses within its main family in a similar way to contemporary children's literature, demonstrating that nineteenth-century children's books did not always present perfect families. What is striking is that the ideal of the family, as in modern children's literature, remains a constant subtext, and it is no surprise that near the end of the first volume Harry returns home and says with a sigh 'There's nothing like home' (Yonge 310). The home may not be perfect, but its attractions remain constant.

Little Women, like *The Daisy Chain*, is a text which addresses the weaknesses of its characters – Jo especially – and then goes on to offer solutions which usually depend on self-discipline. The texts promote the ideal family while recognising and, for the most part, overcoming these complications and both families are left under the guidance of one parent for the majority of the text. *Little Women* and *The Daisy Chain* offer complex representations of family, ranging from what seems all-encompassing family warmth to darker subtexts of power and control. Critics cannot agree about *Little Women*: Elizabeth Keyser, from a feminist perspective, argues that it 'abounds in images of constriction, concealment and pain' (53), while John Rowe Townsend states that it 'marks a relaxation of the stiff and authoritarian stereotype of family life' and goes on to suggest that it has the warmth essential to a family story (*Written for Children* 79–80).

In a broad sense, both critics are right; in many ways it seems a warmer text than *The History of the Fairchild Family*, yet it is by no means a revolutionary story:

> They all drew up to the fire, mother in the big chair, with Beth at her feet, Meg and Amy perched on either arm of the chair, and Jo leaning on the back, where no one would see any sign of emotion if the letter should happen to be touching [. . .] only at the end did the writer's heart overflow with fatherly love and longing for the little girls at home. (Alcott 11)

The family is shown huddled close together as the members sit around the chair by the fire, supporting Townsend's reading. Yet the subtext of power and order evident in the text cannot be ignored. The mother is the central figure; she dictates when to read the letter as she saves it for a 'treat after dinner' and physically she is positioned in the centre as she sits in the big chair surrounded by her children. Beth, being the most submissive, sits at her mother's feet, where she is to stay for her ambition is, 'to stay home safe with father and mother' (Alcott 200). Meg and Amy sit on the arms of the chair, prominent, yet not quite central, and Jo plays her 'fatherly' role as she leans on the back in order to conceal any possible emotion. The children have set positions in this scene which echo their roles within the text, and these positions are very much part of an ordered, somewhat constraining pattern. Let it not be forgotten that the letter they are all sharing is from the hands of their father: it is the father's written words which gather the family together, warrant their actions, and illustrate his powerful position in the family.

This subliminal assertion of patriarchal authority can also be seen in later texts such as Arthur Ransome's 'Swallows and Amazons' series. In *Little Women*, Jo reverts to her feminine role at the mere mention of her father: 'I'll try and be what he loves to call me, "a little woman" and not be rough and wild, but do my duty here instead of wanting to be somewhere else' (Alcott 12). She is constricted. The text implies that, especially for a woman, it is wrong to want to be anywhere other than home and, in so doing, declares its own disciplinary stance. The home is constantly promoted in *Little Women*: Meg is glad to return home after her stay with the Moffats, and while the children do leave home and travel later in the series, emphasis is always laid on their return to the home and family. Child readers are constantly reminded of the advantages of returning home, for this is what the adult wants to remind the child as, from the adult perspective, if the child remains in the confines of home he/she remains under adult control.[3]

Staying with the American theme, *Five Little Peppers and How They Grew* was published thirteen years later than *Little Women* and follows the formulaic story in which the small, poor family is 'saved' by richer relatives whom the family has recently, and rather co-incidentally, rediscovered. But this new encounter is something of a mixed blessing as the family gains wealth but in doing so, sacrifices its feeling of cosiness. In contrast to *Little Women* the Peppers cannot return 'home' to the 'little brown house' after the family has moved into the Kings' mansion, and this is seen as a loss. Essentially, the moral of *Five Little Peppers and How They Grew* is that wealth derives from a happy family:

> "Mother's rich enough," ejaculated Mrs Pepper, her bright, black eyes glistening with delight as the noisy troop filed back to their bread and potatoes; "if we can only keep together, dears, and grow up good so that the little brown house won't be ashamed of us, that's all I ask." (Sidney 28)

Mrs Pepper's eyes still shine as she enjoys watching the 'troop' eat noisily. This is in distinct contrast to *The History of the Fairchild Family* and *Home* as the children are encouraged in their noise and appetites which signify their apparent healthiness. What is constant in all the texts is the unity and love of the family, which is illustrated to the full when they sit down to share food. The mother, while separated from the 'troop' as she overlooks them, talks about the family as a single unit, as she insists on them keeping together. The little brown house is personified into a kind of father figure; in *Little Women* the girls want to be good in order to make their father proud, but here, in the absence of a father, the house shelters the family and must not be shamed. It is an ambivalent situation then when the characters have to 'empty [. . .] the little brown house into the big one' (Sidney 359). On the one hand the family's economic difficulties are over, but on the other the children cannot return, as in *Little Women*, to their idealistic, albeit poor, childhood home. While in a conventional sense *Five Little Peppers and How They Grew* reaches a happy ending, there remains a distinct sense of a lost ideal. Poverty, in the family story, almost always acts as a unifying bond; all have to work together to find a solution. The Peppers are effectively submerged into the richer Kings and, as is suggested by the siblings' quarrels that occur for the first time in the King house, the strength of the Peppers' family, epitomised in their home, is beginning to dissolve.

It seems that children's literature cannot face leaving its families in the reality of poverty. While Avery argues that this outcome would not have been provided by a British writer, the next generation of British children's literature writers like Nesbit and Frances Hodgson Burnett adopt this Cinderella-style story-line in which the 'Fairy Godmother' appears in the form of a rich relative (*Behold the Child* 169). As in 'Cinderella', the story closes with the family's acquisition of wealth, leaving the assumption that the future will only bring happiness. But there also exists a sense of loss as the small family (which in contrast to Cinderella's was a happy one) is absorbed by richer, more powerful relatives.

1886–1914 the Turbulent Turn of the Century

J.M. Barrie's *Peter Pan* (1911), Kenneth Grahame's *The Wind in the Willows* (1908), *Anne of Green Gables* (1908) and several other domestic stories written by Edith Nesbit and Frances Hodgson Burnett represent some of the most well-known children's literature. These texts will be familiar, even if not in literary form, to a large part of the British population, with films, television series and the accompanying merchandise still appearing on our shop shelves. Thacker and Webb suggest that '[r]ather than merely a point of smooth transition, the *fin de siècle* can be seen as a period characterised by disruptions and conflicts that had been building up throughout the late nineteenth century' (50). In the light of this observation we might expect the family structures at the turn of the century to be brought into question, to be shaken from the fairly strong foundations that were established for them in the previous century but, while some changes are evident, they are far from revolutionary.

These texts share a concern for the child and childhood and so it follows that they also imply certain values concerning the group that is meant to preserve and protect the child. As in *Five Little Peppers and How They Grew*, many of these domestic narratives follow a formulaic fairy tale structure as the orphaned or poor children are discovered to be, metaphorically speaking, princes or princesses after all: Little Lord Fauntleroy is assured of his rightful position after a legal case which exposes an impostor; the Treasure Seekers are assured of a secure position in the upper classes as they move in with their rich uncle; and Sara Crewe in Frances Hodgson Burnett's *A Little Princess* (1905) is returned to her privileged position in the upper classes as the Indian gentleman takes her in. These somewhat unlikely conclusions function to reassure, as social boundaries are eroded in this period and as the Empire begins to show signs of fracture, class distinctions are maintained in children's texts.[4] This literature reaffirms the notion emphasised in *The History of the Fairchild Family* that everyone has their place. It just happens that the majority of children's literature's heroes and heroines seem to belong in the middle or upper classes.

While the one-parent family is common in Burnett and Nesbit's texts, the yearning for two adults of authority is apparent as the closure of all the texts except *The Secret Garden* sees the making of a two adult, if not two-parent, family. The eponymous protagonist of *Anne of Green Gables* is eventually welcomed into a two-adult family and, even in the child world of Neverland in *Peter Pan*, Peter and Wendy become the lost boys' adoptive parents for a while. In the light of this parental emphasis it is a little strange that children's literature criticism often argues that parents were becoming superfluous in the twentieth century and that fathers could at best hope for 'ineffectuality' in this period (Dusinberre quoted in Nikolajeva *From Mythic to Linear* 23; Nelson 'Introduction' 98). Certainly, fathers are not always perfect: Wendy's father is presented as a self-centred fool who banishes himself to the dog kennel as he blames himself for errors leading to Peter Pan taking Wendy and the boys away from home to Neverland. Mr Craven in *The Secret Garden* is, like the father in *Holiday House*, travelling abroad after the death of his wife and is therefore absent for the majority of the text. But I suspect that the father has not lost his position entirely. What has happened is that the depiction of the father has developed since the stolid example of Mr Fairchild: the father has human flaws –as is evident in *The Daisy Chain* – but this does not mean that he is not regarded positively in the texts.

The father is, in these turn-of-the-century texts, weaker than Mr Fairchild or Mr Barclay, but his own character is given more consideration than in the early nineteenth century. It is significant that the children in these texts still strongly desire to please their fathers (or stand in fathers who may be uncles or grandfathers), as can be seen when in *The Railway Children*, *The Secret Garden*, *Little Lord Fauntleroy*, and *The Story of the Treasure Seekers* the children seek to alleviate their father's troubles. While a distinct parent/child divide remains in the texts of this period, the children are portrayed as more free to converse with adults. Relationships are becoming increasingly flexible as siblings negotiate and even help to alleviate their parents' awkward situations. The family ideal remains as influential as ever.

From the very beginning, and indeed for much of the story, the main characters in *Little Lord Fauntleroy* and *The Secret Garden* live in what could be termed dysfunctional families: Cedric is physically separated from his widowed mother by his paternal grandfather, and Mary Lennox is orphaned (although we are told that her parents never loved her anyway) and sent to live with her uncle, who leaves both Mary and her 'invalid' cousin, Colin, in the care of servants.

But by the conclusion of both texts we see the beginnings of united, happy families. The narratives are concerned – as they are in the late twentieth century – with how the families transformed themselves, and here we see that these later texts are still tracts that dictate to both adults and children how families should, and more importantly should not, be managed. The family at the turn of the century, and indeed in our contemporary texts, is a location in which adults as well as children grow emotionally, and while many early and mid-nineteenth century conventions remain, the literature in this period is beginning to acknowledge and represent the need for parental growth and development. The influence of Rousseau's writing on Burnett is evident as responsibility not only for restoration of the family but also adult redemption is attributed to the figure of the child. Sara Thornton's argument refers to texts from the 1840s but is equally applicable to Burnett's texts for children. As she explains, in literature '[t]he adult world must be redeemed by the child, who is seen as having access to a primitive or lost state which it can restore to us. The child is considered as a pure point of origin'(130).

This is exactly what happens in Burnett's texts. We see Mr Craven in *The Secret Garden* revived, and thus returned to the heart of family, by the sight of his son healthy and walking in the garden, and Cedric in *Little Lord Fauntleroy* trans-forms his grandfather who 'had been so selfish himself that he had missed all the pleasures of seeing unselfishness in others' and, as a result of this self-realisation, the grandfather resolves his problems with his daughter-in-law and the family is united (Burnett *Little Lord Fauntleroy* 75). The children are given a more central role in the family than in nineteenth-century literature, and they are seen as key to the restoration of the family. In many ways this pattern continues well into the twentieth century with texts such as Nina Bawden's *Carrie's War* (1973) and Anne Fine's *Madame Doubtfire* (1987) where the children also impel the adults to reflect on their own behaviour. Contemporary children's literature makes adult characters re-assess themselves and they do this by giving the child characters the voice of reason, as in Fine's *The Granny Project*. The lessons regarding the importance of the family remain constant as we see the same values being promoted again and again; the family should behave in certain ways but from this moment on the adult should also take note of the virtues and wisdom of the child.

In Edith Nesbit's *The Story of the Treasure Seekers* (1899) this pattern, in which children's virtues redeem their elders, is continued. The Bastable children charm their uncle to such an extent that he asks them and so their father to live with him and thus their father's financial worries are brought to an end. While as in *Five Little Peppers and How They Grew* and *Little Lord Fauntleroy* there exists some regret as the original family home is consumed by the larger, richer one, at the same time the family is seen as whole again: the new house has a portrait of the mother on the wall suggesting that the family is as close to becoming complete as possible. The complete family is seen as the epitome of the happy ending, reinforcing specific ideological concepts of what families should be.

Nesbit's *The Railway Children* concludes with the father's return in what Hunt terms the 'sentimental climax, perhaps the apotheosis of the Victorian mode' (*An Introduction* 92). The conclusions in these turn-of-the-century texts contrast in some ways with what has come before them as the stories make pertinent points about the parent/child divide. Erika Rothwell observes that 'adults and children seem to occupy separate spheres' in *The Story of the Treasure Seekers* (62). Certainly, a definite divide between adult and child is visible as Oswald remarks that adults very rarely say sorry and that they use 'don't' more than any other word (Nesbit *Treasure Seekers* 149, 203). The text is complex then, as it works on many different levels: children and adults are apparently separate, and yet the children seem able to negotiate with adults more than in earlier texts; the adventures focus on the child and yet at times the narrative almost makes an authoritative wink at the adult reader (the adult reader is aware that the 'noble' editor as the children name him, is in fact, a tabloid journalist who patronises the children for example) (Rothwell 62); and children, while quarrelling amongst themselves, still engineer the solutions to the problems facing family unity.[5]

Although the family and its survival remain the priority in *The Story of the Treasure Seekers*, the relationship between parents and children has elements of role reversal. It seems that the children are beginning to take responsibility for their parents in a manner which is particularly reminiscent of later twentieth-century texts like John Rowe Townsend's *Gumble's Yard* (1961) or Gillian Cross' *Wolf* (1990). The father's lack of intervention in the Bastable children's adventures has been read as permitting an increased freedom for the child (Avery 'The Family Story' 340; Tucker and Gamble 16), but it can also be argued that the children do not wish to burden their father with their own problems, that they are protecting him in the same way, though on a far smaller scale, as Cassie cares for her mother in *Wolf*. This change in the father's position is also evident in *The Railway Children*:

> These three lucky children always had everything they needed: pretty clothes, good fires, a lovely nursery with heaps of toys, and a Mother Goose wallpaper. They had a kind and merry nursemaid, and a dog who was called James, and who was their very own. They also had a Father who was just perfect – never cross, never unjust, and always ready for a game – at least, if any time he was not ready, he always had an excellent reason for it, and explained the reason to the children so interestingly and funnily that they felt sure he couldn't help himself. (Nesbit 2)

For a story that is centred on the wrongful imprisonment of the father, it seems strange that he is presented at the bottom of the list of the children's needs. Before him come the clothes, warmth, toys, wall paper, nursemaid and dog, while the mother's virtues had been described in the previous paragraph. Where in *The History of the Fairchild Family* the description began with the parents, here, the father is far down the list of the children's needs and possessions. Indeed, I suggest that to some extent the parents have become the property of the children, emphasising the increasing importance of the child to the family.

Further, changes in literary technique also begin to appear in *The Story of the Treasure Seekers*. The use of the child Oswald as narrator marks a clear contrast from the authoritarian adult-voiced narratives typical of the earlier nineteenth century. Yet in giving the child characters more textual insight and authority than before, the adult world is in fact reinforced and nineteenth century patterns of children's literature reappear. The children, left to their own devices, practise typical adult activities and maintain prescribed power structures and procedures. Dora, as the eldest sister, makes the others sit in an age-defined row on the floor; Oswald lets H.O. be Captain, but retains the role of Lieutenant for himself as he 'is the eldest next to Dora after all', and Dora is often rebuked by Oswald for behaving as the 'good elder sister'(Nesbit *Treasure Seekers* 16; 18; 112). The structures of the adult world and, indeed, earlier children's fiction, remain very much in place. Dora, as the eldest sister, like Katy from the 'Katy' series and Maggie from *The Daisy Chain*, is the one whom mother delegated to take care of the others (Nesbit *Treasure Seekers* 156), and the children's activities are ordered in terms of age and status in the same way as they are in Ransome's 'Swallows and Amazons' series. These patterns are evident in so many domestic children's stories of both the nineteenth and twentieth century that while we see contradictions and tensions we must also recognise that Nesbit's texts conform to the traditional conventions of the domestic story far more than they actually decry them.

The same can be said with regard to *Peter Pan*. As Peter is barred from his, and eventually every, family it becomes apparent that, despite all the adventures in the Neverland, home and family remain the ultimate desires. As with Nesbit's text, *Peter Pan* appears a revolutionary text as it interrogates family ideology, yet it also adheres to many traditional conventions and ideals. The children are separated from their parents as they seek adventure in the Neverland, and yet their lifestyle in the Neverland is clearly based on adult structures. The relationship between Peter and Wendy is somewhat dubious as they adopt the parental roles, bringing an uncomfortable sexual subtext to the narrative. The mother's role is brought under scrutiny as the story vacillates between Peter's negative concept of the mother and Wendy and the boys' rather Romantic ideas of the maternal. The Darlings' own home life is presented in a humorous fashion: Mr Darling is depicted as weak, pompous, and foolish while the children's nanny, who is portrayed as practical and sensible, is a dog. And yet despite this ambiguity and apparent questioning of family the narrator promises that 'it will all come right in the end' (Barrie *Peter Pan* 53) and the closure of the novel sees the return of the children to their family home.[6] The parents may be foolish, insecure, even unreliable, but they remain loving, and the same ideology of family is adhered to as in earlier children's texts, as Wendy, John and Michael are embraced unquestioningly by their mother. Peter is left immortal, perhaps free, but always returning to borrow Wendy or her female descendants in order to experience a period of mothering: even Peter, in a somewhat convoluted manner, has adopted a mother of sorts. Both the adult and child are reminded that all children need a mother and ideally desire a family. Therefore, a regulating ideology is apparent even in this most seemingly liberal of texts. The complications arising from *Peter Pan* are numerous, and in terms of the family it is simultaneously quite unlike its predecessors, and yet retains many surprising similarities: Victorian morals and traditions prove difficult to banish.

Children's literature is often painfully slow to respond to change, and while the beginning of the twentieth century saw a rise in the number of women campaigning for female emancipation, the heroines in the children's literature of the time remain confined to their domestic roles, as a change in their position may threaten the ideal of the family. The heroines are allowed to dream, and are perhaps even given the freedom to experience temporarily a more independent life, but then they are dragged back into a world of self-sacrifice as they are plunged into domesticity – and this, we are told, makes a happy ending. Wendy is given a choice in *Peter Pan* and has the opportunity to escape the domestic world and embrace adventure, but she chooses, or, to re-work Rose's phrase, perhaps ideology chooses for her, the domestic role – to cook, clean and care for Peter and the boys. Similarly, Jo in Alcott's 'Little Women' trilogy travels but returns to her domestic role; Anne of Green Gables has the chance to go away to study, but stays to care for Marilla; for Susan in the 'Swallows and Amazons' series the adventure is her new adult and maternal domestic role, and even as late as *Gumble's Yard* Sandra undertakes the main role of carer. The child-heroine is destined to develop into a mother and in reiterating this pattern children's literature naturalises families in which women adhere to traditional domestic archetypes.

Family, it seems, is the essential happy ending of a great deal of children's literature, from Jo March's compliance to the domestic role to the frequent theme of orphans finding solace in a new substitute family. Indeed, there is positively a fashion in children's literature to follow the plight of an orphan. This may seem to be the complete antithesis of the family story, and perhaps it would be if it was not for the prevalence of the classic ending in which the orphan finds a family. The orphan figure appeals to both adult and child readers: the child is given an opportunity to follow the lifestyle of a character free of parents but they know that by the conclusion, the protagonist will settle down with a hot supper in the comfort of a family home, and the adults are reminded of a child's need to be looked after, encouraging feelings of self-worth and ensuring the security of family structure. Much children's literature focuses on orphans throughout the twentieth century: Mary in *The Secret Garden*, Peter Pan, Anne of Green Gables, Pollyanna, and more recently, J.K. Rowling's Harry Potter, the children from Lemony Snicket's postmodern 'The Bad Beginnings' Series (2002–), James from Roald Dahl's *James and the Giant Peach* (1961), Sophie from Dahl's

The BFG (1982); and although it turns out she is far from being an orphan, Phillip Pullman's heroine Lyra enjoys all the romance of being an orphan at the beginning of *Northern Lights* (1998).

Anne of Green Gables and Pollyanna are the sentimental embodiment of the truly grateful orphans, Pollyanna forever being 'glad' of her selfish aunt's hospitality, and Anne thanking the world for all its beauties; they are the adult's ideal orphans. The Romantic trope where the child revives the adult continues, as Anne's foster mother Marilla softens towards her in the course of the narrative, concluding with Anne taking care of Marilla in a reversal of adult/child relations, and Pollyanna's Aunt Polly is redeemed by Pollyanna to the extent that she becomes likeable enough to be marriageable; the Romantic notion that youth replenishes the old is a recurring theme. But what is crucial is that the making of a family has enriched the lives of all of its members. Children's literature dictates, to adult and child readers, that it is through family that personal salvation can be found and implicitly, those who do not embrace family will be condemned to a life of selfishness and loneliness.

On initial examination *The Wind in the Willows* seems to have little to do with family, in fact, it has no traditional family. There is only one of each species of animal, but like the orphan narrative texts, it begins with the loneliness of an individual (Mole) and concludes with several individuals sharing homes, meals and concerns in a manner that is strongly reminiscent of family. In addition, Toad plays the part of the spoilt child who is constrained for his own good by the 'adult' characters, again emphasising the adult/child divide, while concentration on food and the tension between home and away are themes that are typical of domestic stories. *The Wind in the Willows* is, like *Peter Pan*, an inherent part of British literary culture, and as Hunt notes it 'sums up many shifting features of the period' (*An Introduction* 97). The text abounds in complexities and responds to contemporary social unease: while the Riverbank represents an arcadia where the men can idle time away on boats and indulge in picnics, it is also in danger, for it refuses to include any animals of the opposite sex and is therefore a sterile environment. In addition to this the weasels, who inhabit the Wild Wood and, for a time, Toad Hall, symbolise the threat of lower-class rebellion, and the wide world outside the Riverbank is perceived to be a threatening place. It seems that this arcadia will be short-lived and, with the onset of the First World War in 1914, must disintegrate. What happens to the institution of the family when a large number of the males in it have been lost to war, and what effect this has on the portrayal of the family in children's literature will be discussed in the next chapter. But in this turbulent transitional period in children's literature (1886–1914) there is an emerging sense of the complexity of the family, a more child-centred approach to family and yet also a reluctance to leave the conservative traditions of the nineteenth century very far behind.

Chapter Three
1920–2003 Depictions of the Twentieth-Century Family: From 'Just William' to 'Harry Potter'

If children's literature responds to changes in society, then post-war children's literature would surely focus on the problems faced in the aftermath of war – for example lost relatives: there would be an absence of father figures and an increased number of single parent families. But in the children's literature of the inter- and post-war years there is a tendency to retreat into known worlds of nostalgia: the safe nursery worlds of bears, with 'Rupert Bear' appearing in *The Daily Express* in 1920, and A.A. Milne's *Winnie the Pooh* in 1926; fantasies of talking animals such as Hugh Lofting's *Dr Doolittle* in 1920, and stable reliable nuclear families with Richmal Crompton's 'Just William' series featuring in *Happy Mag* in 1922, and Joyce Lankester Brisley's 'Milly-Molly-Mandy' series first published in 1928.[1] The response of children's literature to cataclysmic world events it seems, was to portray an idealised world that was safer than ever before (Thacker and Webb 109).

Peter Hunt argues

> War, change and the threat of war and change made nostalgia and retreat even more attractive and urgent than before, and it naturally found a place in children's books – at once a place of retreat for adults and of protection for children. ('Retreatism and Advance'195) [2]

There existed a marked contrast between what was depicted in children's literature and what was happening in the rest of the world. In reality many families had lost husbands, fathers and sons, and yet those that we see in the popular children's literature of the 1920s and 1930s tend to be complete nuclear families in which, for the first time since the days of the Fairchild and Wallace families, children enjoy the company of both parents. This reasserts notions of a certain type of idealised family emphasised in children's fiction that almost forms a paradox with the reality of more diverse families who may well be struggling to come to terms with loss and separation. *Just William* can be read as a 'sitcom' in which the family unit is taken for granted; a mark of security in itself. In addition, certain stereotypes are reinforced as the mother seems to be constantly darning socks while invisibly organising and feeding her husband and family, and the father complains that his digestion is ruined if his mealtimes are interfered with, emphasising the solid gender ideology that is implicit in the idealised family at this time (Crompton 26–33). The family share their spaces, sit down together to share their meals, and, while William causes upset, the reader is assured that family life will continue to provide an idyllic, almost utopian backdrop to William's adventures.

Brisley's 'Milly-Molly-Mandy' series (1928) steps even further back into domestic utopia, for while William is mischievous, Milly-Molly-Mandy complies with domestic order and her behaviour sets an example for her female readers; they too are encouraged to be thoughtful, industrious and compliant. While Milly-Molly-Mandy and the Fairchild children may be separated by just over a century and at least one class divide the introductory paragraphs emphasise a continuation of specific ways of managing the family thus emphasising the promotion of a certain ideal which applies to all kinds of families at all times.

> Once upon a time there was a little girl.
> She had a Father, and a Mother, and an Uncle, and an Aunty; and they all lived together in a nice white cottage with a thatched roof. (Lankester Brisley 9)

The fairy-tale beginning marks the retreat into a distant, perhaps fantasised, world, although in contrast to *The History of the Fairchild Family* the little girl is named first, emphasising the centrality of the child in a culture that desires to return to days of 'innocence'. The list that follows maintains a nineteenth-century patriarchal sense of order with father before mother and uncle before aunt. In addition, the extended family all live together, a trend that was beginning to vanish as the nuclear family began to dominate in the twentieth century, and they share a 'nice white cottage with a thatched roof' in a village, rather than a terraced house in the midst of the city: the signs all lead to a constructed world of idealised domestic harmony. This domestic utopia seems far removed from the reality that had survived the First World War only ten years previously, and, as Kimberley Reynolds argues, the family constructed in the 'Milly-Molly-Mandy' series 're-create[s] a world that seems much older – even pre-industrial.'[3]

Traditional gender roles are maintained as the father grows vegetables while the mother cooks, and the map of the village suggests an environment something like that discussed earlier in *The Wind in the Willows*, that is cut off from the wider, more dangerous world. The map firmly encloses the village in a border, offering a sense of security in its containment and allowing few strangers in. Most of the buildings come with an explanation of who lives there and how they relate to Milly-Molly-Mandy's life. Implicit in the village map is a hierarchy of belonging and there seems to be little alternative to this environment. The main characters are surrounded by caring adults in a loving community, and it is made clear that everyone must adhere to their role. *Just William* and the 'Milly-Molly-Mandy' series are unusual in their portrayal of united, content families; the characters encounter little real danger, and live in an almost sepia bygone world. Perhaps in a post-war world the only real alternative was to create a fictional utopian environment as an escape from reality, and the family, I suggest, was essential to this. For as politics and ideology perennially preach, if families conform to the idealised culturally constructed stereotype then individuals would equally conform to rules of government ensuring social control and cohesion. Life in the *Milly-Molly-Mandy Stories* and *Just William* is predictable and regulated; people stay where they belong and families encounter few serious troubles. But alongside this ideal there are darker issues of control, subservience and gender constriction. There is little in either text to remind the reader that women's emancipation had ever happened, and Milly-Molly-Mandy, her mother and aunt are, with William's sister and mother, unlikely to break free of their domestic roles.

While the period 1930–50 may have been full of contrasts it still saw a whole host of family orientated texts. Rather in the same way that children always return home in children's fiction, writers of children's literature facing the reality of war turned to the familiar safety and security of the domestic story. Further, in times of crisis, and this is especially evident in Ransome's work, the focus of children's literature returned to the family; if children's literature had gone into retreat then it had only taken idealistic notions with it. But in some respects the contemporary children's literature had developed away from the idyll of the 'Milly-Molly-Mandy' series: in Noel Streatfield's *Ballet Shoes* (1936) the heroines had to work for their money and in Eve Garnett's *The Family from One End Street* (1937) the plight of a working class family was followed, and yet alongside these innovative, and in some ways radical texts sat the conservative approach of Ransome, whose 'Swallows and Amazons' series was saturated with nineteenth-century notions of familial obedience and patriarchal authority. For all these apparent differences in approach, the importance of family, of mealtimes and of the centrality of home remain implicit in all these texts.

Ransome's retreat from war-time reality was back into the nineteenth century, a nineteenth century glorified by rose-tinted hindsight into an ideal of Empire, domestic order and patriarchal dominance all safely contained in and insulated by a strict Christian framework. Hunt has argued that the family structure and moral codes that are adhered to in the 'Swallows and Amazons' series are 'essentially late Victorian' (*Approaching Arthur Ransome* 164). This Victorian attitude is evident in the portrayal of the father for, quite unlike the portrayal of the weak father in *Peter Pan* or *The Secret Garden*, the female control over 'bringing up' Anne in *Anne of Green Gables* (Montgomery 64), or the children spiritually restoring the adults in several of the turn-of-the-century texts, Ransome portrays a structured, ordered family, with a strong dependable father, an obedient mother, and children who work together to be true to their father's maxims. It is a nineteenth-century form which has moved on from the Calvinistic Fairchild family, but in which the security still rests in the God-given order of the patriachally constructed family.

The father has two important roles to play in the 'Swallows and Amazons' series: as 'Daddy' he is protector of the family, while as Commander Walker he is protector of country and Empire. It is no coincidence that Empire and family are again associated. The father, though physically absent for much of the series, maintains control; the whole adventure series cannot begin until it is sanctioned by his 'Duffers' telegram (Ransome *Swallows* 2). Deborah Thacker and Jean Webb argue that the children in Ransome's work and in that of Blyton achieved 'a sense of self-sufficiency without the assistance of adults (and often despite adult efforts)' (109), yet while the father is physically absent his influence remains key as, like God, and in a sort of quasi-Foucauldian means of sur-veillance, Commander Walker is always with the children in spirit.

> Out there they would be all right. Jim had waited out there himself. This was what Daddy would do. John, in spite of being able to see nothing but fog, in spite of the broken promise, in spite of the awful mess they were in, was surprised to find that a lot of worry had left him. The decision had been made. (Ransome *We Didn't Mean* 146)

This is almost a biblical intertext in its reference to Jesus calming the storm (*Good News Bible*, Mark. 4. 35–41). John, in the storm, listens to his father's advice and in effect the father saves the lives of his children through John, the eldest son. In true Imperial style the decision is based on an elder's advice, quickly and with determination; faith is never brought into question. Metaphorically, if the father is God-like, I suggest that John is Christ, the mother represents the Church and the siblings are his faithful disciples; in fact, the perfect working family. It is significant that in this world there is no Judas, as there is no quarrelling and has been no war; the structure of the family and power relations within the family do not allow for any rebellious behaviour.[4] Hunt emphasises that there is no conflict between children and parents in Ransome's work, and he is right, for there is no need for any conflict; the children respect their parents, and in turn the parents respect their children; it is a paradise of child/parental relations (Ransome *Approaching Arthur* 15). But this paradise is bounded by a male-orientated system of family and Empire; all characters have their designated, often gender-determined, roles:

> John was thinking of the sailing, wondering whether he really remembered all that he had learnt last year. Susan was thinking of the stores and the

cooking. Titty was thinking of the island itself, of coral, treasure and footprints in the sand. Roger was thinking of the fact he was not to be left behind. He saw for the first time that it was a good thing to be no longer the baby of the family. (Ransome *We Didn't Mean* 8)

The children are presented in order of rank. First John, who, as the eldest and the paternal figure, takes on the responsibility of sailing the boat and without him and his father's teachings the adventure could not begin; Susan comes second, and as the maternal figure her duties consist of feeding the family. John and Susan are followed by 'the children', Titty and Roger, who are free to dream and who can play, as their elder siblings have the parental responsibility. The children faithfully re-enact the family patterns exemplified in their 'real' lives. The template is one of order; while the Fairchild children require to be warned not to fall to the temptation of ambition, as each individual has his God given place, the Walkers do not even have to be advised, for their positions are taken for granted; it is John's birthright to be leader and in this way the world in the text is far more an Empire than a democracy. The 'parental' siblings in *Swallows and Amazons* are by no means unique, as sibling duos who take on the roles of parents also appear in *Peter Pan*, as I discussed earlier, and in John Rowe Townsend's *Gumble's Yard* (1961) and more recently in Anne Fine's *The Granny Project* (1983).

When parents are physically absent, the eldest children tend to fill their places, consequently, the family unit is maintained and the children are trained for their adult roles in life. In terms of domestic chores and rank, Wendy from *Peter Pan*, Susan from the 'Swallows and Amazons' series, Sandra from *Gumble's Yard* and Sophie from *The Granny Project* share remarkably similar positions: it seems that when children are left to a certain extent to their own devices, no matter what class they belong to – for Sandra certainly, is from the working class – they will follow the tradition of a text-book parent. This text-book ideal does not seem to have changed greatly in the thirty years between Barrie and Ransome despite women's liberation and two world wars (by the conclusion of the 'Swallows and Amazons' series), or in the second half of the century when we encounter Townsend's Sandra cooking in the 1960s. By the time of *The Granny Project* in the 1980s the chores are no longer divided entirely by gender stereotypes, but Sophie's role as substitute mother remains integral for a period when the children swap roles with their parents. The static nature of the 'Swallows and Amazons' series can either be read as a re-presentation of the period, or as a comment on the retreatist nature of Ransome's work, or, indeed, an amalgamation of the two, but many of its themes and even the textual mechanics of order remain prevalent in late twentieth- and early twenty-first-century children's fiction.

In contrast to the retreatism of Ransome's children's texts, Noel Streatfeild's *Ballet Shoes* (1936) and Eve Garnett's *The Family from One End Street* (1937) addressed economic difficulties with which many people would have been familiar during the depression of the 1930s. In *Ballet Shoes* the family is still solidly middle-class, and the children are poor in the same way as their predecessors; Nesbit's Railway Children and the Bastables. Their poverty precludes them attending school – no state schooling for these socially privileged children – but there is still a cook employed to produce meals for them. Garnett's *The Family from One End Street* was a radical departure from the very middle-class milieu of most children's literature of the period, featuring as it did a working-class family. Poverty here is real, with the family taking in other people's laundry in order to make ends meet. But despite the fact that Garnett's text is one of the first family stories concerning the working classes, it is *Ballet Shoes* that presents the more marked change in the presentation of family in children's literature.

There are several revolutionary aspects to *Ballet Shoes* in terms of family. Quite unlike the linear ancestry that Cedric had to follow in *Little Lord Fauntleroy* or that the Little Peppers were meant to grow accustomed to, the Fossils' experiences emphasise a new beginning as they invent their own family name and are not related by blood. Further, the family disperses at the conclusion of the narrative, the family home is sold and the sisters separate in order to begin careers, disrupting the traditional comforting closure of family cohesion. The adventure of teenage fiction is, in a way, initiated here, but the disintegration of the family home is a rare phenomenon in children's fiction and perhaps acts as a reminder of reality: the days of women staying home to care for generations of children as in *Little Women* seem to have vanished.

Despite the subversive re-writing of family in *Ballet Shoes* Reynolds argues that *The Family from One End Street* is as radical as *Ballet Shoes*. She claims that the Ruggles' disregard for state interference in the family demonstrates socialist sympathies, in contrast to the Fossil family, who happily accede to state authority (Reynolds 'Sociology, Politics and the Family' 34–6). Certainly, the Ruggleses represent a backlash against state interference and the accompanying advice literature but Reynolds' argument that the text also 'undoubtedly celebrates family values' is valid here as, in dismissing and fighting off outside interference, the family, somewhat conventionally, maintains its own safe haven in a way that is reminiscent of the values in *Holiday House* (Reynolds 'Sociology, Politics and the Family' 36). Essentially, we are reassured that the Ruggleses will still be living in the family home until the end of their days for, in contrast to the Fossil family, there is no desire to move or change.

The upper-class Fairchilds would be proud of the working-class Ruggleses; they know their place, and appear to have little ambition to move from their occupations as washerwoman and dustman. The family work together and stay together as the text presents a rather rose-tinted image of the working classes from a privileged higher social position. The text re-asserts notions of ideological control, as the Ruggleses, representing the working-classes, are kept in their place; moreover, their self-reliance and independence is encouraged and thus saves the state's money as they support themselves. As Gillian Avery argues, the text did not 'dwell on the darker aspects of poverty; this is a cheerful book where the struggles of a chronically hard up family are material for picturesque comedy; it is not an exercise in realism' ('The Family Story' 341). In light of the generic family, it merely continues the didactic message evident in the majority of domestic stories. It does not interrogate the concept of family as thought-provokingly as *Ballet Shoes*.

It seems to be something of a leap – perhaps a backward leap – from *Ballet Shoes* to Enid Blyton's *Five on a Treasure Island* (1942). Streatfield's text was radical and innovative, whereas Blyton is seen as conservative and is often accused of sexism, racism, and poor quality writing. Sheila Ray suggests that Blyton reiterated many of the views of the parents of the period and, as one of the best-selling children's authors of all time, her attitude to and representation of family are influential. Blyton herself commented that her success was because the public felt that her texts offered 'a sense of security, an anchor, a sure knowledge that right is right' (Quoted in Hunt 'Enid Blyton' 70). This gives the somewhat misleading impression that her texts simply offer one meaning and one interpretation; that they are, essentially, conduct texts. But I want to suggest that *Five on a Treasure Island* can be seen as a text rich in contradiction. On the one hand, convention is adhered to as the children work in a hierarchical system headed by Julian and George, while Anne ensures that the group are warm and well-fed; middle-class concepts of home and family are central to the story and the economic situation is, as in *The Treasure Seekers*, salvaged by the children. On the other hand, the adventures are rich in secrecy as the children fight strange adults and conceal things from their parents, and for perhaps the first time adults and children are openly pitched against each other within the family.

David Rudd suggests that while parents are often absent in children's texts, Blyton's work goes beyond the normal convention in which children have the right to escape their parents, as it also validates the parents' rights to be free of their children. Rudd then goes on to argue that the parents in Blyton's texts 'are not quite in the same league as Hansel and Gretel's parents, but they are far from exemplary' (*Enid Blyton* 98). As I have argued, while parents are physically absent in other children's texts they remain key figures in the psyche of the child, and while this is true of *Five on a Treasure Island*, it is unusual to depict children and parents in such direct opposition to each other. Blyton's 'Famous Five' series begins with Julian, Anne and Dick being deserted by their parents, thrust on to an uncle and aunt whom they have never met in order for their parents to be 'all by ourselves!' for the holidays (Blyton *Five on a Treasure Island* 1). The unknown Uncle Quentin is presented as the archetypal Victorian father figure, strict, yet out of place and subject to mockery. Both families are run by the men, the women having little say; the child/adult divide is marked and, in Uncle Quentin's family, in contrast to Ransome's texts, there is initially little mutual respect between adult and child – thus secrets are fostered.

These divisions are further illustrated in key areas of Quentin, George and Fanny's family life, notably in the spaces occupied and the gathering together for the family meal. In *Five on a Treasure Island* the father is often locked in his study and the dinner table does not always see the gathering together of the whole family – conventional signs of unconventional families. In addition, economics seems, as in many previous texts, to be of importance; the family is not happy, not even spiritually together, until the economic crisis has been solved. In contrast to *Five Little Peppers and How They Grew*, *The Family from One End Street*, *Little Women* and many others, poverty separates rather than bonds the family in *Five on a Treasure Island*:

> 'You see, Daddy doesn't make much money with the learned books he writes, and he's always wanting to give mother and me things he can't afford. So that makes him bad-tempered. He wants to send me away to a good school but he hasn't got the money', (Blyton *Five on a Treasure Island* 41)

The position of the father is ambiguous. Although Uncle Quentin acts in a somewhat cliché-ridden Victorian manner, he is unable to fulfil the role of the Victorian patriarch: he is neither successful nor rich, he is not considered god-like, as are Mr Fairchild or Commander Walker; he has an unpredictable temper as opposed to the unchanging Commander Walker or the father from *The Railway Children* and, ultimately, Uncle Quentin cannot be depended upon. But this does not mean that the father is insignificant, for when all is resolved George and her father can begin to live the ideal as the two embrace and we feel the secure closure of a happy ending – the adventure, far from finding treasure or capturing criminals, is in fact to repair the damaged relationship between father and daughter and reinforce the prevailing familial ideology.

1945–1970 the Mid-Twentieth Century

The retreatism evident after the First World War had vanished post-Second World War, and as Thacker and Webb argue, it was the threat of nuclear annihilation that 'made the possibilities of a better world more difficult to imagine'(110). After the Second World War there was a proliferation of children's literature which resulted in what many critics have described as a period of great development and some have even gone so far as to refer to it as a 'second golden age'.[5] Much of the literature that emerged during this period explored the darker aspects of post-war life, paving the way for the emergence of teenage fiction in the 1960s and for later social realist fiction. Indeed, Reynolds has a subsection dealing with this period which she calls 'Unhappy Families' in which she argues that Mary Norton's *The Borrowers* (1952), Lucy Boston's *The Children of Green Knowe* (1954), and Philippa Pearce's *Tom's Midnight Garden* (1958) represent wider anxieties concerning the fragmentation of family life in post-war society (*Children's Literature* 36–40). While Reynolds argues that the texts concern themselves with the story of a child cut off from his/her family, she also points out that the texts offer 'a continued preoccupation with the child as inheritor of a fallen world which s/he is capable of (at least partially) saving, healing and restoring' (*Children's Literature* 40).

This returns us to notions of the child as man's saviour so prevalent in children's literature from the mid-nineteenth century to the Edwardian period. Certainly, *Tom's Midnight Garden* and *The Borrowers* take a slightly less idealistic approach to family and its environment, for while the parents again are often absent, the two texts remain framed by the ideal of a cohesive family – Arrietty's family is loving and dependable and *Tom's Midnight Garden* concludes with his return to his immediate family. As always, in this period, a variety of texts were published and contradictions in patterns are evident; the literature of 1945–70 depicts the less stable worlds of family and society in *Tom's Midnight Garden, The Borrowers*, C.S. Lewis' 'Narnia' series (1950–6) and *Gumble's Yard*, but it also sees the publication of Michael Bond's *A Bear Called Paddington* (1958), a text and series dependent on the stability of family and community, and the reinforcement of domestic stereotypes is also apparent in Roald Dahl's *Charlie and the Chocolate Factory* (1964), *Fantastic Mr Fox* (1970), and *James and the Giant Peach* (1961). It is the earlier texts that I will concentrate on here, for while they overtly present an uneasy picture of family, covertly they also fit into the conventional patterns and structures of children's literature inherited from their predecessors.

Lewis' *The Lion, the Witch and the Wardrobe* (1950) follows the paradigm offered by Hodgson Burnett, Nesbit, Blyton and many others, as it begins with the separation of children and parents (Rustin and Rustin 41). In addition, the children comply exactly with the template for family which has been established in the mythology of children's fiction:

> Once there were four children whose names were Peter, Susan, Edmund and Lucy. This story is about something that happened to them when they were sent away from London during the war because of the air raids. (Lewis 76)

The children are named in order of age, a conventional pattern similar to that of the Ransome's Walker children, the Famous Five and Marjorie Lloyd's *Fell Farm Campers* (1960). There are four children who are old enough to play; two boys and two girls, the eldest is male, and therefore the leader, and the second eldest, being female, acting as the substitute mother.[6] In addition to the template of the family, Hunt has argued that in terms of literary language and imagery, many of the phrases are recycled, borrowed from the traditions of earlier children's literature, reaffirming the argument that the text has nothing particularly new to offer.[7] Far from being a story concerning the erosion of family, which the children's separation from their parents might support, *The Lion, the Witch and the Wardrobe* promotes a conventional familial ideology.

Most simplistically, the narrative can be read as the fight of good against evil, personified by the White Witch. Her evil status is figured in anti-familial terms: she does not have a husband or children and she has rejected the domestic. In contrast, the good characters – Mr Tumnus and the Beavers – are surrounded by family and by domestic signifiers. Mr Tumnus repents of his allegiance to the White Witch as he looks at the picture of his father 'over the mantle piece', reiterating the connection between the positive values of home, family, and loyalty. Equally, the Beavers feed the children wholesome British food and emphasise the relationship between mealtimes, family and again implied goodness. While the children are from a middle-class background the Beavers symbolise the working class; their name signifies their hard-working natures and they can be seen as servants and protectors to the children as Mrs Beaver feeds them thus fulfilling her adopted role as a mother who serves and Mr Beaver ensures they are safe. Good in *The Lion, the Witch and the Wardrobe* is represented by the family, home and food, and this is pitched against evil, which is represented by a single, childless, sexualised temptress who offers sweet foreign food in the form of Turkish Delight. Family is the epitome of goodness, and while Edmund betrays his family after he has fallen victim to the wiles of the White Witch, his sins are atoned for by the lion, Aslan, and the family overcomes the White Witch as it is re-united. It is not new to suggest the Biblical intertexts of Narnia, but what is important regarding the family is that it is the family and their loyalty that defeat the evil rule of the White Witch. Parallels of war in fantasy and war in reality are clearly apparent, but the strongly British family prevails; the Christian defeats the Pagan other. The family fights evil, and here we could read evil as Fascism, and wins, but it does so in a British, elitist manner, as it dictates that the family should stay loyal both to itself and to its culture and so demonises those who reject that culture and the domesticity which supports it.[8]

The social instability arising from the Second World War also overshadows *The Borrowers* (1952) and *Tom's Midnight Garden* (1958); we are reminded of war-time evacuation as the Clocks in *The Borrowers* and Tom in *Tom's Midnight Garden* are forced from their homes and have to live with other relatives (Rustin and Rustin 173). But where Thacker and Webb see this as a representation of the stateless family, Kimberley Reynolds recognises that the Borrowers' metaphorical and literal eviction is needed in order to instigate a new and more positive beginning (Thacker and Webb 130–1; Reynolds *Children's Literature* 37–8). What is significant here is that although these texts have often been regarded as possessing a certain uneasiness in tone resulting from post-war anxieties, the texts still adhere to and advocate traditional notions of the cohesive family: there might be evacuation, separation, the loss of homes and yet it is always the family which provides the all-important backdrop to events – it is there no matter what.

At the conclusion of both texts the families are re-united: in *The Borrowers* the Clocks have found their relatives and so their family future is assured and the boy living with Aunt Sophy returns to his family in India, while in *Tom's Midnight Garden* Tom rejoins his beloved brother and parents. I contend that, responding to the contemporary social reality, in children's fiction the preservation of the family now entails more sacrifice than before as there are more obstacles to overcome. As is made clear by Arrietty's education and apparent sexual equality with her fictional male companions, the world is beginning to offer new perspectives and ways of life. But as the closures of these texts show, this affects the family only superficially, and social and cultural irritations never really threaten the power of the family and its ideology. The difficulties that face the families can only strengthen the ideal of family; family, we are told, is always worth fighting for and the battle must involve some sacrifice. The heroism of the characters is demonstrated by the extent of their sacrifice – in *Tom's Midnight Garden* Tom leaves Hatty and his garden; in *The Borrowers*, Arrietty's mother Homily is forced to leave her cherished home. This sacrifice is comparable to those of Meg or Jo in *Little Women* or Anne in *Anne of Green Gables*, who all relinquish something held dear in order to maintain the status quo of their families, and it is partly this that constructs their status as heroes/heroines. While the themes of eviction, evacuation and relocation emphasise a less stable world the family still maintains its centrality and idealism: sacrifices are made as they have always been, and children's literature continues to privilege and promote the sanctity and importance of family.

The 1960s saw the emergence of teenage fiction and social realism, but the argument that the 1960s saw the beginnings of the breakdown of parent-child relationships is questionable, as textual patterns still reveal that the ideal family remained the ultimate goal.[9] The children in post-1960s texts might not have this ideal family as the parents may have left, been abusive, or been unable to support the children, but the child characters still entertain fantasies of a perfect family constructed not only in the mythology of children's literature, but by all aspects of contemporary culture now and then. I suggest that the major change from the 1960s onwards is that the texts tend to focus on, rather than pass over, the uncertainties and instabilities of the family unit for, as I have shown, historically the family in children's literature has always had its problems.

John Rowe Townsend's *Gumble's Yard* can be read as questioning the family, parents and familial ideals as Kevin and Sarah are deserted by their guardians and left to care for themselves and their younger cousins. Nicholas Tucker and Nikki Gamble have argued that *Gumble's Yard* represents a turning point in children's literature in its interrogation of family relationships, and Avery suggests that it presents the child 'alone in the world'(Tucker and Gamble 26; Avery 'The Family Story' 341). Similarly, Peter Hollindale and Zena Sutherland argue that in *Gumble's Yard*:

> not only the topographical, economic, and social setting but also the systematic demythologizing of parental adequacy, the ruptured cliché of

family harmony, point the way to a more observant, sceptical, and candid social fiction for young children. (279–80)

Certainly the demythologising of parental authority is evident, as Doris and Walter simply vanish with no thought of the children, yet to suggest that *Gumble's Yard* 'ruptures the cliché of family harmony' may be a little extreme, for the fantasy of the perfect family remains at the forefront of the text. This is most apparent in its closure, when, as the parents return and the moral of the text is clearly articulated: '[e]ven an unsatisfactory family is better than none' (Townsend *Gumble's Yard* 100). There are highly conventional aspects of the text: there are four children, two girls and two boys, the eldest being male, and the two eldest children take on the parental roles.

Following the pattern of some nineteenth-century texts such as Hesba Stretton's *Jessica's First Prayer* (1867) or Richard Henry Horne's *Memoirs of a London Doll* (1846), in *Gumble's Yard* Kevin, while alone and looking for his uncle in a new town, finds great community support. The Harrisons feed him, and there is a sense that the wider community, in the absence of parents, takes on family responsibility, acting as a safety net. So, far apart from being 'alone in the world' as Avery suggests, the child in Townsend's text is surrounded by a wider network of trustworthy adults and by his sibling/cousin family. Sandra, like Barrie's Wendy and Ransome's Susan, becomes the substitute mother but there is a difference in tone, from the adventures of *Peter Pan* or the 'Swallows and Amazons' series, as the narrator, Kevin, tells us:

> "Somebody's got to have their head screwed on right," retorted Sandra. She looked more like my mother than ever. Mother had been dead for three years, but I remembered her well. She'd had a hard life, and watched her pennies like a hawk. Sandra is well set for the same life. She'll never be a romantic girl, but after all there isn't much romance in the jungle. She'll know which shop to buy her potatoes at, and that's more important. (Townsend *Gumble's Yard* 39)

There is a difference, I suggest, between choosing to take the maternal role and having it thrust upon you. There is no playful aspect to Sandra's role, as domesticity is the only possible path open to her, and yet she is also celebrated for being like her mother. Sandra is a positive role model, and readers are expected to recognise her heroism.

The domestic is celebrated at the same time as it is questioned, for in presenting the guardians as the bad examples of family and Sandra and Kevin as the good, Townsend adheres to the patterns established in previous generations of children's literature, where bad is contrasted with good and children are meant to redeem and teach the adults who surround them. In *Gumble's Yard* it is significant that there can be no closure to the narrative until the family is reunited, in whatever shape. The children's literature of 1945–70 does articulate a change in the representation of family, responding to the contemporary social anxieties and concerns about the erosion and potential disintegration of the traditional family unit. But again, the ideals, patterns and belief in the importance and intrinsically beneficial nature of the family remain: the ideology of family triumphs, in fictional form, over the reality.

1970–2000 Approaching the Millennium

This period, I suggest, recognises the fragility of the nuclear family. Several of the texts published between 1970 and 2000 depict single-parent families and discuss issues of divorce and abuse. Many critics have commented on this superficial change: Peter Hunt argues that '[b]efore 1970, it might be said, adults were, on the whole reliable: since then they have not been' ('Anne Fine' 14). Gillian Avery observes that the texts show children isolated from their parents ('The Family Story' 341–2), and Nicholas Tucker and Nikki Gamble note that the greatest change in children's literature of the period is to be seen in its representation of the nuclear family (26). Certainly, there has been a distinct increase in the number of texts addressing complex domestic issues. But, in terms of my argument, the key difference is the focus on the darker recesses of family life. In previous children's literature adults have rarely been entirely reliable, for example the fathers in *The Secret Garden, Holiday House, Peter Pan,* and *Five on a Treasure Island,* and children have often been physically separated from their parents. However these issues were often pushed to the margins in earlier children's texts – pushed out of sight and therefore, presumably, intended to be out of mind. The challenge in children's literature of the late-twentieth, and indeed into the twenty-first century, is the untangling of strained relationships and family dilemmas. The texts which I analyse in this section are all primarily domestic stories, yet all address the complexities of late twentieth-century family relationships and I will suggest that through the texts' representation of these complications the ideal of family is strengthened rather than weakened. In foregrounding the complications and variations of family and family life, the ideal of family is not weakened, but in fact made stronger by negative example.

It is fitting to begin with Nina Bawden's *Carrie's War* (1973), not just because of its position in the wider chronology, but because I feel that the later works of Anne Fine, Jacqueline Wilson and Michelle Magorian build on the foundations put in place by Bawden's text. What makes *Carrie's War* a crucial text is its inclusion of the adults' stories; in the nineteenth century the adult story was often told to the detriment of the child's; for most of the twentieth century the child was the main protagonist, but in *Carrie's War* we are told Mr Evans' history, why he is so 'ogre-like', and this need on the part of the child to sympathise and relate to adults' problems is then adopted by Fine in texts like *Madame Doubtfire.* The parents might not be god-like. They might not even be satisfactory, but they are becoming human, and to become human, feelings have to be portrayed. Lissa Paul argues that *Carrie's War* is a transitional text which marks the move from what she calls the 'cosy adventures of children on their own (in the Nesbit tradition)' to the more complicated domestic issues evident in teenage fiction (58). Certainly, this is a text about adults and children, and the adults are more fully rounded characters who experience and articulate emotion; real people who invoke the sympathies of a child readership.

But while *Carrie's War* can be argued to be a transitional text, in its inclusion and dependence on traditional motifs it also shows that the strict patterns of children's literature are inescapable. *Carrie's War* is concerned with family but, like other domestic stories, it is also concerned with the theme of separation: a grown-up Carrie and her children are separated from their husband/father after his death; Carrie and Nick have been separated from their parents in the evacuation necessitated by the war; Mr Evans and his sister have long been separated after a family dispute and finally Carrie is separated from Hepzibah and Albert for several years after the war until the reunion at the text's conclusion. In children's literature reunion ends separation; in the past of the narrative Carrie and Nick return to their parents after their evacuation, and then in the present of the text, not only does Carrie return to the place of her evacuation to find that Hepzibah and Mr Johnny are still alive and living in the same house, but the reader is given hope of a reunion between Carrie and Albert. The family, as in *Tom's Midnight Garden*, *The Borrowers*, and *The Secret Garden* among many, is reunited, thus enabling narrative closure.

Following earlier patterns of children's literature, the position of the child is seemingly weak in *Carrie's War*, as Albert's statement that 'it is a fearful *handicap* being a child' when he cannot buy Druid's Cottage and save Hepzibah and Mr Johnny from homelessness shows (Bawden 116). But in the conclusion the reader learns that Hepzibah and Mr Johnny live in the same house because Albert has grown up and bought it for them (p.140). Traditional patterns are also evident as the child, following the example of *Anne of Green Gables* or *The Story of the Treasure Seekers*, saves the family. Equally, what makes Carrie a heroine is her concern with maintaining relationships and trying to be loyal to her substitute families; her desire to maintain the status quo of the family is privileged above all else.[10] While the text acknowledges family problems, and more specifically addresses the divides between children and adults, it still prioritises family relationships, and it does this through using traditional conventions of children's domestic fiction. *Carrie's War*, like Michelle Magorian's *Back Home* (1985), recognises the complexities of families, and undermines the myth of a golden age of family during the Second World War, but the text, in its focus on the past of the adult as well as in the present of the child, opens the way for the texts of the 1980s to address further the intricacies of family relationships from dual perspectives.

This progression is evident in Anne Fine's *Madame Doubtfire* as the eldest daughter, Lydia, builds on Carrie's heroic role; Lydia, like Carrie, is concerned with family relationships, but Lydia, as a girl experiencing childhood forty years later than Carrie, is able to assert her independence and rights to family by openly questioning the adults who surround her. Fine's texts can be read as tracts or conduct manuals in the same way as many nineteenth-century texts, as the changes in the portrayal of the family are only evident at a surface level; what is inherent in the texts is the constant promotion of the idealised, respectful, loving, cohesive family. In many ways Fine's work attempts to teach children and adults how to deal with family conflict. Although most of Fine's texts concern the family, for the purpose of this study, I will concentrate on two of her most popular texts which, on the surface, may seem to be very different: *The Granny Project* (1983) and *Madame Doubtfire* (1986).

One text describes a traditional nuclear family, while the other follows a newly separated family, yet the two are remarkably similar in their adherence to the values and narrative strategies of traditional children's literature. Anne Fine has been praised for being able to combine humour and topical issues, yet in *Madame Doubtfire* the tone is one of black humour.[11] Ray's statement that divorce was not covered in the children's fiction of the 1970s was no longer valid by the time Fine began to be successful, for separated families from the 1980s onwards have become a common feature of children's literature (79). In addition, Avery suggests that in the latter half of the twentieth century 'domestic security is seemingly unknown and children survive against a background of problem parents' ('The Family Story' 338). But, in contrast, I suggest that what is particularly telling about Fine's work is its constant return to the family; certainly despite the variety of families presented, all her texts seek to resolve family problems, to strengthen the family, to understand adults' shortcomings. Avery's remarks would perhaps be more apposite if they simply stated that children and adults learn to work together in the children's literature of this period, for family, paradoxically, can, I suggest, be argued to be at its strongest in its depiction of problematic issues.

Madame Doubtfire is perhaps the perfect example of a text in which the family is shown as something to fear rather than to embrace:

> "See?" Daniel crowed triumphantly. "See? She only lets you wear my coats when she's afraid the coats *she* bought will get scorched, or ripped, or filthy, or –" [. . .]
>
> The taut grey look around his eyes intensified, and seemingly without noticing what he was doing, he lifted an imaginary rifle down from an imaginary rifle rack on the wall and, tilting his head slightly to one side, took imaginary aim through imaginary sights.
>
> "What are you doing?" Lydia asked him. "Have you got cramp in your neck?
>
> Embarrassed, Daniel made to hang the weapon back on the rack before, even more embarrassed, coming to his senses. (Fine *Madame Doubtfire* 5)

The father consciously enacts shooting the mother, murdering an essential part of the traditional family unit. His actions are childish in the repetitions of 'see' and the possessiveness over the coats. There is something deeply disturbing about the grey look around his eyes, and in his alienation both from the family and from reality as he mimes murder 'seemingly without noticing'. It is Lydia, the eldest child, who takes on the parental role here as she chastises her father so that he is embarrassed. Furthermore, it is Lydia who becomes independent enough to catch the bus across town on her own at the conclusion of the text in order to save the family, to negotiate and understand her rights, the rights of her siblings and those of her parents. As Tucker makes clear, it is the 'worldly-wise' children who are the embodiment of maturity in Fine's texts, whereas the adults act in an irresponsible fashion ('Writing off Mum and Dad' np).

This neglectful behaviour of the adults, however, is not really new: the father in *Holiday House* goes away after the death of his children's mother, unable to cope, as does Mr Craven in *The Secret Garden*. This returns us, then, to the concept that it is often the children who force the adults to redress their childishness: in both Fine's *The Granny Project* and *Madame Doubtfire* the children still have the ability, in a manner reminiscent of the Victorian and Edwardian Romantic texts (*Little Lord Fauntleroy*, *The Secret Garden*, *Pollyanna*) to encourage the adults to reform, but what is different about Fine's texts is that now this reform demands that children understand their parents:[12]

> Sophie and Ivan stood side by side on the grass a few feet from the grave [...]
> Sophie said:
> "Ivan, if Granny hadn't died, and we could start again, would you still vote for keeping her at home?"
> "Yes," Ivan said.
> "Just the same?"
> "No, not just the same. Not with the system where they did all the work, and hated it. Or with the one where I did. I'd opt for the final negotiated settlement, that plan you all had just worked out together before she got sick."
> "That's compromise?"
> "That's right. That's what I would have voted for." (Fine *The Granny Project* 123–4)

The Granny Project, like *Tom's Midnight Garden*, *Carrie's War*, or *The Railway Children* among others cannot close until the family is re-united. But the *Granny Project*, in its narrative technique and plot mechanics, goes back even further than this: as, in Sinclair's *Holiday House* or Sedgwick's *Home*, the children face a rite of passage as a family death brings added maturity and awareness of the importance of family life to the characters. The family and its relationships, as Tucker and Gamble note, is becoming the adventure as the children learn to compromise with their parents (67). The desire to 'get it right' is inextricably entangled in the mythological construction of the 'natural' family and, while parents and children may behave badly to each other, the notion that parents love their children and vice versa is never seriously questioned. Families still love, and Fine's texts chart parental and child reform, so that by the conclusion there exists the rekindling of respect and also the hope that the family may return to being nuclear and 'natural' and therefore happy. The texts may question behaviour, but they cannot stray into the realm of parents and children not loving each other, for this I contend is too radical: it would break the traditions of family as represented in children's literature, for this literature, despite its apparent changes is inherently conservative.

In a vein similar to Anne Fine, Jacqueline Wilson's texts have been much acclaimed for dealing with family problems, but they are far from revolutionary. The notion that the family is the most important relationship is, as in *Madame Doubtfire* and *The Granny Project*, at the heart of both *The Bed and Breakfast Star* (1994) and *Double Act* (1995). In a recent interview Jacqueline Wilson commented that, 'Lots of children look on me as someone who understands, which is a wonderful feeling but also a great responsibility. I can make things turn out OK for children in my books but, although I try to be helpful, in life I haven't got any answers at all' (Kellaway np). Wilson's texts do have a tendency to reach satisfactory closure, not perhaps in a classic 'happy ever after' way but in a content, happier-than-at-the-start manner, again somewhat reminiscent of Fine's novels.[13] What is also noteworthy is the construction of the 'normal' family, both by the narrative and by the child characters. Elsa's introduction of her family is significant in this context:

> Pippa and Hank aren't my proper sister and brother. They're halves. That sounds silly doesn't it? As if they should look like this [picture of a half a brother and sister]. We've all got the same mum. Our mum. But I've got a different dad. [. . .] My dad didn't come back after that. Mum said we were better off without him. Just mum and me. That was fine. But then mum met Mack. Mack the Smack. That's not a joke. He really does smack. Especially me. (Wilson *The Bed and Breakfast Star* 10–11)

It is difficult to determine from Elsa's terminology whether it devalues half siblings or simply mocks the term. What is clear is that the half siblings' diluted blood ties are deemed important, constructing the family as something 'other' rather than 'normal'. Similarly, the 'otherness' of the twins' current family life in *Double Act* is enhanced by the twins' constructions of their past 'normal' family life, which focuses on a time when their mother was alive:

> Once upon a time a man called Richard fell in love with a girl called Opal [. . .] They got their own flat. They got married. They had twin daughters [. . .] The twins started school, and Opal and Richard went to work and at the weekend they did fun things like going swimming and shopping and they had nice days at the seaside. All the normal nice family things. But

then everything stopped being normal and nice. Opal got a bit sick. Then she had to go into hospital [. . .] Gran had to meet the twins from school. Richard stopped working and looked after Opal. But she couldn't get better. She died. So they stopped being a family. (Wilson *Double Act* 18–23)

Accompanied with illustrations of the parents' first flat, wedding and new born twins, the history is a stereotypical one; it even begins in the manner of a fairy tale. The fairy tale intertext is appropriate since the 'normal' and normative family is privileged above 'non-normal' families. The family that the twins have in the present of the narrative is devalued; deemed not normal precisely because it is set against the idyllic vision of the family of the past which did 'normal nice family things'. It seems that much recent children's literature emphasises breaks within the family because it compares itself with a mythological past family, but still it is this mythological family that remains the most desirable goal in the majority of children's fiction, whether nineteenth or twentieth century in origin.

In *Double Act*, while the blood mother cannot be resurrected, the reader is shown that the family can change, but in a far from revolutionary way. In classic fairy-tale fashion, the twins' father meets a new woman whom he marries; the children resent her at first, but the traditional family is reborn as eventually the children accept their stepmother. This acceptance is emphasised by typical signs of domestic contentment, as the family is pictured sharing food and space in an aesthetically acceptable home – all signifiers of the mythology of family. Such cultural signifiers are powerful, and in not conforming to these, families in Wilson's texts are constructed very much as the deviant other. Problem families are confronted, rather than hidden away, but the traditional ideal of the family is very much apparent in Wilson's work; the heroes and heroines constantly yearn for a loving, two-parent family, for the house with four windows, a chimney and a central door.[14] In reality, parents are unlikely to return to the pedestal on which Mr and Mrs Fairchild or Captain Walker were elevated, but parental importance never fades. The family at the end of the twentieth century is as central as ever as children's texts attempt to guide their readers through the complexities of family relationships, which continually advocate and privilege the traditional, clearly outdated, conventional nuclear ideal.

In this period, while authors such as Fine and Wilson explored serious social questions through entertainment, Roald Dahl was writing his perennially popular fictions for children, fictions which, superficially at least, seem to have no serious messages at all. The texts span the apparent changes in children's fiction: the perceived breakdown of family and the beginnings of teenage fiction. They exist alongside those of Fine, Townsend and Wilson and yet Dahl's texts resist easy categorisation. *Charlie and the Chocolate Factory* (1964) or *Fantastic Mr Fox* (1970) transmit traditional messages about the importance of the parentally constituted nuclear family, and yet Matilda's family in *Matilda* (1988) leave her as they flee to Spain and George in *George's Marvellous Medicine* (1981) blows up his grandmother. Dahl is notorious for emphasising the divide between parents and children, insisting that adults and children fight against each other rather than live together in harmony. Subverting this apparent opposition is a didactic notion of what families should ideally be like, and this is illustrated in Dahl's work by positive and negative examples.

In *Fantastic Mr Fox* the reader is presented with a perfect family where the parents and children work together and defeat the farmers who destroy their home. In *Matilda* the reader is given the antithesis of the Fox family as, while the nuclear family initially remains intact it does not conform to the 'signs' of a good family: the family eats ready-made meals and takeaways, does not dine at the table, watches too much television, and the members fail to share their domestic space in a conventional manner. Both *Fantastic Mr Fox* and *Matilda* expose the highly constructed nature of family in children's literature; the family can only work successfully in one acceptable manner and this is the archaic traditional one. Aspects of *Fantastic Mr Fox* read like a dated family manual:

> And Mrs Fox said to her children, "I should like you to know that if it wasn't for your father we should all be dead by now. Your father is a fantastic fox."
> Mr Fox looked at his wife and smiled. He loved her more than ever when she said things like that. (Dahl *Fantastic Mr Fox* 30)

This is a highly traditional and conventional scene which is reminiscent of the parental relationship in *The History of the Fairchild Family* or *Home*. The mother plays a gender-specific role as she stands in the background in order to admire and promote her husband's bravery. The father is the hunter, the mother the nurturer, and the small foxes are not even differentiated in the text, having no individual names but simply referred to as 'small foxes' or 'the children'. Again, as in *Home* or *The History of the Fairchild Family* this is the story of the parents, or more specifically here, of the father.

It could be argued that the family is less relevant in *Matilda*. Mr Wormwood as the father is the antithesis of Mr Fox, lacking bravery, largely ignoring his children, and running away leaving Matilda behind at the first sign of trouble. But the ideal of the respectful loving family remains at the forefront of the text. In many ways *Matilda*, like *Fantastic Mr Fox*, reads as another traditional tract:

> There are many things that make a man irritable when he arrives home from work in the evening and a sensible wife will normally notice the storm signals and will leave him alone until he simmers down. (Dahl *Matilda* 38)

Mrs Wormwood tactfully leaves her husband alone and so conforms to stereotypical constructs of wifehood and this passage is distinctly reminiscent of the marriage conduct books of the first half of the twentieth century. A pattern is set, then, for in some ways the Wormwoods adhere to family traditions and the father is the head of the family, 'the wage earner', yet he is mocked (Dahl *Matilda* 59–60). This mockery is not limited to the depiction of Mr Wormwood, but is extended to the Wormwood family and, by implication, the concept of family itself. The representation of the nuclear family, revealing all its faults and the flimsiness of its façade, actually works, by negative example, to advocate what it seems to despise.

This concept can be further explained by analysing the oppositions between good and bad characters in the text: the goodness of Miss Honey is in part defined by the 'badness' of the Wormwoods and, within the text positive and negative traits are deeply rooted in Victorian constructions of convention. Mr Wormwood is 'bad' because his career is rather dubious, verging on the illegal; he is not a Commander (Mr Walker), an upper-class gentleman (Mr Fairchild), or a teacher (*The Granny Project*), but a used-car salesman; physically he is repellent, being skinny and rat-like, and in a telling comment on the value of literature, neither he or his wife read books, but simply watch television. Mrs Wormwood is 'bad' because she is fat; she is fake with platinum blonde hair and excessive make-up; she plays bingo rather than doing the housework, and she provides ready meals rather than home-cooked delicacies.

In short, the Wormwoods are presented as unloving and unnatural because they do not conform to middle-class sensibilities of how a family should behave. Dahl produces here a very black and white portrait of family life. There is an acknowledgement that bad families exist, but there are no grey areas, and, unlike Anne Fine's patterns, bad parents like the Wormwoods are never recuperated. But what is intriguing about *Matilda* is the role of Miss Honey. In many ways she is the archetypal Madonna figure; she is maternal, slim, and yet virginal. She is the perfect mother, but she has no partner. So while family convention seems to be adhered to in most of Dahl's work, in *Matilda* he does something quite unusual, as the reader is shown that the best conclusion for Matilda is a life with unmarried Miss Honey rather than with Matilda's blood-related nuclear family. It appears that Dahl's text here departs from the normative traditions of fictional families in children's literature. But it must be remembered that Miss Honey is surrounded by all the domestic signifiers that indicate the good family – her mealtime routines, cooking, the family house and so-on. The only real change here, I suspect, is the recognition that families do not have to consist of the two-parent, two-children model any more, but the conventions of family life as constructed in the myth must still be maintained and followed. The ideological infrastructure of family continues to support and contain the variations that are appearing in society, and this is represented in late twentieth- and early twenty-first-century children's literature.

Inevitably there have been changes in the portrayal of the family in children's fiction over the last two centuries. The Fairchild family's rule of fear and discipline has been replaced with a more sympathetic analysis of complex family relationships. Yet, there have been fewer changes than might be imagined: there has, I contend, been no revolution in children's literature. Families, as I argued in Chapter 1, are a means of controlling individuals, and children's literature complements this as it functions as a means of disseminating the ideology of family. Children reading books in the last two centuries have internalised and replicated the ideologies inherent in those texts, and as a result the family has maintained its centrality and significance. Patterns repeat themselves constantly in children's literature, from the representation of the child as saviour of the adult to the cliché of the four children who constitute the ordered family – although in more recent literature the four children are more likely to be two in response to the fall in family numbers after the advent of effective birth control. It is these patterns that I will explore further in Part 2, for the themes of home, spaces and food are integral to the cultural construction of family. What will become evident is the conservative nature of children's literature, for when it comes to what adults hold dear, the family and childhood innocence, there are few authors who are really willing or able to challenge the status quo.

Chapter Four
There's No Place Like Home:[1] Home and Family in Children's Literature

The home, like the family, is central to children's literature. Indeed, home and family here are almost inseparable; the term 'family home' barely needs to be voiced, for home *is* essentially family. John Tosh argues of the nineteenth century that 'at a symbolic level the family became indistinguishable from the domestic space which it occupied', and certainly with regard to children's literature this remains the case: if the image of the home remains riddled with cliché and adult ideals then so does the image of the family (*Masculinity and the Middle-Class* 4). This idealised image can be demonstrated by asking anyone, child or adult, to describe the depictions of homes in children's books, for it is more than likely that he/she will describe homes with warm kitchens where hams hang up, beamed ceilings, log fires and Welsh dressers; images that abound in the homes found in texts from Kenneth Grahame's *The Wind in the Willows* (1908), Katherine Holabird and Helen Craig's *Angelina Ballerina* (1983), Roald Dahl's *Fantastic Mr Fox* (1970), to Hagrid's hut in J.K. Rowling's 'Harry Potter' series and many others.

The home is the haven of the family and, like the family, the ideal of the home remains intrinsic to children's literature throughout the nineteenth and twentieth centuries. This literature defines what constitutes a good and bad home and judges the family accordingly, dictating a correct mode of behaviour both to its child and adult readers. But the home is not simply a cottage-like haven. It is a place of disciplinary control and as such can be both enriching and stifling, a sanctuary and a prison, a place to return to and to escape from. This chapter looks at the history and theoretical ideology of the home before turning to examples of homes in children's fiction. It charts the depictions of seemingly perfect and then imperfect homes throughout the last two centuries, analyses characters' returns to the home and also considers the difficulties they have in escaping it, and goes on to offer a reading of the home as the site of maternal love and influence and hence a place of womb-like retreat.

History and Theory

The retreat to the home is clearly articulated in Aidan Chambers' *Tell Me*, in which an example of classroom discussion is cited. When the children are asked 'What would you do if you had had a bad day, or a horrible experience, or felt the world was against you, where would you go?' they all replied in unison 'Home' (106). Home is meant to be a sanctuary, a place to retreat to away from the cold outside world, or at least this is how it has been constructed and has therefore been instilled in individuals from the nursery to the nursing home. Part of the definition of home comes from what it is not; most simply it is the antithesis of away, and therefore the word 'home' becomes culturally loaded as it invokes a nostalgia for warmth and comfort. The ideal home, like the family, is so entangled in myth that it has, in a Barthesian sense, become naturalised and consequently, any home that does not conform is classed as unnatural (Barthes, *Mythologies*). This ideal and ideology have developed, in the main, from the nineteenth century, especially the Victorian era, when the home and the family became increasingly important symbols of moral and social wellbeing.

Children's literature and the mythology of the perfect sanctuary of the home grew up together during the nineteenth century. Then the interest in the home was developed to new levels: the Industrial Revolution and urban growth led to an increasing number of the population working outside the home and so the home's importance increased as, instead of being a place in which people lived and worked, it became, for the man of the house at least, an alternative place to the outside world and work – a place dedicated to family. Judith Flanders argues that 'as the Industrial Revolution appeared to have taken over every aspect of working life, so the family, and by extension the house, expanded in tandem to act as an emotional counterweight' (*The Victorian House* xxxxi). Countless journals for the middle classes regarding the home became common: the *Gardener's Magazine* was founded in 1826 (Tosh *Masculinity and the Middle-Class* 33); the first citation of the word 'homesick' appeared in the *OED* in 1798 and phrases like 'Home Sweet Home' expressed what Tosh calls the Victorians' 'deep commitment to the *idea* of home' (*Masculinity and the Middle-Class* 27). While this may have been initiated by the middle classes the nostalgic impact of the home and the idealistic images that emphasise how a home should be run are apparent in the majority of children's fiction and thus apply across the social scale. Hagrid's hut and the children's home in *Gumble's Yard* are made just as homely as Badger's house in *The Wind and the Willows* because they all aspire to a similar image of what the home should be. Similarly, despite essentially being homeless, Elsa in Jacqueline Wilson's *The Bed and Breakfast Star* constructs a conventional ideal home as she imagines where she would like to live. The working-class families in children's literature then adhere to what was originally a nineteenth-century middle-class ideal of the home and this notion punctuates much of our children's literature.

Accounts of home and its pleasures are frequent in nineteenth-century literature: John Ruskin's father wrote 'Oh! How dull and dreary is the best society

I fall into compared with the circle of my own Fire Side with my Love sitting opposite irradiating all around her, and my most extraordinary boy' (Quoted in Flanders xxiv). Similarly, the French philosopher Hippolyte Taine commented on the Englishman's obsession with the home as a type of fortress against the evils of the world, stating that

> Every Englishman has, in the matter of marriage, a romantic spot in his heart. He imagines a 'home', with the woman of his choice, the pair of them alone with their children. That is his own little universe, closed to the world. So long as he has not achieved this he is ill at ease. (Taine 78)

The concept of the home as complete retreat 'closed to the world' was a popular one, for in this small world the inhabitants are able to exercise complete power; it is a navigable, controllable world. More recently, Gaston Bachelard argued that 'our house is the corner of the world. As has often been said, it is our first universe, a real cosmos in every sense of the word' (4). The image of the home is focused upon in many aspects of culture and society, but in children's literature the home is central and is constantly referred to as it represents the location in which family matters are dealt with.

Accordingly, the home in children's literature has been subject to a great deal of critical attention. Maria Nikolajeva emphasises the importance of the home in a variety of texts from J.R.R. Tolkien's *The Hobbit* (1937) to Michelle Magorian's *Back Home* (1985), arguing that 'Home in idyllic fiction is the foremost security. Home is where the protagonists belong and where they return to after any exploration of the outside world' (*From Mythic to Linear* 24–5). I would add that even in non-idyllic fiction the home remains central to the text as the desire for the ideal home has already been initiated by previous generations of texts: the dream instilled in the reader by the text is always to return to the ideal of home as depicted in *The Hobbit* or *The Wind in the Willows*. Sarah Godek also recognises the home as a 'symbol of stability' but simultaneously argues that texts like Mary Norton's *The Borrowers* (1952) show that stability is becoming increasingly unobtainable and concludes by suggesting that modern children's literature has seen a shift from sheltering children by means of household stability to preparing them for future instability (89–107). But this shift is not as revolutionary as it might appear, for even in the most seemingly radical texts there remains a desire to return to an ideal of home and family, and that ideal is still, I suggest, caught up in images of nuclear families living in symmetrical houses with roses around the door. In addition, even in preparing children for instability children's literature still dictates a certain way of living; it demonstrates that ideals still exist, that readers should strive for a 'good' home and family.

Nowhere is this desire for home better illustrated than in the pattern of returning home after a journey that is prevalent in children's fiction. This return to the home is crucial as it ensures that the child characters and therefore the child readers recognise and internalise the importance of returning home, for it is in the home where adults have complete control. Jon Stott and Doyle Francis argue that children's literature tends to chart the child characters' move 'from a setting which is "not home" to one which is "home"' (223). They use Maurice Sendak's *Where the Wild Things Are* (1963) as an example, explaining that Max moves from a place which he does not see as homely to the world of the 'wild things' but then, having had his adventure, returns to a true home 'where someone loved him best of all' (np).

For Stott and Doyle the home is a mental attitude and it is Max who changes rather than the fabric of the home. The purpose of the text then is to indoctrinate Max into an adult system of belief, to ensure that he returns to the home and family, and to the policed adult society in which food, homes and families dominate.[2] In short, to study children's literature is to analyse an adult ideal (Hunt, *Introduction to Children's Literature* 3). Consequently, in analysing the home in children's literature the position of the adult must be acknowledged, as it is the adult who moulds the concepts of home for the child. As Nodelman notes:

> As Orientalism is primarily for the benefit of Europeans, child psychology and children's literature are primarily for the benefit of adults [. . .]. By and large, we encourage in children those values and behaviours that make children easier for us to handle: more passive, more docile, more obedient – and thus more in need of our guidance and more willing to accept the need for it. It's no accident that the vast majority of stories for children share the message that despite one's dislikes of the constraints one feels there, home is still the best, the safest place to be. ('The Other' 30)

Even in troubled family stories the children are encouraged to return home and to the family. The message at the conclusion of John Rowe Townsend's *Gumble's Yard* (1961) is 'Even an unsatisfactory family is better than none' (100). For home is where the family is, and, as Nodelman makes clear, where adults exercise power, but also where the child should be in order to fulfil the life of the parent.

Nikolajeva argues, in her explanation of the popularity of domestic stories, that 'they fulfil the child's need to confirm the stability of the childhood world' (*From Mythic to Linear* 49), but I contend that the utopian element in domestic fiction fulfils the adult and parental need for the stability of home as much as it does the child's. Children's literature is dominated by adults and the images of homes, and the emphasis on returning home is an adult-orientated perception. Virginia L. Wolf suggests that 'our desire for home, rooted in our infantile perception of reality, is so strong that we cannot do without the myth' (66). Surely this is something of a chicken and egg dilemma: the desire for home is rooted in the adult psyche in part because of the constant reinforcement of the ideal of home that adults encountered in the texts they read as children, and as a result adults continue to produce children's books which show idealistic homes, and so children's literature remains trapped in a circular pattern. This circularity appears in different forms; Nodelman calls the times when characters leave home for an adventure and then return the home/away/home pattern (*Pleasures* 147). This is a circular pattern which serves the adults as it sees the return of the child to the confines of the home.[3] The pattern re-emphasises the static problem of children's literature; change, if it even exists with regard to home and family, is a very slow process since children's literature is forever trapped in adult-orientated nostalgia.

Home as Haven

In the editor's preface to *Children's Literature: An Illustrated History* Peter Hunt explains that the 'most common view of children's literature is that the books have progressed steadily from didacticism to freedom, or from strictness to corruption' (xii). Hunt then goes on to argue that while the earliest children's fiction was heavily influenced by religion and didacticism, 'even the most modern liberated book cannot escape the adult-child relationship' (xii). The conduct-book style evident in Catherine Sedgwick's *Home* (1835) and Mary Martha Sherwood's *The History of the Fairchild Family* (1818) promotes a strict concept of the idealised home and, while the tone of address may have changed, the ideal concept of the home which underlies the majority of children's fiction has hardly changed at all.

This is clear in the descriptions of characters returning to the sanctuary of home having completed an adventure in which they discovered the dangers and vanities of the world. Meg, in Louisa M. Alcott's *Little Women* (1868), returns from her stay at the Moffats' house declaring that 'Home *is* a nice place, though it isn't splendid' (134). Forty years later, Anne in *Anne of Green Gables* (1908) insists that while she had 'a splendid time,' at Diana's Aunt Josephine's 'the best of it all was the coming home' (Montgomery 285). Bilbo Baggins in *The Hobbit* (1937) comes 'back again' to find that the 'sound of the kettle on his hearth was ever more musical than it had been even in the quiet days before the Unexpected Party' (Tolkien 288). In Judy Blume's *Superfudge* (1980), during a family discussion concerning whether or not to return to the home city of New York, baby Tootsie's first words are, rather conveniently, 'Nu Yuck', and so the family return and Peter rejoices in going back (140). And more recently, Lyra, in *Northern Lights* (1995), desires the comforts of her admittedly unconventional home when she is in hiding on the boat: 'then she wished passionately that nothing had ever changed, nothing would ever change, that she could be Lyra of Jordan College for ever and ever' (Pullman 151). Happy endings in children's literature often consist of homecomings, and this is a disciplinary technique for it instils in children that home and the family it represents is the only place in which to find solace and that, ultimately, the successful character and family can be recognised by the return to a happy home.

As well as promoting the ever-clichéd homecoming, children's literature also tends to deal with the home in general in a rather saccharine way. In Sedgwick's

Home, the home is presented as the epitome of security and love as Mr Barclay tells his wife:

> You could make the happiness of any home to me, Anne. Shifted about as I have been from pillar to post, I scarcely know what home is, from experience; but it is a word that to my mind expresses every motive and aid to virtue and indicates almost every source of happiness. (5)

Mr Barclay articulates the powerful ideology that surrounds the home; he has no experience of the ideal secure and stable home, yet he has internalised the ideal. Moreover, Mr Barclay's experience of the unstable home serves to emphasise further the 'normal' desirable home. The image of the home is a peculiarly idealistic one which, in conjunction with the title of Sedgwick's novel, emphasises the centrality of the home in the text. The reader is told what a home should be, rendering this text as much of a guidebook to family life as it is a children's text.

In *The History of the Fairchild Family* the Fairchild family's home is also depicted as a haven and is described in pre-lapsarian imagery: 'Mr and Mrs Fairchild lived very far from any town; their house stood in the midst of a garden, which in summertime was full of fruit and flowers' (Sherwood 7). The house is separated from the town and stands surrounded by nature – not wild nature like a forest or field, but a tamed respectable garden, and in fact the garden serves as a sort of buffer surrounding and protecting the home. In addition, this garden is fertile enough to produce fruits and flowers, rendering the family self–sufficient; ideally the family should be able to live off the fruits of their labour. The symbolic perfection of the family home implies the perfection of the Fairchild family.

The fantasy of the home as an Edenic retreat is reproduced in several children's texts: in *The Wind in the Willows* Mole and Ratty, while on their journey home in the cold, stumble upon a home which corresponds to the stereotypical constructed fantasy of home:

> But it was from one little window, with its blind drawn down, a mere blank transparency on the night, that the sense of home and the little curtained world within walls – the larger stressful world of outside Nature shut out and forgotten – most pulsated (Grahame 86).

The description reasserts the opposition between inside and outside and associates home with warmth and belonging and the outside with the cold sense of isolation. It illustrates Hippolyte Taine's comments on the Englishman's obsession with home in the nineteenth century and reinforces conventional notions of what constitutes a good home. Depicted as a cosy place cut off from the cold outside world, home is symbolised by domestic signifiers: dressers, beamed ceilings, log fires, lighted windows and countless other indicators, and these are evident in children's literature from *The Wind in the Willows* to the 'Harry Potter' series and the 'Angelina Ballerina' picturebook series.

The centrality of the home in children's fiction is frequently demonstrated by its location at the beginning of the texts as in *The History of the Fairchild Family* (1818), Edith Nesbit's *The Story of The Treasure Seekers* (1899), Noel Streatfield's *Ballet Shoes* (1936), *The Hobbit* (1937) and *Harry Potter and the Philosopher's Stone* (1997). By placing the home at the beginning of the narrative it is shown to be integral to the text; it is the foundation of the story regardless of whether it is a good or bad home. The solidarity of the family is shown by the illustration in *The Family from One End Street* (1937) where the family is pictured on the doorstep of a terraced house; the family members sit close together as the house is small, but this affords a sense of cosiness. While the father goes out of the house to work as a dustman it is implied that the mother and children work together as they stand united under the sign for the family laundry business. Furthermore, this business, like the family, is not a normal run-of-the-mill business, but an 'ideal' one. The home serves to unite the family and also to cement its identity beneath the family sign.

Identity and the home are also entwined in *The Story of the Treasure Seekers* as Oswald describes the home before even giving his readers the family name: 'Our ancestral home is in the Lewisham Road. It is semi-detached and has a garden, not a large one. We are the Bastables' (Nesbit 10). In addition, while the style of narration may be different from Mary Martha Sherwood's, the fact that the story is initiated with a description of the home, and that the situation of the house is semi-detached with a garden is emphasised shows that similar ideals and traits are evident. The house is not entirely detached, does not stand buffered by a garden, but it is only attached in one place and though the garden is 'not large' it still exists. The ideal of living in a house like the Fairchilds' is certainly evident since Oswald, in his narration, describes the Bastable home in relation to the desirable ideal. The desire for a specific type of home is promulgated in children's fiction; homes should be welcoming places that can be returned to and desired at every turn, and the family that achieves such a home is considered to have reached the epitome of good, moral domesticity. It is necessary then to turn to the not so perfect, and those families that cannot achieve such levels of domesticity are dismissed as failing, and consequently, in their 'failure' they promote, by negative example, ideologically constructed notions of normality.

The Not So Perfect

Just as much attention has been paid by critics to the loss of the family in children's literature, so there has also been criticism regarding the loss of the home. Lucy Waddey, for example, argues that the home is losing its cosy image:

> But in more recent fiction attitudes toward home and parents have changed; indeed, one mark of contemporary realism for children is its ambivalent description of home and family life. (13)

Superficially, at the level of the narrative this appears to hold true; contemporary fiction often portrays homes that are unconventional. But, it seems to me, that the home remains important even in texts which are ambivalent about it: the image of the bad home only serves to enhance its opposite. The classic traits of children's literature are still present, and in order to accentuate the good homes it is essential to depict the bad ones. Good families, it seems, rarely live in 'bad' homes and while these exist in children's literature, the ideal and hope to return to a good home remains a constant didactic subtext. In Gillian Cross's *Wolf* (1990), Cassy's mother lives in an untidy squat, and while she saves Cassy in the end, her home reflects her style of parenting: somewhat erratic, at times bordering on neglectful, and generally unpredictable. In Jacqueline Wilson's *The Bed and Breakfast Star* (1994) the text is structured around the number of beds Elsa has slept in, and the family is trapped in the one room where the stepfather often smacks the children. In *Back Home* Rusty's little brother Charlie refuses to acknowledge that his grandmother's house is home because of his dislike for his unloving and unjust grandmother.

Children's literature insists that the home, like the family, should be a place of love, benevolence and warmth, and anything that falls short of this is at best described as a 'house', and depicted as a place which the character is passing through on his/her journey to somewhere better – that is, the quest for a real home. But it is also important to recognise the variety of homes that exist in children's literature, for contemporary literature represents homes such as those in *Wolf* or *The Bed and Breakfast Star* in parallel with the idealised homes in Jill Murphy's 'Mrs Large' series or the Weasleys' home in the 'Harry Potter' series.

It is too simplistic to suggest that homes fit into a pattern of being bad in modern stories and good in the golden days of children's literature: there are deviations and variations in both periods. This variety can be seen in the early twentieth century, Misselthwaite Manor in Burnett's *The Secret Garden* (1911) is a 'queer place,' a 'grand big place in a gloomy way' (14). In Burnett's *Little Lord Fauntleroy* (1886) Cedric's grandfather's house ensures that mother and son are separated until near the conclusion of the text, and it is again a threatening, unconventional home, yet these texts were published in the same period as *The Wind in the Willows* and *Anne of Green Gables*. As we have seen, the home that deviates from the constructed norm does not necessarily simply respond to cultural change but rather reasserts notions of normality. Texts like the 'Mrs Large' picturebook series which focus on the homely activities of a happy family of elephants and *The Bed and Breakfast Star*, which concentrates on a far less idyllic family in the depths of poverty, work together in constructing a mythology of home and family; rather than contradict each other they do in fact complement each other as they combine to restore the fantasy of the happy home and family.

While homes are often presented in idyllic terms in children's literature, these literary homes are not simple havens. They are part of a disciplinary ideology that works on the characters in the text and by proxy on the reader. Nikolajeva argues that there are few threats in domestic fiction:

> The utopian elements we find in domestic stories are once again the isolated setting allowing for an autonomous micro-society (in *Little Women* also a mono-gender), the absence of serious threat, and a general sense of security, happiness and harmony. (*From Mythic to Linear* 41)

I concur that this is how children's literature seems to be, sometimes is, and is perhaps how the adult would like it to be, but further analysis reveals underlying tensions within even the most seemingly placid home in children's literature. Sometimes the threats come from within, from not being able to escape the utopia. *Little Women*, with its images of the sisters and mothers working together and sitting around the fire to read the father's letter, seems to promote an idea of domestic utopia, but concealment and restriction are also evident. Jo's comment, after listening to Marmee read the letter, illustrates the powerful hold of domesticity:

> 'I'll try to [. . .] do my duty here instead of wanting to be somewhere else,' said Jo, thinking that keeping her temper at home was a much harder task than facing a rebel or two down South. (Alcott 13)

This is the first indication that Jo would rather be 'somewhere else'; that the home, rather than nurturing her, confines her. Subverting the positive images of a home in which all the sisters love and help one another is the desire to escape.

Elizabeth Keyser argues that Jo is 'confined within the uncomfortable role of little woman' (54), limited by gender, and I would further suggest that it is also partly the domestic sphere that confines Jo. Eventually she marries and only gains acknowledgement in the title when she has her own family – *Jo's Boys*. Identity is still entwined with the home and family, and Jo is unable to escape either. The home in *Little Women* becomes a threatening place since in not allowing escape it can only stunt growth and ambition. There is a certain ambiguity with regard to the home; of necessity the home must provide security, but that security can become confining and limiting. Children's literature promotes the fantasy of the good home at every turn and yet there are instances when the home is depicted as a stifling place. Of course, Jo conforms to the path that society has laid down for her, and the contemporary readers were perhaps meant to admire this, and yet, there remains something troubling, to the twenty-first-century reader at least, about her submission. In short, Jo has returned home, and she, like Max in *Where the Wild Things Are*, has been 'civilised'.

Home, for all its constriction and confinement, is still promoted as the place where all belong, and this, according to children's literature, is especially so for women and children.

Home Is Where the Mother Is

Jo, in the course of the Alcott trilogy, is made into a mother and accordingly is confined to the home and school. Mother and home, like mother and family, are constantly linked, and as a result the motherless home is something of a contradiction in children's literature. In those texts in which the mother has died or is absent it is common practice for the eldest daughter to take on her role and this occurs in Susan Coolidge's *What Katy Did* (1872), Charlotte M. Yonge's *The Daisy Chain* (1856), Edith Nesbit's *The Story of the Treasure Seekers*, John Rowe Townsend's *Gumble's Yard* (1961), and, to a certain extent, in Anne Fine's *Madame Doubtfire* (1987). But generally, when the mother is absent from the home, the family suffers: in *The Secret Garden* for instance, Misselthwaite Manor is described as a loveless place until Mary discovers her deceased aunt's garden and life returns to the environment; in *Peter Pan* Wendy, as mother, creates a home; and, in *Little Lord Fauntleroy* the grandfather's mansion is sterile and unhomely partly because of his refusal to allow Cedric's mother to live there until the happy conclusion. More recently in Jacqueline Wilson's *Tracy Beaker* (1991) Tracy dreams of the perfect home, but her mother has left her and consequently Tracy has no home and is forced to grow up in care.

The home, especially in the nineteenth and early twentieth century, responds to popular concepts of women and home during these periods:

> 'Home was not a place, but a projection of the feminine, an encircling encouraging, comforting aura that was there to protect a husband and children from the harshness of the world: "wherever a true wife comes", Ruskin wrote, "this home is always around her". (Quoted in Flanders xxxi)

The home encapsulates pre-conceived ideas of mothers and families, and even the homes in which the elder daughter takes over the maternal role are still portrayed as having complications, as essentially the mother is always presented as the key symbol of the home, and therefore, the family. Nowhere is the association of mother and home clearer than in Kenneth Grahame's *The Wind in the Willows*:

> Now, with a rush of old memories, how clearly it stood up before him, in the darkness! Shabby indeed, and small and poorly furnished, and yet his, the home he had made for himself, the home he had been so happy to get back to after his day's work. And the home had been happy with him, too, evidently, and was missing him and wanted him back, and was telling him

so, through his nose, sorrowfully, reproachfully, but with no bitterness or anger; only with plaintive reminder that it was there and wanted him.

The call was clear, the summons was plain. He must obey it instantly and go. (88–9)

The home is personified; it becomes the mother. In a text devoid of key female characters it is noteworthy that the need for the maternal is still apparent and moreover that this need is articulated in the depiction of the home as it becomes the substitute mother. In turn, the call of the mother returns us to the very physical connection of mother and child which is entirely uncontrollable on the part of Mole; his destiny is in the power of the mother/home. The return to the mother/home is naturalised; it is something that cannot be avoided and as a result it is implied in the tone of the text that it should not be avoided. The home, like the idealised mother, is not bitter or angry, but patiently awaits the character/child's return; it is always there offering security and stability. The text reminds its readers that the home and by proxy the mother and family will always await the return of the adventurer.

In Edith Nesbit's *The Story of the Treasure Seekers* ambivalence about the home can be located in anxieties about the absent mother as, unlike the summons that Mole receives, the Bastable children have to live with the knowledge that their mother has died, and consequently this disrupts their faith in the security of home. While the home in *The Story of the Treasure Seekers* contains some idyllic conventional images of family life as the children meet their father at the door in the evenings, it also offers an ambiguous representation of the family:

And when I went back into the dining-room I saw how different it was from when Mother was here, and we are different, and Father is different, and nothing is like it was. I am glad I am not made to think about it every day. (Nesbit 150–1)

The home is a source of unease as it is incomplete in the absence of the mother. The text moves through a number of positions with regard to the home: it is described positively and proudly initially, as shown by its prominent position in the opening sentence; becomes uncomfortable, as the quotation demonstrates, and then finally, the family move out of their 'ancestral home' into 'one of those jolly, big, ugly red houses with a lot of windows, that are so comfortable inside' (Nesbit *Treasure Seekers* 234). Oswald's choice of language here adds to the ambiguity as he fails to give either a positive or negative portrait of the house. It is appropriate that Oswald describes the new house as 'the most comfortable one I have ever been in' and then goes on to say that his father's sitting-room in the new house contains a 'beautiful portrait of Mother' (Nesbit *Treasure Seekers* 238). The mother has returned, even if only in a painted representation, and so on the one hand the conclusion remains positive as it portrays the reunited family but, on the other hand, the original home has been lost to the family and they are unable to be self-sufficient.

While *The Story of the Treasure Seekers* superficially presents an ideal home and family, this is subverted by the many complexities and ambiguities it depicts, and in many ways it is very similar to Anne Fine or Jacqueline Wilson's late twentieth-century stories in which a parent leaves or dies. Though the children talk less of their mother in *The Story of the Treasure Seekers* than perhaps in Wilson's *Double Act*, the earlier text's influence remains important. Moreover, in both narratives the families move house and set up home with an additional adult, the uncle in *The Story of the Treasure Seekers* and a stepmother in *Double Act*, but neither really acts as a satisfactory replacement for the mother. In contrast, rather than the absence of mothers in *The Story of the Treasure Seekers* or *Double Act*, substitute mothers are a strong feature of J.M. Barrie's *Peter Pan* (1911).

Peter Pan addresses many issues with regard to the house, home and mother. It adheres to other forms of children's literature in its emphasis on the sanctuary of home and the departure from and return home, and yet at times seems to mock the cliché of home. The depiction of the mother is particularly complex, as the conflict between the child's desire for freedom and the need for security and love is symbolised in the opposition between the home/mother and Peter Pan. With the home comes constraint, and when considered in these terms, *Peter Pan* is not so different from *Little Women*: the homes appear secure and loving, yet they also confine and stifle the individuals within them. Peter Pan, unlike Jo, is able to escape these constraints, but in doing so he is forced to deny his need for home and family and to reconcile himself to the sacrifice that independence demands.

There are two homes in *Peter Pan*: the conventional one in Kensington Gardens that belongs to Wendy, John, Michael and their parents, the home that they must ultimately return to; and the home in the Neverland where Wendy, Peter and the boys reside. In many ways Wendy and Peter's home in the Neverland is managed in a very traditional way as both Peter and Wendy conform to prescribed gender roles; the boys meet Peter at the door; Wendy supervises at dinner time and ensures all the 'children' have taken their make-believe medicine; and Peter and Wendy have 'adult' conversations:

> 'Ah, old lady,' Peter said aside to Wendy, warming himself by the fire and looking down at her as she sat turning a heel, 'there is nothing more pleasant of an evening for you and me when the day's toil is over than to rest by the fire with the little ones nearby.' (Barrie *Peter Pan* 144)

This is reminiscent of Ruskin's comments discussed earlier as it idealises the concept of home and family. Peter's comment is a cliché, and further, is contained in another cliché as the chapter is entitled 'The Happy Home'. This over-use of cliché urges caution, for while Gillian Beer suggests that 'cliché assures us that we all belong together' (29) it can also be used in order either to satirise or cover something up. Peter's words appear to parody the stereotypical home so often idealised in nineteenth-century literature and art. In addition to this, Peter's words add ambiguity to his and Wendy's status; they are simultaneously mother and father and girl and boy. The home under the ground is presented as a haven of good parenting and yet the tensions between Peter and Wendy regarding the status of their relationship render it a less idyllic home than it first seemed: ultimately Wendy desires, or is meant to desire, the domestic, whereas Peter, although happy to imitate 'the family circle', is destined to choose the life of adventure.

It is Wendy who brings with her the ideal of the home; before her appearance in Neverland there were only houses. In *Peter Pan* the distinction between the two is subtly made; the house, it would seem, simply accommodates people, whereas the home brings people together. It is appropriate then that the Wendy house is built in the chapter that is entitled 'A Little House', as opposed to the chapters entitled 'The Home Under the Ground', 'The Happy Home' and 'The Return Home', for the Wendy house is really just for Wendy.[4] But in constructing it for Wendy the boys work on conventional ideals of what a house should look like as it is built to a traditional cliché-based design:

> The little house looked so cosy and safe in the darkness with a bright light showing through its blinds, and the chimney smoking beautifully, and Peter standing on guard. (Barrie *Peter Pan* 101)

The house built for Wendy seems idyllic but it serves to separate the 'family': Peter stands outside, Wendy sleeps inside and the boys sleep in the home which is the hole underneath the tree.

The traditional appeal of the house is deceptive. While the house was built as something of a labour of love in order to protect Wendy, it is never described as a home; the home remains under the ground. In building the house around Wendy, the boys metaphorically confine her inside the walls of domesticity and so the connection between femininity and domesticity is reiterated, and it is fitting that the boys ask Wendy to be their mother when she is admiring her new house. But conversely, the Wendy house becomes redundant once Wendy takes on her role as mother, for she moves in with the lost boys and she and her brothers 'grew to love their home under the ground; especially Wendy' (Barrie *Peter Pan* 104). Wendy, like Ruskin's idealised mother figure has, metaphorically speaking, become the signifier of home. In *Peter Pan* the house is built for Wendy, but the home is the place in which the family are together; the home under the tree illustrates this since it 'consisted of one large room, as all houses should do' (Barrie *Peter Pan* 104). The distinction between house and home, and the significance of Wendy's role in this, is clear when Peter tells Mrs Darling that he will live with Tink in the 'house we built for Wendy': home, without Wendy, is simply a house (Barrie *Peter Pan* 230).

Wendy and the narrator enhance the unchanging and inextricably linked image of the home and mother by emphasising that a window will always stand open as it represents 'a mother's love' (Barrie *Peter Pan* 153). Moreover, the difference between Mr and Mrs Darling is marked when Mr Darling asks her to close the window to prevent a draught, to which Mrs Darling responds that the window 'must always be left open for them, always, always' (Barrie *Peter Pan* 220). A mother and home, it seems, can always be relied upon. In contrast, Peter Pan's view on mothers and homes is less conventional:

> 'Long ago,' he said, 'I thought like you that my mother would always keep the window open for me; so I stayed away for moons and moons and moons, and then flew back; but the window was barred, for mother had forgotten all about me, and there was another little boy sleeping in my bed.' (Barrie *Peter Pan* 153)

Here, Peter destroys the cosy images and ideals of homes and mothers illustrated by much of children's literature, as he tells the readers that the home might not always be there or be open to them.

This is in complete contrast to the majority of children's literature, which tends to over-emphasise the importance of returning to the unchanged home. Peter's home has changed, he has been replaced, and he is unable to return. Jacqueline Rose suggests that Peter has challenged Wendy and broken up her happy rose-tinted story and in the Neverland, after Peter has added ambiguity to both the home and mother, the underground family break up and can be captured by Captain Hook (34). Rose goes on to argue that one of the major conflicts in the story is that between the nursery and the Neverland (34). Certainly, this would seem true as this conflict between the Neverland and the nursery divides Peter and Wendy, as the Neverland is fought for by Peter, and the nursery by Wendy.

In light of this, Peter's interruption of Wendy's story can be seen as simply spiteful and not, as the narrator tells us, entirely reliable: 'I am not sure that this was true, but Peter thought it was true; and it scared them' (Barrie *Peter Pan* 153). While Peter addresses the characters' and possibly the reader's, certainly the adult reader's, greatest fears that the home and mother will no longer be there waiting, the narrator reassures the reader by bringing Peter's story into question. While different houses and different homes are addressed in *Peter Pan*, and Peter's image of the home contrasts with the majority of children's fiction, the narrator refuses to endorse Peter's story and this is because the story is too unconventional and too threatening to allow it to be presented without suspicion in a children's book.

The conclusion, then, leaves us with as satisfying an answer as possible: the children return home to grow up, but Peter is forever locked out from this home as he 'looked through the window at the one joy from which he must be for ever barred' (Barrie *Peter Pan* 225). But it must be remembered that this was Peter's choice; he was invited to live and grow up with the Darlings, but chooses instead his house with Tink and the loan of a temporary mother, a Wendy, for spring cleaning. Peter can choose the life he desires but Wendy's choice is bound in domesticity; she can stay in the Neverland and be mother to Peter, or return to London and be mother to her own biological children. If the mother represents the home, then *Peter Pan* re-asserts notions of normality as the home and family are secured by the knowledge that the good mother will always be at the beck and call of her family; essentially, she is given no other option.

Womb-Like Homes

In finding that the home in children's literature is embedded in maternal imagery it is reasonable to take this a step further and consider the home as a metaphor of the womb. The perfect home as described in children's literature should be cosy, safe and warm with a constant food supply and this can be interpreted as a Freudian desire to return to the womb. Of course there are other possible readings of homes in children's fiction, but the psychoanalytical approach is helpful because it goes some way to explaining the static nature of the family in children's fiction. The womb symbolises the body of home; it is the ultimate home, where life begins, where the foetus is safe and nourished, and if the foetus is in the womb then the adult always knows where he/she is.

In representing the home as a womb-like environment, adult readers/writers/publishers reiterate the theoretical ideal, for if the family could only live in an all-encompassing womb-like home then the children would be safe and controlled and the home would epitomise the idealised hidden retreat from the outside world. The texts in which womb imagery is most manifest tend to be written in the early twentieth century, a time when individuals were looking back towards childhood for salvation, but I suggest that in the depictions of homes, even disreputable homes, writers, even now, never really break away from this ideal of home. Moreover, in attempting to maintain this fantasy, children's literature remains static as it emphasises the need to keep the child in the body of home and so under the control of the family.

The imagery which links the home and womb causes inevitable complications because, while there might be a desire on the part of the adult to return to the sanctuary of the womb, this is contradicted by the child's need to move away from the womb: to be born into the outside world. Roderick McGillis observes that 'children's books both collectively and in each work of fiction, present a rite of passage from dependence to maturity' (77–8) and Pauline Dewan argues that all childhood homes are 'stepping-stones to other places' as a child must eventually leave home (134). I would agree that most children's books follow this pattern, and add that this pattern fits with the imagery of wombs/homes and births – the child must leave. McGillis also recognises the significance of the symbolism of the womb imagery to children's fiction as he refers to its use in

Charlotte's Web and in *The Hobbit* and, with regard to the latter, explains that Bilbo Baggins' journey from his womb-like home is a formative one.

The home, in children's literature, nurtures and protects, and then the child changes and feels the need to leave, metaphorically to be born. Allowing the parturition of the child is a troublesome issue for children's literature, since rarely do the children leave home entirely. Often, as Nodelman suggests, they leave home briefly and then return. This may seem problematic, for obviously in reality the return to the womb is not physically possible, but there is a sense of self-indulgent desire in allowing fictional characters to return to the home/womb after an adventure. Children's literature permits the possibility of returning to, and perhaps hiding in, the security of the womb/home and this, I suggest, is partly in response to the fantasy of returning to a mythological golden age of family; the ideal is promulgated at every step.

But there are instances when characters manage to leave home for good: in A.A Milne's *The House at Pooh Corner* (1928) Christopher Robin leaves home when he breaks the definite boundaries of the woods as shown by the border around the map at the front of the text and emerges into the real world. Here, though, Christopher Robin leaves a part of himself in the home in the toys that are conserved in a static womb-like environment from which they will never be freed. Further, the narrator informs the reader, that magically, 'in that enchanted place on top of the Forest a little boy and his Bear will always be playing' (Milne *House at Pooh Corner* 316). There remains a need, perhaps on the part of the author and readers, to be able to return to the home/womb and find it unchanged; in short, to immortalise it. This need to return to the womb adds complexity and a sense of awkwardness and tension to children's literature; the child, who tends to want to grow up, is set in conflict with the adult who wants to return to the idealised safety of childhood. Consequently, texts like *The Wind in the Willows*, *Winnie the Pooh* and to a certain extent *Little Women* create a sense of repression in conjunction with an idealistic notion of home and protection. The conflict between preserving offspring in the cultural construct of childhood and liberating him/her into the world away from the immediate family is integral to children's fiction and the womb-like homes reassert these complexities.

Although the characters in *The Wind in the Willows* leave the Riverbank periodically, their lives of retreat are never seriously threatened, as the Riverbank provides for all their needs. The Riverbank is, like the garden in other texts, an extension of the home. It remains a safe haven which Mole and Rat are destined never to leave. As Rat makes it clear, there is no need to move away from the Riverbank and consequently the animals can never emerge into, or meta-phorically be born into the Wide World:

'Beyond the Wild Wood comes the Wide World,' said the Rat. 'And that's something that doesn't matter, either to you or me. I've never been there, and I'm not going, nor you either if you've got any sense at all. Don't ever refer to it again please. Now then! Here's our backwater at last, where we're going to lunch.' (Grahame 16–7)

It is possible to read this passage in terms of birth imagery. The animals are protected on two levels from the Wide World: first, the animals retire to lunch in the backwater, representing the nutrition afforded by the amniotic fluid and constant food supply in the womb; second, in order to reach the Wide World the animals would have to travel through the Wild Wood, a metaphorical passage through the vagina. Mole and Rat's harrowing experience of the Wild Wood emphasises the brutality of the transition, as the two were 'aching with fatigue and bruised with tumbles', an image that is evocative of birth and the move away from the warmth of the womb/home/family where the text insists the characters belong (Grahame 58).

It is the framework of maternal imagery that constructs the home or garden as being womb-like and comforting, and those places that do not correspond to this tradition, like Misselthwaite Manor in *The Secret Garden* or Toad Hall in *The Wind in the Willows*, are depicted as cold and unhomely. Conversely, Parsons argues that Colin's room in Misselthwaite Manor in *The Secret Garden* is also representative of a womb, 'yet it is stifling rather than nurturing, and Colin has become both physically and emotionally crippled within it. The house disables, discourages and hides life away' (Parsons 259). I would argue that it is precisely because of the lack of maternal signifiers within Colin's room that it cripples him both emotionally and physically:

> It was a big room with ancient, handsome furniture in it. There was a low fire glowing faintly on the hearth and a night-light burning by the side of a carved, four poster bed hung with brocade, and on the bed was lying a boy, crying pitifully. (Burnett *The Secret Garden* 124)

The description of the room is distinctly masculine: it is not small and cosy like the homes of Badger, or Mole or Rat, but big and ancient: the four poster bed and the heavy brocade add a sense of grandness; the furniture is 'handsome', a masculine descriptor, and although the fire gives comfort, it is surrounded by male, upper-class signifiers. If this is a womb, as Parsons suggests, then it is oxymoronic. It is a male womb; the surroundings are part of the patriarchal tradition as opposed to the images of nature evident in the secret garden which are perceived to be part of the feminine tradition. It is not surprising that Colin lies crying and stunted in the midst of this, for this is not a womb in the traditional sense. There is an absence of feminine imagery in Colin's room: even the portrait of the mother is covered and it is a room without love, friendship or any contact with nature. Dark, stifling and devoid of life, it results in Colin's illness, it is as Pauline Dewan observes an unhealthy indoor place (55). The happiness of the story comes with the discovery of the garden and its impact on the children's health.

If there is a womb-like place in *The Secret Garden*, then it is the garden. The feminine imagery in *The Secret Garden* has been noted before by various critics: Barbara Almond argues that the description of the garden is imbued with imagery of female genitalia: the 'tendrils of ivy, budding plants and blooming flowers' (491); Shirley Foster and Judy Simons comment on 'the womb-like seclusion of the garden' but fall short of an in-depth analysis (187), and Linda Parsons, in a celebration of the feminine influence in the garden, also emphasises the links between Colin's recovery in the uterine-like garden and the renewal and rebirth that Spring brings with it in the text (259).

These critical viewpoints all reference the idea of the garden as womb-like but they do not develop this symbolism to encompass the idea of birth and the move away from home. In order to return to a normal healthy life in the house Colin must move from the house to the maternal influence of the garden; he needs the gestation period that the time in his mother's garden allows him. The garden is also attached to the house and as such it is a transitional area that remains controlled, walled and thus, like a womb and ideal home, safe from the outside world. It is within Colin's mother's garden that Colin is nurtured and returned to health rather than in the masculine seclusion of the sickroom. But all pregnancies must end, and it seems appropriate that he is met by his father in a scene reminiscent of birth:

> And then the moment came, the uncontrollable moment when the sounds forgot to hush themselves. The feet ran faster and faster – they were nearing the garden door – there was a quick, strong, young breathing and a wild outbreak of laughing shouts which could not be contained – and the door in the wall was flung wide open, the sheet of ivy swinging back, and a boy burst through it at full speed and, without seeing the outsider, dashed almost into his arms. (Burnett *The Secret Garden* 294)

In contrast to the metaphorical birth experienced in *The Wind in the Willows*, this birthing passage is a positive and exciting event filled with running and laughter; it is something natural that is out of human control. Here, Colin moves on and away from the garden. As he and his father walk on together, he is given his full title and as he walks towards the Manor he is taking steps towards manhood. Accordingly, after the birth the story disintegrates; it is no longer considered a children's story but an adult's narrative. The children are released from the confinement of home/womb and as a result of this the story ends, for children's fiction remains the story of 'unborn' children, those who stay at home under parental observation.

The place of the womb/home is less secure in some texts after the Second World War since the womb becomes penetrable. In Mary Norton's *The Borrowers* (1950) and Roald Dahl's *Fantastic Mr Fox* (1970), while the homes remain womb-like, they also come under threat as the characters are forced to move out. *The Wind in the Willows* retains a contented conclusion because the characters stay in the safety of the womb; *The Secret Garden* has a positive end for Colin at least, as he chooses to leave the womb, but in *The Borrowers* and *Fantastic Mr Fox* the home is violated and the enforced eviction from the home can be read as a kind of induced premature birth. The home in *The Borrowers* is again redolent with womb-like imagery.

> It was Pod's hole – the keep of his fortress; the entrance to his home. Not that his home was anywhere near the clock: far from it – as you might say. There were yards of dark and dusty passage-way [. . .] It was only Pod who knew the way through the intersecting passages to the hole under the clock. And only Pod could open the gates. There were complicated clasps made of hair-slides and safety-pins of which Pod alone knew the secret. His wife and child led more sheltered lives in homelike apartments under the kitchen far removed from the risks and dangers of the dreaded house above. (Norton 15)

The home itself seems less secure, the passages to it are described in war-like masculine imagery; it is a keep, a fortress, it is dark and dusty and guarded by a clock, emphasising the passing of time and enhancing the idea that a threat/invasion is near. Pod, like Mr Fox in Dahl's text, and later Arrietty, is able to move from the womb to the outside world, yet the home is always the place to return to and anything else is a risk for borrowers or for foxes. The tunnels can only be negotiated by Pod, as the passage to the womb is reserved for the male; when Arrietty does join her father she must follow him closely. The home in *The Borrowers* is placed in opposition to the outside world; it is the place where the women and children should remain, usually by the fire, safe and sheltered, in a 'bright and cosy' room (Norton 17).

But in order to progress and survive both as a family and as a race, the borrowers need to be 'born' into the outside world; stagnation is no longer a possibility and the womb is too confining for Arrietty's growth. The child needs to mature, but what is disturbing about the borrowers' move from the womb is that, unlike Colin in *The Secret Garden*, the borrowers have no choice as to the moment of departure since they are smoked out of the home, and I suggest, metaphorically induced. It seems a logical leap then to consider *The Borrowers* as a text highly influenced by the harrowing events of war; the home has become less secure as the characters' violent eviction demonstrates. Deborah Thacker and Jean Webb argue that many post-Second World War texts emphasise complications and a shift towards a more complex way of portraying the world to children:

> What is more, the narrative relationship embodied in many of these texts [post Second World War] suggests a disruption of adult confidence in providing a sense of the world for children which at times approaches a postmodern sense of fracture and decentring. (110)

This is helpful in considering the change from the womb-like imagery in *The Wind in the Willows* and *The Secret Garden* to *The Borrowers*. *The Wind and the Willows* completely discourages the move away from the home; *The Secret Garden* celebrates Colin's time in the womb but also encourages his move away from it, and furthermore his move away is only really back to the estate, and so he does not leave his family; and finally, *The Borrowers* is more ambiguous, as the nuclear family is violently evicted, and yet it is this birth into the outside that saves them and reunites them in the second volume with their extended family:

> Kate was silent a moment, looking down. "So that *is* the end," she said at last.
> "Yes," said Mrs May, "in a way: or the beginning . . ."
> "But" – Kate raised a worried face – "perhaps they didn't escape through the grating? Perhaps they were caught after all?"
> "Oh, they escaped all right," said Mrs May lightly. (Norton 110)

The conflict between the desire to stay in the womb/home and the need to move away is reiterated, for it constitutes both an ending and a beginning. Ideally, the home/womb/family is depicted as the place in which children should stay in children's fiction, for it is perceived that the home can protect the culturally constructed innocence of childhood. But alongside this runs the acknowledgement that childhood cannot be preserved, and, consequently, texts like *The Wind in the Willows* no longer necessarily fulfil all the needs of children's literature, as such literature has, at some stage, to allow the child to leave. This is a tricky business though and in conflict with the knowledge that children should leave home is the desire to keep them and the ideal family preserved in a womb-like environment. The fantasy of the return to the womb underlies much of children's literature in its desire for the idealised tranquillity of the perfect home and family. But, as the next chapter will demonstrate, everything is not always well within the womb-like home, for divisions emerge in the way in which the space within it is ordered, categorised and controlled.

Chapter Five
A Room of One's Own?
Spaces, Families and Power[1]

As I suggested in the last chapter, images of the home in children's literature have become something of a literary and cultural cliché. In this chapter I will interrogate this cliché by looking at the construction of space within the home as a process heavily invested with issues of power and control. While we might expect the home to bring individuals within a family together, the different rooms and spaces within a house also serve to separate those individuals: stereotypically the father in his study, the mother in the kitchen and the child in his/her bedroom. The home is at once a place of security, a haven from the outside world, and a place of constraint. A common childhood punishment is when the child is sent to his/her bedroom, or 'grounded', like a prisoner. The home, it seems, is a complex environment essentially controlled by adults and increasingly, we find the child occupying a liminal and powerless position on the borders of the family. Before looking specifically at space in children's literature it is useful to discuss the theory and history of domestic space in general as this will help to illustrate the importance of space and homes to our sense of self and social position, while challenging what we see as 'natural'. Indeed, it becomes apparent that the same practices, in domestic architecture and in children's literature's depiction of space, have continued for the last two centuries thus illustrating the consistent relationship between space and adult power in British children's literature.

History and Theory

In the 1970s Foucault argued that a 'whole history remains to be written of *spaces* which would at the same time be a history of *powers*' ('Power/Knowledge'149). This argument is appropriate here, as in children's literature the power of the adult over the child is a constant subtext. In Foucault's argument disciplinary power is intrinsic to space in literature and in reality, as space is always organised in relation to power and control. The dominant ideology that is apparent in the children's story which sees the main protagonist return to the sanctuary of home has already been discussed, and yet this didacticism and power over the child is also evident in the way in which homes are physically presented. The ideological and the physical presentations of the home are intrinsically linked. An analysis of what Inga Bryden and Janet Floyd term the 'interior architectures' of homes reveals that inanimate objects like Welsh dressers, teapots and table cloths signify an idyllic representation of the home (1). This idealised literary cliché is deconstructed by the representation of space within the home in children's literature. The conflict between the adult and child is made clear in these spaces, for while adults are free to roam around the house, children are restricted to certain rooms – rarely, for example, are they allowed to play in the study. By looking at space in children's literature it becomes apparent that the seemingly united family, while celebrated on the one hand, is simultaneously broken down and questioned on the other, and this occurs across a range of texts from the nineteenth to the twentieth century.

To understand the centrality of the home to children's literature it is necessary to consider the importance of home to our sense of identity and security. Homes are invested with a strong sense of nostalgia. The house in which we live is not just a shell. The way we organise it, the possessions we place in it, and the memories we attach to previous houses emphasise the importance laid on the places we inhabit. Gaston Bachelard's analysis of the emotional investment we make in our childhood homes illustrates this nostalgia:

> But over and above our memories, the house we were born in is physically inscribed in us [. . .]. We would push the door that creaks with the same gesture, we would find our way in the dark to the distant attic. The feel of the tiniest latch has remained in our hands. (14–15)

While this is a somewhat indulgent account, the power invested in the house is clear. Bachelard's observations are redolent with a sense of the past and research has shown that 'patterns of domestic space have been consistent since the Industrial Revolution' (Lawrence 90).

If, as Johnson argues, '[o]ur attempt to make sense of the old, the traditional, the past, thus merges with our attempt to create and maintain a sense of place, of location'(70) then it is logical that spaces within homes remain remarkably similar, as the home and its structure are crucial to our sense of belonging. It is not simply a sense of belonging and a commitment to nostalgia that engineer the reproduction of certain interior designs. The continuity of domestic patterns also stems from a continuing need to separate individuals. Basically, this separation of bodies is performed on two levels: the private domestic sphere is separated from the public and, within the family, the adult space is separated from the child space. In terms of public and private space, Tosh points out that '[s]tyles may have been transformed [since the nineteenth century], but the home is still imagined and equipped as the antithesis of the workplace and as a refuge from it' (*Masculinity and the Middle-Class Home* 197). As well as being a refuge from the workplace, the nineteenth-century home interior was also constructed as a haven of privacy away from the public eye, and this was reflected in the decoration and architecture of the houses. As Judith Flanders observes, the 'English became ever more inward turning' as the openness of Georgian balconies disappeared and thick curtains were drawn over windows, emphasising the privacy of the home (xxiv). O'Malley argues that this separation of public and private was initiated by the middle classes as early as the late eighteenth century and that it coincided with an increasing interest and focus on the importance of families and the children with them (9–10).

But this exclusion of the outside world and the creation of an insular private world produced, and still produces, a rather schizophrenic situation; the house was and is at once both a symbol of wealth and class to be displayed to the public and at the same time a private sphere.[2] Similarly, the house was viewed both as a place in which the family could be pictured living together harmoniously and as a building in which members of the family were constantly regulated and separated. The division of space and ordering of the house became increasingly important to the nineteenth-century middle classes. Flanders sees this division as one of private and public: as outsiders were seen in drawing, dining and morning rooms, but separate rooms were designed for servants, and parents and children were less likely to share space as the nursery developed as a child-specific locus (xxv, 28). The physical divisions between adults and children that arose as a result of changing definitions of childhood during this time have already been discussed in Chapter 1, but the implications are intrinsic to an understanding of the segregation of domestic space; the child became idealistically central to family and yet at the same time was physically pushed to its margins. In the late twentieth century parents and children have begun to close this gap, but, as children's literature shows, the void has by no means vanished.

Theories regarding the home and moral wellbeing in the nineteenth century are still relevant with regard to twentieth-century homes and the depiction of domestic space in literature for children. Flanders argues, of the Victorian house, that Mrs Beeton's '"A place for everything and everything in its place" [. . .] was very much a feeling for the time: something that was out of place was something that was both practically and morally wrong' (23n). This maxim also applies to children's literature for, on the whole, it is the untidy, unclean homes that represent the bad families across the represented social scales; tidiness, especially with regard to the adult spaces, is the epitome of order and goodness and a poor and worthy family will maintain this system of order and cleanliness as is apparent in *Five Little Peppers and How They Grew*. Further, Flanders argues that 'what the house contained, how it was laid out, what the occupations of its inhabitants were, what the wife did all day: these were the details from which society built up its picture of the family and home' (xxxvi) and with regard to children's literature this remains the case; the presentation of the house represents the moral wellbeing of the home and in turn the family. In addition, the spaces which the adults and children inhabit remain divided and while divisions are perhaps less marked in contemporary children's literature than in that of the nineteenth century, their existence, though easily overlooked, is an indicator of the power discourses that are inherent in children's literature and which are in effect naturalised.

These systems of power are constantly apparent as in discussing space it is impossible to avoid the terminology of confinement and, implicitly, a sense of power structures. Tosh refers to the inhabitants of the nineteenth-century home as 'inmates'(*Masculinity and the Middle-Class Home* 27); Moira Donald argues that the Victorian nursery was viewed by some children as a prison (107) and Stephen Taylor notes that while the Englishman's home was his castle, for his wife it was 'too often her gaol' (235). The division of space is an exercise in control and it is not entirely surprising that Tosh argues that the house 'is integral to masculinity. To establish a home, to protect it, to provide for it, to control it, and to train its young aspirants to manhood have usually been essential to a man's good standing with his peers'(*Masculinity and the Middle-Class Home* 4). The use of the word 'control' here is most revealing, and seemingly, in providing and protecting a divided house, power is maintained by the 'head' of the house. Furthermore, a connection between identity and place is formed as the father's reputation is maintained partly by his control over his house.

The effect of domestic setting on identity cannot be overlooked, for it emphasises the importance of place and if, as Tosh suggests, the male controls the space (and certainly in children's literature it is the adult, if not necessarily the male who controls the space) then identity is also implicitly controlled by the adult/male. Radhika Mohanram observes that while place is often perceived 'as a passive, abstract arena [it is] saturated with relations of domination which are relevant to the construction of identity' (xv). Though Mohanram concentrates her arguments on racial difference, her theories concerning space and identity can equally be applied to children's literature; a divide of power still exists and whether it separates different races or adults from children is inconsequential since it is the use of space to exercise power that is significant.

Foucault's theory that spaces are always invested with power is explained by Markus and Cameron. According to their reading, power is exercised not only in disciplinary institutions like prisons and schools but also in places concerned with domesticity and leisure. They contend that 'power is always at issue in the articulation of space' (68). It is not only prisons that are policed, but our entire culture, and within this the home is most commonly the first encounter that we have with controlled space. The child, in literature and reality, is constantly monitored, separated, and directed within the boundaries of the home. In literature, even if the child is essentially free to meddle in the mother's or father's possessions or spaces, there remains a sense that the child character is always being observed, ensuring that the unwritten rules are still obeyed.

The child character, like the prisoner in Foucault's reading of Bentham's Panopticon, 'knows himself to be observed' regardless of whether an individual is actually watching, and it is this that ensures the general good behaviour of the child character and encourages him/her to remain in the designated space (*Discipline and Punish* 201). To stray into others' spaces is, in children's literature, to face danger and invite punishment. Characters in children's literature usually only delve into the private spaces of 'bad' characters, or wrongdoers, for it is those questionable, often seedy characters who, because of their refusal of the normal rules of society, lose the right to their own space: they are often, as in 'The Famous Five' series, criminals, and so loss of privacy is their just punishment. Paradoxically, the child character who has broken the rules is normally sent to the confinement of his/her room, where he/she becomes the criminal and is, in a sense, watched by the invisible adult narrator who exercises power and informs the reader of the character's every move, whether through description or dramatisation. The spaces within houses in children's literature, then, conform to an 'all seeing' order which reconfirms adult control.

The presentation of space within children's literature responds to contemporary use of space in our everyday lives, for space is always governed by those who exercise control, and so it is appropriate that adults manage space within the home. If, as Jacqueline Rose suggests, 'children's fiction sets up a world in which the adult comes first', then the environments in which the texts are set are a re-working of adult control; the child character is constantly surrounded by very adult settings (2). These settings are the detailed descriptions and illustrations of homes that are presented in children's fiction: the tidy dresser, the tablecloth, the beamed ceilings; the signs of adult domesticity that surround and engulf the child protagonist who sits with his/her mess in the midst of adult order. It would be useful to analyse how many of these domestic details escape the notice of the child reader, to consider if they are just taken for granted and are therefore naturalised themselves acting as part of the controlling ideology of home and family.

Yet, whether noticed in a conscious fashion or not, these settings are important since they lay the foundations of a domestic ideal. They correspond to a set of unwritten rules that direct how a home should be presented. Children's literature constantly re-emphasises these guidelines, and the stereo-typical comfortable home with roses round the door and a beamed ceiling becomes a goal that the successful adult must achieve in order for the child to prosper and in turn to imitate this situation. The perfect home is not an ideal confined to the pages of children's literature; it occurs in all parts of our culture. Nonetheless, in children's literature it seems more prevalent. Therefore, while the presentation of space and the home in children's literature does, to an extent, represent everyday concerns, the exaggeration employed in children's fiction ensures that a specific ideology of domesticity is imposed on and internalised by child readers.

Writing Family: Making Spaces

Children's literature tends to follow fairly strict narrative and plot structures. This rigid form evident in children's literature replicates the disciplinary structures evident in ideology. Space in children's literature is important because of what it tells us about the wider relationship between adults and children. Houses in children's literature have changed in appearance from the 'handsome old mansion' illustrated in the frontispiece of *The History of the Fairchild Family* (1818) to the cottage-like beamed ceilings depicted in *Angelina Ballerina* (1983) but the change, I suggest, occurred in the main at the beginning of the twentieth century, when homes began to be depicted in the rustic style seen in Badger's house in *The Wind in the Willows* or the Wendy house in *Peter Pan*. The illustration of the Fairchilds' house offers a fixed-point perspective which directs the gaze of the reader and this is indicative of the strictness and orderly nature of the text. Nothing is out of place in the outward display of the Fairchild family's house and with the straight path that leads through the garden to the house it is implied that there is little room to stray from order. Even the garden is beautifully landscaped and pristine for here nature is controlled in the same way that the nature of the children will be tamed in the text. Further, a church spire overlooks the house thus suggesting in line with the text that the eye of God is always upon the family home. The initial illustration of the house and gardens, like the introductory descriptive passage of the text, takes a moral, evangelical stance; it suggests that the house is a haven of godliness and self-control.

While the house is depicted in a way which might seem remote and alien to a modern reader, the fact remains that, like more modern illustrations of houses in children's literature, it is still presented as a goal to which its readers might aspire. A slight shift is evident in the description of the house in *Holiday House* (1839) and this is reflective of the nature of the text, which presents a Romantic rather than Evangelical reading of childhood. The house, though still majestic rather than cosy, is described as being comfortable:

> Holiday House was not one of those prodigious places, too grand to be pleasant [. . .] it was a very cheerful modern mansion, with rooms large enough to hold as many people as one could desire to see at once, all very comfortably furnished. A lively dashing river streamed past the windows: a small park sprinkled with sheep, and shaded by fine trees, surrounded the house; and beyond were beautiful gardens. (Sinclair 95)

The house is again depicted as a pastoral object of desire. It sits comfortably in nature with the sheep 'sprinkled' around the park and the river 'lively', and yet order is established by the reference to gardens, the 'comfortably furnished' rooms and the warnings later in the text directed at Laura who has to learn to keep her frocks clean (Sinclair 95–6). There exists a distinct relationship between order and idyll in children's literature: the ideal home, like the ideal family, while usually presented as comfortable, must also impose control both over its characters and its adult and child readers. The presentation of a house as an object of aspiration is in itself a didactic and culturally weighted statement, since it promotes a certain way of living.

In *The Wind in the Willows* (1908) the description of Badger's home emphasises the significance of the interior architecture of homes as symbolic of domesticity:

> A couple of high-backed settles, facing each other on either side of the fire, gave further sitting accommodation for the sociably disposed [. . .]. Rows of spotless plates winked from the shelves of the dresser at the far end of the room, and from the rafters overhead hung hams, bundles of dried herbs, nets of onions and baskets of eggs. It seemed a place where heroes could fitly feast after victory, where weary harvesters could line up in scores along the table and keep their Harvest Home with mirth and song, or where two or three friends of simple tastes could sit about as they pleased and eat and smoke and talk in comfort and contentment. The ruddy brick floor smiled up at the smoky ceiling; the oaken settles shiny with long wear, exchanged cheerful glances with each other; plates on the dresser grinned at the pots on the shelf, and the merry firelight flickered and played over everything without distinction. (Grahame 67)

Even the objects within the house are personified to promote a sense of familial warmth; a circle of happiness is described between inanimate objects as they smile up at each other, producing the effect of being an impenetrable group. Although Badger's home is not grand or as prosperous as Toad's, it is wholesome and comforting; it is warm, clean and full of food – a refuge in the midst of the wild wood.

The description of Badger's home has become something of a literary cliché, since various aspects of the portrayals of the rafters, dresser, open fire and herbs hanging from the ceiling can be seen in children's books throughout the twentieth century. The 'Milly-Molly-Mandy' series (1928) depicts the family eating at the table with the dresser in the background, a beamed ceiling just evident and flowers and food on the table. Mr Tumnus and the Beavers' houses in *The Lion the Witch and the Wardrobe* represent the ideal home through their domestic signifiers; these include the depiction of a dresser, a cosy setting and a roaring fire. Domestic signifiers are evident in countless twentieth-century texts from *Fantastic Mr Fox* to *Angelina Ballerina* or Jacqueline Wilson's *Double Act*. A definite sense of belonging is inherent in the texts as, by constantly reiterating the domestic clichés, the literature ensures that the child becomes embedded in an adult-orientated ideology. With regard to homes in children's literature, this evokes desire since both adult and child are engulfed in images of a seemingly perfect domestic ideal.

But as I have suggested, the myth of the perfect home is open to deconstruction. Domestic spatial divisions are most noticeable in picture books. The materiality of picture books allows for the spatial divisions to be depicted in the separation of pages, the use of borders to surround illustrations, and in the way in which text and illustrations are presented on the page. In the case of Jill Murphy's 'Mr and Mrs Large' picture book series, the home overflows with traditional symbols of domesticity: the dresser is displayed, neat and tidy, in the background, the children's pictures are pinned in the wall, and the children are shown huddled together at the lighted window at night time, yet, when we analyse the use of space and boundaries within the home, divisions between the family become significant. In *Five Minutes Peace* (1986) the adults and children are often separated; the adults frequently appear on the left hand page looking on at the children on the facing right hand page. In addition, the adults and children are usually separated both by the text on the left page and by the frame that exists on the right hand page. This division is especially evident in *All in One Piece* (1987) when the mother 'bellows' at the children "'Can't I just have one night in the whole year to myself?'"(Murphy np). The mother stands on the left hand page, above the text, while the children stand in decreasing order of size in a framed illustration on the right hand page. The mother's space has been determined. She stands above the children, signifying an adult and superior space rather than a child's.

Perhaps the most cliché-ridden image in *All in One Piece* is the one in which the children and grandmother are pictured in the window, waving goodbye to Mr and Mrs Large who are going out for the evening. The contrast between inside and outside is here emphasised, and the reader is reminded of the insular nature of the series in which all the action takes place within the safety of four walls. In the picture the background glow of yellow light signifies a cosy world of warmth within the home as the young elephants are pictured in a portrait style, cuddled together. In contrast, the mother is wrapped in a shawl as she steps into the dark night on the facing page. Again in the illustration the mother and father are placed opposite to the children. The vocabulary is also significant: "'We've escaped," said Mr Large with a smile, closing the front door behind them. "All in one piece," said Mrs Large, "and not a smear of paint between us"' (Murphy *One Piece* np). This is reminiscent of the language of confinement that is often used to describe homes as I suggested earlier. While Mr Large is able to 'escape' the home and close that world behind him, paradoxically, although Mrs Large also escapes, she remains tied to the home, marked by her family with the paint that is pictured on her dress in the final illustration. The home then is for women and children, a constricting, clichéd and controlled space in *All in One Piece* and *Five Minutes Peace.*

In children's literature the divide between outside and inside is crossed most frequently by the father since, in the majority of texts it is he who leaves the house in order to work. The trope of the children meeting the father at the door on his return from work is evident in texts such as *The Story of the Treasure Seekers*

(1899), *Peter Pan* (1911), and *The Borrowers* (1952). Of course, it is not only the father figure who ventures into the outside world, but the fact remains that it is the father who has most links with the outside; it is the father who crosses the boundary between outside and inside most frequently, it is the father who tends to watch television (in those rare texts that feature a television), and it is the father who reads the newspaper.

The majority of the information about the outside world is first passed through the father as the head of the household, preserving the traditional ideal of the home as a refuge which needs constant protection in the form of the patriarch, from the outside world. This adherence to stereotypical gender roles is not confined to texts written pre-1970, but is evident in more recent works such as Anne Fine's *The Granny Project* (1983), Jan Ormerod's *Sunshine* (1981), Anthony Browne's *Piggybook* (1986) and in J.K Rowling's 'Harry Potter' series (1997–2007). The father usually reads the newspaper at the breakfast table, separating himself from the rest of the family. The newspaper then seems to signify and delineate the male space. Whereas in many nineteenth-century texts the father had a study, in twentieth-century texts this space has been reduced to the area defined by the size of a newspaper. This relates back to the point that it is the father figure who occupies transitional space between home and work, as the newspaper is also a way in which to bring the printed, authoritative, outside world into the sanctuary of the home. The survival of the father's designated space, however altered, is significant as it reveals the apparent timelessness of the boundaries established, perhaps unconsciously, within the families in children's literature.

A dichotomy with regard to space is established in children's literature: on the one hand the family that eats, plays and works together is positively promoted yet, on the other hand, private spaces are celebrated. The family home is a complex mixture of private and communal and issues of power and control are consequently inevitable subtexts. The father's space often seems entirely impenetrable, and it remains a space to which he can retreat. The rather distant and old-fashioned father in Michelle Magorian's *Back Home* (1985) is able to hide away from the family in his study, and is a little alarmed at his daughter's invasion of this space: 'He drew himself up. "I did ask, Virginia, that I wasn't to be disturbed. I'll see you at dinner." He gave a short wave of his hand indicating the door, and leaned over his papers again' (279).

As his defence of space shows the father is portrayed in a generally negative light in *Back Home* since he is represented as the archetypal Victorian patriarch who when Rusty does not leave in this scene resorts to ordering his daughter to leave the room. The power at this point in the text is vested in those who own the space – the father and grandmother, with the mother and children silenced and constricted:

Supper was a polite affair. Rusty's father sat at the head of the table, her grandmother at one side, and Rusty and her mother opposite. Charlie was in bed. Most of the conversation took place between her father and grandmother, while her mother remained almost silent. (Magorian 280)

While the text in no way condones this separation, since the divisions at the dinner table are echoed later in the text by the separation of the parents, the manner in which space is used cannot be ignored since much of children's literature emulates this pattern and usage of spaces and divisions.

Space within *The History of the Fairchild Family* is organised in a traditional, patriarchal manner, partly because it represents the time in which it was written, but it is significant that such spatial organisation, though more subtle in the twentieth century, is still apparent. Mr Fairchild, after the death of Augusta, is 'affected' to the extent that he 'hastened into his study and shut the door' – even the most god-like of fathers makes use of his own male space (Sherwood 83). Henry takes lessons with his father in the male domain of the study while his sisters, Lucy and Emily, attend to their needlework in the parlour (Sherwood 170), and it is in the study where Mr Fairchild chastises Henry for refusing to learn his Latin – it is a place where the father can exercise complete control. The patriarchal space is also emphasised in Burnett's *Little Lord Fauntleroy* (1886) where mother and son are initially separated by the grandfather and Cedric has to meet his grandfather in the adult male domain of the library. Similarly, in Nesbit's *The Railway Children* (1905) the children and adults are separated when the father calls the mother into his library/study to explain the 'bad news' that he has received: the divisions of space and parents and children encourage and respond to the secrecy that divides the family (7–8).

While the libraries and studies have, for the most part, disappeared in both contemporary children's literature and in reality, fathers still maintain areas of separation from the children. The fathers in both *Sunshine* and *Angelina Ballerina* are regularly described grasping newspapers which they can use to form a barrier between themselves and the family, effectively hiding in their own private space. In more recent texts fathers are sometimes actually forced out of the house in order to maintain some private space: in *Double Act* (1995) the father escapes the house after an argument with his daughters and mother concerning his new girlfriend, and his slamming of the door and the 'horrible silence' that follows it re-emphasises the separation of the family (Wilson 30).

Divisions within the family are reflected by physical divisions of space within the home; even when the family members seem content in their customary habits, they still adhere to politics of space. The father will be relaxing in *his* chair, the mother in hers, and as in 'Goldilocks and the Three Bears' each member of the family has his/her set position in which internal power is structured and invested in this. Spatial divisions tend to be more marked during times of emotional crisis: a death in *The History of the Fairchild Family*, a family argument in *Double Act*; or they imply a more lengthy separation as in *The Railway Children* and *Back Home*. Spaces that traditionally have been categorised as male, such as the library and study, have largely disappeared, as they have no place in smaller modern homes, and while male spaces are less easy to find in contemporary children's literature they still exist in the margins of the texts. The adult male in the household is automatically given a set amount of space in literature and this, whether a conscious authorial decision or not, re-asserts his power.

The space given to the adult male is most evident in those texts in which he, as a potential or actual stepfather, is at first unwelcome; Kitty in Anne Fine's *Goggle Eyes* (1989) 'hated the whole house whenever he was in it [. . .] it just didn't feel like home anymore if he was ambling from room to room in search of a pencil' (35) and Elsa in Jacqueline Wilson's *The Bed and Breakfast Star* complains that 'We only had a little flat and Mack took up so much *space*' (14). The intrusion of the non-family male or the substitute father figure is unsettling; as a stranger he poses a threat and this is shown by his colonisation of the family space, for if space equates to power then the power remains with the father figure, no matter how new or temporary he might be, even in contemporary texts. While mothers are still often depicted in the kitchen they have never had a 'room of their own' and even in middle-class nineteenth-century children's texts few of the mothers enjoyed the privacy of their own parlours or drawing rooms. Women in children's literature, as I have suggested, belong to the home, but within this home they have no private space, not even, as is evident in Murphy's *Five Minutes Peace*, in the bathroom.

If the male space is the study/library and the space most associated with the female is the parlour or kitchen, then the child's space has always been his/her bedroom/playroom. The child's bedroom is an intriguing space for it is both a sanctuary to run to in times of emotional distress and a cell in which children can be isolated and punished. In Roald Dahl's *Matilda* (1988), the heroine escapes her family by retreating to her bedroom with a variety of books; in *Back Home*, Rusty runs to the privacy of her room where she barricades the door and reads her letter from her American family; in Maurice Sendak's *Where the Wild Things Are* (1963) Max is sent to his room, but in it finds adventure and solace; and in *The History of the Fairchild Family* Henry takes solace from the Bible in his bedroom after arousing the wrath of his father.

It seems that the bedroom is a place in which children can hide from the family and also discover new worlds through books or letters; a space in which they can learn and develop. This space, though, is controlled: the bedroom, while being the child's own room, remains part of the house, and the ownership and control of it is still vested in the adult. In Frances Hodgson Burnett's *The Secret Garden* (1911) Colin's bedroom has a portrait of the mother hanging on the wall, and while the curtain may cover her, the theme of surveillance remains prominent. In Bawden's *Carrie's War* (1973), while Carrie and Nick's bedroom remains a retreat, there is a stark reminder on the wall that the space is not a private sanctuary in which the children can do as they please:

> It was a small room with two narrow beds and a hooked rug between them.
> A wardrobe and a wicker chair and a large, framed notice on the wall. The
> black letters said, The Eye Of The Lord Is Upon You. (Bawden 22)

This suggests Foucauldian surveillance. The children are reminded that they are
constantly under supervision subverting the concept of the child's bedroom as
sanctuary. The children, even if they are not actually observed, believe themselves to be, and thus the power of the adult becomes absolute since the children,
having internalised the possibility of surveillance, regulate their own behaviour.
This system of control and fear permeates into all sections of the home, often
subliminally, but nonetheless constant and powerful.

Similarly, when children are sent to their rooms as a punishment, they are
separated and barred from the immediate family – Wallace, in Catherine
Sedgwick's *Home* (1835), is told that he has 'forfeited' his right to be among the
family and this again re-asserts adult control; the child is sent away from the
family room into the confines of his own section of the house. Yet this section
of the house is not the child's own since it remains under the control and
surveillance of the adult. This returns us to correlations between the family and
society; children who have misbehaved, like adults who have misbehaved, are
guilty of having broken the rules of either the family or society and are sent to
the margins of family/society. Children are sent to their bedrooms and adults
are sent to prison. The prison cell and bedroom are, then, used for similar
reasons, and both of these systems of punishment re-assert control and order.
The family here is a microcosm of society, with a head and a hierarchical order
and it is the organisation of space within the family that keeps the children, as
the lesser beings, under control, since they remain on the margins of the home
and are essentially powerless.

In the same way that children have very little to do with the actual organisation
of their literature or homes and families, child characters often occupy liminal
spaces within those homes. Not only are children often confined to their
bedrooms, but they are regularly shown to be on the boundaries of rooms as they
search for a place in which to belong. This does not just occur in texts that we
might think of as obvious, for example where an orphan is taken in as in *Anne
of Green Gables* (1908), but is equally evident in texts which seem to present an
ideal family. In *The History of the Fairchild Family* the use of space emphasises
that the divide in the family is most apparent when Henry has been chastised by
his father for refusing to learn Latin:

> Mr Fairchild got up, and walked up and down the room in great trouble;
> then turning to Henry he said [. . .] 'I will have nothing more to do with
> you; so go out of my study immediately.' [. . .] Mr Fairchild walked away
> with a terrible look and went out of the house. Henry stood at the study
> door, to which he had followed his father, for some minutes, not knowing
> what to do, and wishing he had not been so obstinate. (Sherwood 149–50)

Henry is left on the margins of the family, trapped in the liminal space of the doorway, ignored by everyone: Lucy runs past him and goes upstairs, Emily sees him and goes back out into the garden and his mother closes the parlour door in his face. Henry then goes out of the 'back gate' and to the top of the hill where he can observe the rest of the family preparing to go for a walk.

In disobeying his father Henry is cast out of the family and this is evident by his inability to stay in any one room other than his bedroom, in which he weeps. Henry is left on the boundaries of rooms, on the boundary of family and here he exists in a kind of limbo. The power of the father and family is emphasised by this passage since Henry is left with no comfortable space other than outside the walls of the home or in his bedroom. Mr Fairchild, though, leaves a point of entry; his study door is 'half-open', but again the space is the father's and its authority proves too much for Henry for when 'he should have run up to his father and knelt down before him [. . .] he ran away into the garden'(Sherwood 153). In order to gain forgiveness, power and control must be returned to the father and this is emphasised by the physical submission that Henry must give in kneeling to him. It is important that when Henry does obtain his father's forgiveness it is in the garden before the entire family; the garden is a more neutral setting than the father's study, yet it is also where nature is tamed. Henry's wild disobedience is brought under control, and it is deemed a natural progression.

This division of space is also apparent in more recent texts. In *The Granny Project* (1983) the children meet on the fringes of the home, specifically the garage, in order to discuss their secret project and again secrecy and disobedience are articulated in spatial boundaries. In *Angelina Ballerina*, although Angelina is not disobedient, the family are not pictured in harmony together until her ballet lessons have begun and the chaos that her dancing has caused is reduced. Instead Angelina is pictured in doorways or on stairways, frequently separated from her parents by a room. The family in *The Granny Project* are spatially separated because of the strain of living with their senile grandmother. After an 'accident' in which the parents are forced to clean the grandmother's soiled sheets, the tension is realised and diffused in the dispersal of the family into different areas:

> One by one, as the children finished eating, they left the table and the room. Though the large plastic tub of ice-cream sat, still half-full, on the draining board, nobody asked for more. Tanya and Nicholas went into the back room and switched on the television set. Ivan went out of the front door. Sophie went up the stairs and into her bedroom. (Fine 19)

The children are separated from the parents, who remain in the kitchen, and to a certain extent from each other, showing how family problems can force a family apart rather than together. It is appropriate that by the conclusion of the narrative the family is pictured coming together again, albeit in the graveyard at the grandmother's funeral.

At this point Sophie and Henry have already resolved that they were wrong in their 'granny project' and that negotiation within the family is the way forward; while Henry and Sophie still go away with a secret, the family are reunited. The reunification of the family in the freedom of the outside emulates the regrouping of the Fairchild family in the garden. In both texts lessons have been learnt and characters have been taught to reflect on their own behaviour. Boundaries are also set between adults and children in picture books. In *Angelina Ballerina*, while the text has been described as an 'exercise in charm and nostalgia [with illustrations that demonstrate] an elusive, hard-to-describe quality of affection and commitment' the unity of the family is subject to subtle questioning by the location of the characters in indefinite spaces (Hunt *Criticism, Theory* 186).

Certainly, the charm and nostalgia is produced by the traditional domestic signifiers discussed earlier, but the placement of characters in liminal spaces is telling; on the first page the mother and father are in the kitchen, father behind his newspaper, mother clearing the table, while Angelina is pictured through the doorway dancing down the stairs; on the second page mother and child are separated by the window as mother looks out on her daughter in the garden from Angelina's untidy bedroom; in the third illustration Angelina's dream moves outside the frame, emphasising the liberation that it brings, and in the fourth illustration the mother is again pictured looking at her daughter from the doorway. In the two illustrations in which the adults and Angelina are pictured in the same room prior to Angelina attending ballet lessons, Angelina knocks the food from the table on to the floor as she dances and also dances on top of the knitting basket, thus she constantly disrupts traditional domesticity.

But when Angelina becomes 'the happiest girl in the world today' after she has attended her ballet class, the family is pictured together without chaos; father's newspaper is even rolled up and the barriers are removed (Holabird np). Angelina cooks with her mother, tidies her room and, although one illustration still shows mother and child on different levels (separated by the stairs), the text remedies this by insisting that 'From that day on, Angelina, came downstairs when her mother called her' (Holabird np). Angelina has won her happiness through attending her ballet classes, but systems of parental control are still present as Angelina is tamed into a domestic, tidy, punctual little girl. It is only when she has gone through this domestic process that she is allowed to be pictured in harmony with the family; she has, effectively, earned her place in the room and thus in the family.

Children are often found on the fringes of the home and this perhaps accounts for some of the successes of the camping adventure genre in which the children are given their own space and control over its organisation. Often this new-found liberty reflects the children's move into adolescence; as they grow up they gain increased freedom and power. What is significant about the children's organisation of their space is its complete replication of adult domestic space. The 'Fell Farm Campers' series shows the characters performing traditional gender roles as the girls wash up and cook while the boys collect firewood, and later they even invite the adults to take afternoon tea with them. Rusty, in *Back Home*, builds shelves, paints, makes a table and finds books and ornaments to place on the shelves in order to make her cabin 'feel more like a real home' (338). The children in *Gumble's Yard* put up a shelf, have a table, put rugs on the floor and have shiny pans hung up in an ordered fashion to create an effect that 'was not luxurious, but it was really quite cosy' (Townsend 40) and the children in *Swallows and Amazons* also make their tents home-like, in an adult-inspired ordered fashion:

> In the middle of it were the biscuit tins, with the food in them. These tins made two seats. Then at each side of the tent, where their beds were going to be, they had spread out their blankets and folded in the tops of them. The cooking things were neatly arranged in one corner, just inside the tent. Outside the tent, on the rope on which the tent was hung, two towels were drying. (Ransome 55)

The domestic detail and order described surely presents us with an adult perspective on how children should behave: they should emulate the ideal adult home – pans should be washed up and tidily stacked, the washing should be hung out, beds should be properly prepared. In Rusty's ramshackle cabin in *Back Home*, traditional signs of domesticity are displayed; the shelves with ornaments represent a Welsh dresser. To make something 'home-like' the child has to subscribe to archetypal signs that maintain the myth of the ideal home. The home and the ordering of spaces and objects within it remains static, and this is because children internalise the adult ideal. In literature the ideology of the perfect homely home is constantly established as something to which the child should aspire. Therefore, while the children are apparently given their own space in these adventure texts, this space is monitored and controlled by the adult writer and narrator and an adult ideology. This returns us to issues of adult domination over children: the adult feels safe in knowing that the children will simply emulate their examples of what homes should be and the circular pattern of ordered homes continues. Further, the pattern established in the fiction and internalised by the child ensures the continuation of such patterns in society, ensuring that the child subject will grow up to become the obedient adult.

The style, order and power evident within the home reflect familial systems of control. The home is a complex place; it is a place to return to – a sanctuary – and yet it is a place of constraint; it is a place of security and timelessness which is emphasised by common traditional signifiers of home, and yet this myth of cosiness is deconstructed by the organisation of space and boundaries within the texts. It is both a private and public sphere, and conflict can be seen between the home's retention of its supposed idealised image and the adult powers that are invested in it. The home, like the family in children's literature, is an adult ideal, often invested with nostalgia and a sense of didacticism, since old ideals recur, and the circular pattern of perfect homes and families goes on, for the most part, unchallenged.

Bad homes, like bad families, have always been evident in children's literature and the stark black and white attitude towards them seems to prevail, with an untidy house usually representing a morally untidy family. It is only in breaking down traditional images of family homes that we can see the power structures invested in them, for these systems of control are such a part of our culture that they have been internalised and naturalised, and so we often remain oblivious of the child who sits at the edges of the home and in the margins of the text. The child, it seems, has been marginal to the family for some time, and is destined to remain there, for the adults create and monopolise the texts, investing them with their own needs and nostalgia, incorporating, probably unconsciously, an adult-orientated ideology in which to immerse, and therefore control, our – and the possessive pronoun is fitting here – children.

Chapter Six
Edible Fictions: Fictional Food –
The Family Meal in Children's Literature

Children's literature itself, the way in which family is represented, the emphasis on the return home, and the divisions of space within the home, which I discussed in the previous chapters, are all primarily concerned with issues of power and control. This chapter considers food and its functions within and in relation to the power structure of the family. Having looked at the construction of the family and the environment in which it is contained, it is important to turn to that which both literally and figuratively develops the individual within the family – that is, the food which the family consumes and the significance of food and the spaces in which it is eaten. Both the home and the food that is consumed within it act as cultural signifiers of the wellbeing of the family, for to argue that food is only a form of nourishment would be equivalent to arguing that the home's only function is to provide shelter.

Children's fiction dictates what types of food should be eaten and where, and how the family should go about preparing and consuming them. It tells us what family meals should be, and in turn reinforces notions of idealistic families: a good family, no matter where it sits in the social scale, in children's literature will eat home-made food round the dinner table at set times, a bad family will eat takeaway or at different times, or in different rooms. These notions of constructed normality are present in children's literature from the nineteenth to the twenty-first century. But underlying the cultural institution of the family meal are rituals concerned with power and control, for to feed someone is to exercise power, to penetrate metaphorically the body of another and to gratify desire. The first part of this chapter considers both the significance of the kind of food presented in children's literature, focusing on issues concerned with nationality, belonging and sexuality. The second half analyses how and where the food is eaten, looking at the history of the family meal and the importance of the mealtime as a constituent of family in children's literature.

Food for Thought: History and Theory

Food occupies an ambiguous place in society. It can nourish or poison; it can be both sexualised and wholesome, and its refusal, whether on the part of the child it is presented to, or the adult in refusing to prepare it, can be a means of empowerment. The consumption of food is a biological necessity but it is also a cultural practice as the type of food, the method by which it is prepared, and the people with whom it is shared suggest an adherence to specific ideologies, families, and even nations; eating has become, as Margaret Visser notes, a 'carefully cultured phenomenon' (ix), and this is clearly evident in children's literature.

Roland Barthes argues that food is 'a system of communication, a body of images, a protocol of usages, situations and behaviours' and as a result it comes to represent part of the cultural identity; traditionally roast beef symbolises Englishness while red wine equates Frenchness ('Towards a Psychosociology' 21–2).[1] Of course, this does not mean that all the French drink red wine every day or that the English eat only roast beef any more than the continued representation of the dream of the nuclear family means it really works for all individuals, but such associations of food and nationality emphasise the cultural investment in food and its importance to perceptions of belonging, on both national and familial terms. Food and its central role in family life invokes in individuals from childhood onwards a sense of belonging. But this is not just a cosy, warm image, rather it is invested with ideologies of discipline and control:

> The choice of what is acceptable to eat plays a major role in defining the culture – whether of a nation, a tribe, a class, or a family. Thus one of the first things that the child learns is what is eaten in the group(s) to which he or she belongs. Accepting these strictures as absolute is a formative experience in childhood, both in terms of the development of the individual and of that individual's membership in the group. (McGee 15)

The child must conform to his/her family diet in order to belong to the group. When the child becomes an adult it is more than likely that he/she will return to the memory of childhood food with some nostalgia and thus replicate certain recipes: for him/her, the home and family will be associated with certain types of food.[2] This loyalty to familiar food is emphasised in children's literature. This is especially prevalent in texts such as those by Blyton and Ransome, as characters are seen eating traditional English food, showing their membership both of family and of nation and so, in part, constructing identity. Foreign food in children's literature is often viewed as threatening, for if food plays a part in creating identity and if it is something that connects individuals, then children should always be encouraged to remain with the family hearth rather than embrace the unknown other.

The threat of the 'other' both in terms of foreignness and sexuality is often symbolised in food. If, as Diane McGee argues, the sharing of food in adult literature leads to 'revelations [being] made, intimacies exchanged, and seductions attempted' then those with whom the food is shared with become increasingly important (4). This also applies to children's literature: Edmund, in C.S. Lewis' *The Lion the Witch and the Wardrobe* (1950), as I will show later, will be suitably punished for his desire to share food with the White Witch rather than his own family; he is essentially, seduced by the foreign. The linking of the sexual other with food is far from new or consigned to children's literature, for forbidden or exotic food from the fall of Eve in the Garden of Eden onwards represents temptation and desire, and the consequences, as we see in Edmund's case as well as Eve's, are often concerned with expulsion. In Western culture advertisements have played with images of food and sex as temptations for several years; sex has been used to advertise chocolate from the seventeenth century to today (Day 'Teatime' 108) and Elspeth Probyn argues that the language of food has become the language of sex (6).[3] Food within the family, in children's literature in particular, is very controlled and thus desire and temptation are kept under constant check but the threat of the sexual always underlies family food rituals.

The nineteenth century saw an increasing concern about food and its relationship with sexuality; what was eaten and how much was eaten became important matters for the middle and upper classes. Red meat was thought to stimulate sexual development and activity; women often thought that they could dissociate themselves from sexuality by avoiding animal flesh (Brumberg 166). Similarly, anorexia began to appear because the 'thin body not only implied asexuality and an elevated social address, [but] was also an expression of intelligence, sensitivity and morality' (Brumberg 173–4). Margaret Visser argues that the late twentieth-century trend of *nouvelle cuisine* with its beautifully presented but tiny portions is a product of Victorian times when, as now, successful people ate expensively but crucially were expected to be thin (204). Fragments of these ideas are still evident in twentieth-century children's literature. In Dahl's *Matilda* (1988), Miss Honey and Mrs Wormwood are antithetical to each other: Miss Honey is the thin, frugal, virginal, intelligent character as opposed to Mrs Wormwood who has an 'unfortunate bulging figure' and is rude, unintelligent, and implicitly immoral (27). A similar contrast is exercised between the thin servant-like Harry Potter and his obese spoilt cousin Dudley for children's literature frowns on excess at every level. Indeed, as Carolyn Daniel points out food in children's literature imparts important rules about society and proper behaviour (12–15). Food has always been carefully regulated and what and how much is eaten signifies whether the individual has an insatiable appetite or can control his/her desires, and further symbolises social position.

In the nineteenth century the man of the house would be served the best food while any leftovers would be given to the servants, and similarly the divide between adult and children was re-emphasised by the plain but nourishing food that was given to the children in contrast to the meat-heavy feast presented to their father.[4] This can be seen in Nina Bawden's *Carrie's War* (1973) where the children are fed the remains of Mr Evans' meals minced with bread and gravy; the term Auntie Lou uses for this, 'DoneDown', signifies the children's position in the household (35). Food plays a significant part in identity and social position; power is invested in the individual who provides the money to buy the food, hence the term 'breadwinner', and, in the nineteenth century in particular, the head of household was signified and rewarded by his position at the table and the quality and quantity of food he received and could give to guests.

Food, like the home and the family, can be placed on social display. But, again like the home and family, there often exists a marked difference between the image and the reality. The importance attached to the image of the provision of food for the family is illustrated by the account given by an East Londoner recollecting a 1900s childhood. On a Sunday dinner time, he tells us, his mother rattled the plates to ensure that the other tenants heard, regardless of whether or not she actually had any food to serve (Quoted in Ross 20). By giving the impression that she had provided a meal for the family this woman maintained her reputation as a good, respectable mother. Food, then, becomes a way of measuring the worth of the mother of the house, for a home with good domestic values is expected to provide a 'proper' meal. Davidoff *et al.* argue, with regard to the nineteenth century, that 'the putting of food in the children's stomachs was the ultimate test of motherhood, as preparing food acceptable to the man was the ultimate test of wifehood' (120).

This notion is also apparent in the letters of working women from the beginning of the twentieth century, as accounts exist of women who starved themselves in order to provide for their families (Davies 34). The woman here makes the ultimate sacrifice for her family. A woman's identity and image in the nineteenth and early twentieth centuries was deeply dependent on the food she prepared; William Cobbett in 1822 went so far as to suggest that a woman who could not bake was 'unworthy of trust and confidence [. . .] a mere burden upon the community' (Quoted in Hall 84). To a far lesser extent there remains today a pressure on mothers of all social standings to provide good food for their children; culture inserts into individuals the ideal of the family sharing home-cooked food, and this becomes a powerful, naturalised image. Children's literature plays an important part in promoting the myth of the perfect mother with her roast dinners and homemade cakes and reaffirms its tirelessly conservative stance on the image of family. Daniel observes that in both children's literature and popular literature '[. . .] food is used to make implicit judgements about a woman. Her mothering skills, including her capacity to love and nurture, and her willingness to sacrifice herself for her family, are thus put on trial' (108). Certainly, the idea that a family can be judged by the food it shares is implicit in several media, but it is particularly apparent in children's fiction as it dictates the sort of food that good, and, by implication, bad families consume.

Food in Children's Literature: The Critics

What most critics seem to agree on is that children's literature is saturated with food-related images and that food occupies a semiotic place in children's fiction. Wendy Katz argues that food in children's literature represents 'hospitality, gluttony, celebration, tradition, appetite, obesity' (192); Maria Nikolajeva reminds us of food's ambivalent status as both nourishment and potential poison (*Mythic to Linear* 16), and Claudia Nelson describes how both J.R.R. Tolkien and C.S. Lewis use 'food to indicate character, making divisions among the homely, the exotic, and the unwholesome according to racial boundaries (animal, human witch; hobbit, elf, orc)' (*Boys will be Girls* 204 n73).

All these points demonstrate the marked division between the safe food of the home and food's potential, when taken from the wrong hands, to threaten order, initiate desire and therefore destroy the controlled institution of the family. Katz's 'hospitality', 'celebration' and 'tradition' evoke images of belonging that are then contrasted with the dangers of 'gluttony', 'appetite' and obesity. Nikolajeva emphasises that the food of the home is regarded as secure and safe, like the mother's milk, whereas the move away from home brings about the threat of the unknown (*Mythic to Linear* 15–16), and Nelson, again, demonstrates that food and home are powerfully linked as they are regarded as safe and comforting. The sharing of food acts as a metaphor for family relationships; to eat the same food emphasises a sense of belonging, it is an act of union, for the word 'companion' literally means to 'break bread with', and the good family, as it shares blood, should share the same food (Visser 3). Consuming food given by a stranger often symbolises a betrayal of the family and simultaneously signifies a fall into otherness, into the unknown; essentially, into the sexual.

Feeding someone can be seen, in Freudian terms, as a penetration of the body (Freud 117).[5] It is also a deeply sensual activity. The institution of the family is one that regulates sexual activity and desire by adhering to social conventions and installing social rules and conventions in its young, and feeding the family the right food is an important aspect of this. But the conflict between desire and socialisation can be complex, and it returns us to concepts found in *The History of the Fairchild Family*, where the child is animal and the adult is tamer. Katz insists that children's literature often uses food to demonstrate how the child has succumbed to family order. She goes on to cite Anne of Green Gables' drunken, and therefore disastrous, cake-making activity as an example of how uncivilised Anne was on first arriving at Marilla's. Katz also suggests that while the readers are expected to approve of Anne's spirit they are also asked to condone her social conditioning; by the conclusion of the narrative Anne is the main carer; proficient in cooking and manners, she has made it into the adult world (Katz 193–5).

The journey to adulthood is seen to be one in which children must learn to repress and control desire and food plays a useful role in this, as can be seen in

Maurice Sendak's *Where the Wild Things Are* (1967). Max is too much of a 'wild thing' to be accepted at the dinner table; he is pictured chasing a dog with a fork, and threatens to eat up his mother who sends him to bed without any supper (np). Max represents the animal other, as he represents something of a threat to the adult; he embodies the child's desire for power over his parents, the need to consume his mother, to defy parental order, to become larger than his mother.[6] But, conversely, Max's journey is one to adulthood, for power is reversed as Max tames the wild things and in a neat twist sends them to bed without supper; in doing this he achieves the power he desires as he is the adult in the wild world. Tellingly, it is the smell of 'good things to eat' which is coupled, not coincidentally, with the place 'where someone loved him best of all' that entices Max's return home (Sendak np).

This text has produced much critical interest as it addresses the struggles between adult and child, human and animal, wildness and civilisation. It also sees the continuation of adult control and Max's all-important return to family, food, and the civilised society that the two represent.[7] Roderick McGillis gives a psychoanalytical reading of *Where the Wild Things Are*, arguing that the warm food is Max's reward for learning to control his phallic aggression: Max has learnt to repress his desire to consume his mother and this is replaced with the desire to eat the socially acceptable home-cooked food (80–2). Max's journey has taught him to opt for the safe option as again the home symbolises ultimate security. In addition to this Daniel argues that the food that awaits Max's return is to be expected, for it is only 'bad' mothers who would leave their children, no matter how naughty, without a wholesome meal. Thus while on the one hand Max has returned to a controlled society and as such the mother regains her authority, on the other Max's mother is always constrained by her role as food provider and absolver (Daniel 56). Children's literature then adheres to the deeply conservative and didactic both in its emphasis on the mother's role and on the protagonist's need to return to the social construct of family; in order to do this, desire and animal instincts must be repressed.

Food is an important signifier of the development of the child character in children's fiction, and both Max in *Where the Wild Things Are* and Anne in *Anne of Green Gables* are shown to have matured in consequence of their initial experiences with desire and the inevitable repression that must follow. But the family can only police the sexual; it cannot banish it entirely, and in the same way food can be monitored but it has to be provided. Freud argued, the sexual is first experienced at the mother's breast, sex is always already inherent within the family and further, 'the satisfaction of the erotogenic zone is associated, in the first instance, with the satisfaction of the need for nourishment' (Freud 98). The majority of criticism concerning food in children's literature concentrates or at least draws on these links with sexuality. As Peter Hunt observes of children's literature: 'No sex, no violence: what are you left with? Food' ('Cold-tongue 9). Keith Barker has used the word 'orgy' with regard to the scenes concerned with food in Dahl's work (4). A paternal reader of C.S Lewis' 'Narnia' series remarked that the narrative gave the children food in place of forbidden sex as 'the little blighters like plenty of good eating' (Quoted in Nikolajeva *Mythic to Linear* 129).

McGillis, Daniel, Nikolajeva and Katz have all emphasised the link between sex and the oral gratification that comes from food in children's literature.[8] Certainly, the gluttony and lack of resistance to temptation emphasised in children's literature point towards an expression of the sexual, as does the fact that these slips often occur outside family control, when the child is in the company of the ever-threatening other. But the cosy, food-related images prevalent in texts by Blyton or Grahame suggest a sense of self-indulgent desire, albeit one that is socially controlled. David Rudd, though, contests the trend of linking food and sex in children's literature, drawing instead on Kleinian psychoanalytical theory where 'the provision of food is associated with the offer of the breast' (*Enid Blyton* 103). This is a credible perspective, especially when considering the crucial role of the mother as the figure who makes the food and, as Rudd points out, can also withhold the food (*Enid Blyton* 103). Nikolajeva also emphasises the importance of the child's reliance on breast milk to children's literature, arguing that the child sees this as a safe unlimited supply and that problems and fears only occur once the milk has dried up (*Mythic to Linear* 15–16). Certainly this goes some way to explaining the desire in children's literature for warm, wholesome creamy foods but it also reasserts notions of the good mother and bad mother. The majority of adult females in children's literature are categorised by their ability to feed; the good woman feeds the child and is loved, whereas the bad woman seduces the child through food but later withholds it, and consequently, is rendered evil.[9]

The mother in children's fiction has her identity constructed partly by the food she does or does not provide, marking the difference between Aunt Fanny's picnics of plenty in the 'Famous Five' series and the miserly (step)mother in 'Hansel and Gretel'. To suggest that the tie to the mother's breast milk is significant in children's literature is valid, but to do this at the expense of sexual imagery in the same literature is questionable. For, if food represents the sexual, then this explains partly why it is so policed in children's literature, why good families are distinguished from bad by the type and quantity of food that they consume. Food, like desire, must be checked, and if there are to be any banquets and gorging then, as will become clear, they should be confined within the rules, with the 'right' type of food under the proper rituals of dinner. The family in children's fiction is all about control and adherence to a certain way of life, and it directs children to the conservative even when it seems at its most sensual, for the literature and the food it features remain policed by custom and tradition.

False Food and Impostor Mothers

Equally, by custom and tradition and not by biological necessity, food, in children's literature, as for the most part in reality, is first and foremost provided by the mother. The mother is expected to sacrifice herself to feed her children: first through the placenta, second through breast milk and finally through preparing good wholesome food to allow the children to grow healthily. The mother is empowered by her control over food as the health and growth of the family depend to a large extent on her ability to nourish. It is significant that the dark and frightening female characters in children's literature are identified partly by their use and abuse of food and the ability it gives them to feign motherly traits. The deviant mother defines the normative here, for, in opposition to the 'good' mother, the deviant mother in children's literature embodies fears of the ever-threatening other who has the potential to cause the disintegration of the family through betrayal and seduction.

The figure of the stepmother in the Grimms' nineteenth-century fairytale 'Hansel and Gretel' epitomises the ambivalent position of the mother in children's fiction. The stepmother was, by and large, a nineteenth-century addition to the fairytale, as many earlier versions focused on the blood mother (Warner 211–12). By re-identifying the mother as stepmother, it can be claimed that the 'good' mother has died, leaving only the evil as epitomised by the stepmother and witch. Bruno Bettelheim observes that the 'fantasy of the wicked stepmother not only preserves the good mother intact, it also prevents having to feel guilty about one's angry thoughts and wishes about her', emphasising that the tale encourages readers to acknowledge the good and evil side of the figure of the mother (69). From the first picture in Anthony Browne's illustrated version of the Brothers Grimm's *Hansel and Gretel* it is clear that the stepmother is regarded as other. She sits apart from the rest of the family as she watches the aeroplane flying away on the television while the rest of the family sit at the table and her clothes are clean, tidy and colourful as opposed to the bland unclean clothes of the father and children. The stepmother is further vilified through the illustration of her chest of drawers. The top of the chest is cluttered with material objects and quite apart from ordinary expectations of good mothers, the stepmother's lingerie hangs out of the drawers untidily; the woman's sexuality far from being hidden is almost flaunted. This indulgence in cosmetics and lingerie helps to construct her both as a sexual being, a taboo subject for the 'good' mother in children's literature, and as a consumer who refuses to conform to the ideal of the self-sacrificing mother. The lipsticks and Oil of Olay bottle also reveal the stepmother's identity as a fake; she is not the 'real' blood related mother, but an impostor who indulges her vanity at the expense of her family's nourishment (Paul 34).

The stepmother, or the mother who refuses to conform to her conventional nourishing role, is often constructed as being witch-like. In Browne's illustrations there is little to tell the stepmother and witch apart: the stepmother is pictured looming over the children asleep in their beds; the gap in the curtain adds a witch's hat to her shadow suggesting her unconscious self. The stepmother wears black, and black witch hat shapes can be seen on the church spire, in the skirting board and on top of the wardrobe. The children are surrounded by symbols of witchery, and in contrast to this are pictured sleeping under pastel-coloured bedding. The stepmother and the gingerbread house witch are also given a whole illustration each in which both women are pictured behind a window which looks as if it imprisons them. Both women wear cosmetics, and the witch appears to be an older version of the stepmother. The 'evil' side of the mother/witch is shown in animalistic terms; the stepmother is pictured wearing a leopard print coat as she abandons the children in the midst of the forest; the witch uses food as a bait to capture the children, and later, in a reversal of convention, tries to feed off the child as she fattens Hansel up for the pot. The bad mother is constructed as unnatural and animal-like as, in her attempt to destroy the family, she defies all that has been naturalised by society. Furthermore, both witch and stepmother die before the closure of the narrative. They are, I suggest, constructed as the same threatening being.[10]

Food literally marks Hansel and Gretel's downfall. The trail of bread left by Hansel is eaten by the birds, emphasising the unreliability of the bread of home, while it is a house of bread, cake and sugar which tempts the children into the witch's hands. Lissa Paul suggests that the house represents 'a dream turned nightmare' as it embodies a common dilemma in children's literature, that is, the conflict between the 'wish to eat and fear of being eaten' (33–6). It is not only the food that tempts the children: the witch also plays on the children's need for a good, kind mother. The narrative tells us that the witch 'took the children by the hand and drew them indoors' and gave them 'a meal of milk, pancakes and sugar, apples and nuts' and put them to bed. Food is used to entrap the children, for in taking the witch's food into their bodies the children fall into her power. She has seduced the children by offering them comfort in a very maternal manner, and this acts as a warning to readers not to accept food from the hands of strangers, however apparently benevolent.

Browne's illustrations complement this, offering a Biblical intertext: the witch is portrayed as the devil offering temptation. In the illustration of Hansel putting a chicken bone out of the cage for the witch to feel, the shadow behind forms the shape of a snake. In 'Hansel and Gretel' the figure of the bad mother/witch is depicted in a particularly frightening way, for not only does she seduce the children with food, but she threatens their existence in her cannibalistic desires. The mother/witch defies and defines the normative laws of motherhood in her attempt to consume the children: such a reversal of the nurturing role of the mother demonstrates by negative example what the good mother should be. But the subtext of this depiction is the message that the nurturing mother can also represent a cannibalistic threat, and therefore food and its provider cannot always be taken at face value.

The impostor mother in literature constitutes a threat to the family. Children's literature constantly warns children about these dark figures, and as in 'Hansel and Gretel', food almost always acts as an indicator of character. In *The Lion, the Witch and the Wardrobe*, when Edmund takes food from the impostor mother, again a witch, it leads to the breakdown of his family loyalties as he is seduced by the foreign other and the consequences of this endanger all. The witch in 'Hansel and Gretel' uses food in order to seduce the children into her power and similarly, in reality parents expect to hold authority partly because it is they who 'put the food on the table'. The witch in *The Lion, the Witch and the Wardrobe* is empowered when she gives Edmund the food he desires:

> . . .he stepped on to the sledge and sat at her feet, and she put a fold of her fur mantle round him tucked in well.
>
> "Perhaps something to drink?" said the Queen. "Should you like that?"
>
> "Yes, please, your Majesty," said Edmund whose teeth were chattering [. . .]
>
> Edmund felt much better as he began to sip the hot drink. It was something he had never tasted before, very sweet and foamy and creamy, and it warmed him right down to his toes [. . .]
>
> The Queen let another drop fall from her bottle to the snow, and instantly there appeared a round box, tied with green silk ribbon, which, when opened turned out to contain several pounds of the best Turkish Delight. Each piece was sweet and light to the very centre and Edmund had never tasted anything more delicious. He was quite warm now, and very comfortable.
>
> While he was eating, the Queen kept asking him questions. At first Edmund tried to remember that it is rude to speak with one's mouth full, but soon he forgot all about this and thought only of trying to shovel down as much Turkish Delight as he could, and the more he ate, the more he wanted to eat, and he never asked himself why the Queen should be so inquisitive. [. . .] she knew, though Edmund did not, that this was enchanted Turkish Delight and that anyone who had once tasted it would want more and more of it, and would even, if they were allowed, go on eating it till they killed themselves. (Lewis 85–6)

Power relations are quickly established as Edmund sits at the witch's feet. She, like the witch in 'Hansel and Gretel', apparently begins to 'mother' Edmund: 'she tucks him in well' like a mother putting a child to bed and gives him a warm drink, thus making him 'quite warm and very comfortable'. But the maternal role is misleading and it reminds the child reader that figures who act in a motherly fashion cannot always be trusted. Flaws in the witch's maternal act soon become evident: the witch is reminiscent of the stepmother/witch's predator image in 'Hansel and Gretel' as she wraps her fur cloak around Edmund, trapping him within it; she feeds him sweet and exotic foreign food rather than the wholesome British food such as fish, potato, milk and tea, that his brother and sisters later consume at the Beavers' house, and she does not chastise him for speaking with his mouth full.

The witch takes advantage of Edmund's vulnerability by acting in a maternal manner and then subverting this role in providing him with the food he desires rather than the foods he needs. The reader is forewarned of the witch's evil intent by the sensuous description of the food; it is sweet, foamy, creamy, light and delicious. Edmund is seduced by the White Witch's promise of plenty, of 'rooms full of Turkish Delight': food leads to the downfall of Edmund as surely as it did for Eve and for Hansel and Gretel. Almost immediately the enchanted food results in Edmund forgetting his manners: he is losing his purity as a child as he lusts over the sweet forbidden food and begins to lose control.[11] In opening the silk, ribbon-wrapped box, Edmund, like Pandora in classic mythology, releases problems into the world, here, the world of Narnia: his own problem is that he is now the willing captive of the White Witch, and his captivity creates the subsequent problems faced by his siblings. That Edmund chooses Turkish Delight emphasises his moral weakness: the word 'Turkish' denotes the foreign other, more specifically, the Eastern other which opposes Christianity, and which suggests a rejection of the values of his own Christian family. Further, the sensuous language used to describe the sweets and Edmund's greedy reaction to them suggests sexual and perhaps animalistic desire rather than nutritional need, subverting adult concepts of childhood asexuality and innocence.

Edmund's enchantment with and lust for the White Witch's Turkish Delight results in the betrayal of his family. Driven by the insatiable desire that the sweets incite, Edmund will do anything to eat more of them. He is not suffering from ordinary hunger, as he has already eaten at the Beavers' house: he is impelled by magically-fuelled lust. As the narrator reminds us, 'there's nothing that spoils the taste of good ordinary food half so much as the memory of bad magic food' (Lewis 102). The opposition between good and evil is central to the text; the evil witch manipulates Edmund's weak character, feeding him 'bad', enchanted, sensuous food which leads him to reject his nutritious food and consequently to betray his 'good' family. Traditionally, in children's literature and in reality, the family, especially the mother, controls food and implicitly desire. In Lewis' text, Edmund's seduction by and subsequent allegiance to the White Witch parodies the traditional norm as he succumbs to the temptations offered by the sexualised female figure. Daniel suggests that the sexual construction of the White Witch is linked with aspects of *vagina dentata* as Edmund attempts to fulfil his pre-oedipal desires (125):

> Lewis's White Witch is a fascinating evocation of all that is culturally and psychologically fearful about the figure of the woman from a phallocentric patriarchal viewpoint. She is clearly fetishized, evokes the *vagina dentata* and notions of abjection. She seduces poisons, assimilates, and castrates. Her powers induce horror but she is also alluring. (129)

The White Witch is the woman of all good mothers' nightmares as she tempts away sons with her wiles. For children's literature one of the factors that constructs her as the epitome of the bad mother is her blatantly sexual sensuality: mothers, like their children, should be asexual.

The impostor mother is a common figure in children's fiction. She embodies the fears of the bad mother and yet also strengthens the cliché of the good mother through her deviance. From the fairy story of 'Hansel and Gretel', to the Narnia series in the 1950s and to Philip Pullman's *Northern Lights* (1995), the fake mother, like Eve, has always used food to entrap her victims. Ironically, considering Philip Pullman's own criticisms of C.S. Lewis (Ezard 8), Mrs Coulter in *Northern Lights* is depicted in a strikingly similar way to the impostor mothers in 'Hansel and Gretel' and *The Lion, the Witch and the Wardrobe*, thus emphasising the power of tradition as even writers who try to resist it are still entrapped by it:

> The kind lady saw him settled on a bench against the wall, and provided by a silent serving-woman with a mug of chocolatl from the saucepan on the iron stove. Tony ate the rest of his pie and drank the sweet hot liquor without taking much notice of his surroundings. (*Northern Lights* 44)

The narrator tells the reader that Tony 'is lost' and emphasises his passivity as he followed 'the beautiful young lady' through to 'Hangman's Wharf' (Pullman *Northern Lights* 43). The chocolatl is reminiscent of the foamy drink given to Edmund and like Edmund, the more he consumes, the more Tony becomes unaware of his behaviour and surroundings. Further, Mrs Coulter's beauty constructs her as a sexual predator, and her power, like the witch's, revolves around her ability to seduce her victims through the arousal of desire, be that for food, for maternal love, or for sexual gratification. The construction of the mother/witch as a sexual figure leads to the downfall of the boys in both Pullman and Lewis' texts, invoking their Biblical intertextuality.

It is boys in children's literature who are greediest, who can eat the most and are most concerned about food. In turn it is boys who fall easily into temptation and who succumb to their desires most readily. And it is the impostor mothers who offer temptation and promise gratification, usually, in children's literature, in the form of food, but implicitly there are sexual undertones. The impostor mother is the sexual seductress of adult literature and the future sexual partner of the adult male. But the boy cannot, or cannot be allowed, to see the mother in sexual terms, hence her sexuality is transposed on to the bad mother, and her sexual wiles are translated into the provision of exotic food and drink that both arouses and temporarily sates masculine appetite. These impostor mothers embody masculine fears of the *vagina dentata*, the consuming female.

In 'Hansel and Gretel' it is Hansel, not Gretel, who is destined for the witch's supper, and Mrs Coulter seems more interested in boys than in girls. But her kidnapping coterie is nicknamed 'the Gobblers', suggesting that the children who are their victims see them in terms of consumption. Child characters in texts such as 'Hansel and Gretel', *The Lion, the Witch and the Wardrobe*, *Northern Lights*, and indeed, many fairy tales, are in ambivalent positions. They are faced with mother figures who fulfil the traditional requirement and offer nourishment; the children are expected to eat. But equally, child characters are shown interacting with superficially good mothers who seem to adhere to conventional nurturing roles, but who are in fact bad mothers who seek not to feed the child, but to feed on him/her. And this is the ambivalence of the mother: she can both give life, but equally, it seems, take it away. But there is no ambiguity in the deciphering of good and evil in children's literature. An experienced child reader will read correctly all the signs of good and bad mothers in the examples above, for the sensual food offered by, and the exotic beauty of, the witches signify their threatening otherness, reinforcing existing cultural stereotypes of normality and deviance.

Good Mothers and False Fathers

In contrast to a literary world where the females entice the male characters to their downfall through food, in *Peter Pan* it is the male who tempts the Lost Boys as Captain Hook attempts to murder Peter, his arch enemy, and the Lost Boys by leaving them a poisoned cake. But there exist two crucial differences here: Captain Hook just leaves the cake, he does not attempt to mother and seduce in the way that the female figures did, and Wendy, representing the traditional good mother, saves the boys as she polices their desires through forbidding them to eat the cake. Wendy embodies the ideal of the perfect mother as she acts as the controlling force who saves the boys from their downfall: without her, as Captain Hook predicts, the boys would have 'gobbled' it up:

> "To return to the ship," Hook replied slowly through his teeth, "and cook a large rich cake of a jolly thickness with green sugar on it [. . .]. We will leave the cake on the edge of the mermaids' lagoon. These boys are always swimming about there, playing with the mermaid. They will find the cake and they will gobble it up, because, having no mother, they don't know how 'tis to eat rich damp cake." He burst into laughter, not hollow laughter now, but honest laughter. "Aha, they will die." (Barrie *Peter Pan* 84–5)[12]

Here temptation is placed in front of the Lost Boys in the form of sweet food. Sexual undertones are apparent as the 'rich, damp' cake is to be left on the edge of the mermaids' lagoon. If the cake represents temptation, and taking it would represent the fall, then leaving it on the edge of the mermaids' lagoon enhances the link between the eating of sensuous food and sexual awakening as mermaids often symbolise sexuality; the lost boys are on the cusp of purity and impurity, childhood and adulthood.

Family, as I have argued, functions to police desires and sexuality, and control over food plays a key part in this, so it is appropriate that it is Wendy who 'saves' the boys. As the mother figure, Wendy takes her traditional place as the provider of nourishment: she controls the food that the Lost Boys consume and any other figure who tries to feed them is portrayed as a threat. The text insists that children should only take food from the hands of the trusted good mother: to eat 'rich damp cake' without knowing its origin is to succumb to desire and to break away from the mother. Following from this it is apt that when Wendy seized the cake, 'in time it lost its succulence' (Barrie *Peter Pan* 112). Placing the tempting, forbidden cake into the safe hands of the good mother destroys its temptation: the pleasure promised by the forbidden is negated. The mother figure prevents the metaphorical sexual fall of the boys and saves their childhood lives. Indeed, Wendy transforms the use of the cake, as instead of it poisoning the boys it 'became as hard as stone, and was used as a missile, and Hook fell over it one night in the dark' (Barrie *Peter Pan* 112). The cake, once in the safe hands of a good mother, changes; it loses its sensual appeal but it also transforms from being something that would kill the boys to a weapon they can use against Captain Hook and the pirates.

Food can work as a weapon because it is invested with power and control; while food empowers the adult when children accept it, when they refuse it, as they so rarely do in children's literature but frequently in reality, the children become empowered as they control what goes into their own bodies. The reader is reminded that the good mother is one who controls the child's intake of food, protecting him/her from the shadowy father figure, in this case represented by Captain Hook. But in controlling food, the mother figure also polices desire, sexuality and behaviour. Food becomes a disciplinary tool as it can signify a reward for good behaviour, or children can be threatened with its withdrawal for bad behaviour, and the parental figures are judged by the quality and amount of food they give to the children. The children in 'Hansel and Gretel' are left to starve in the woods; in Burnett's *A Little Princess* Sara is allowed to go hungry under the care of the cruel headmistress and in the 'Harry Potter' series Aunt Petunia always feeds Harry less than Dudley, marking Harry's subordinate place in the pecking order of family. Further, she threatens to stop feeding Harry if he does not finish his chores.

In contrast, good families are symbolised by their fairness with regard to food. While the children in *Home, Anne of Green Gables* and *Where the Wild Things Are* have been disobedient and are sent away from the dinner table, they are still, sooner or later, given a good meal for, as Aunt Marilla in *Anne of Green Gables* states, 'When did you ever hear of me starving people into good behaviour? [. . .] She'll have her meals regular'(Montgomery 82). Food in good families remains a constant but the threat of its withdrawal empowers the adults. In contrast, the provision of an excess of food signifies Miss Trunchbull's power in *Matilda* when she punishes Bruce Bogtrotter for stealing food by forcing him to eat an entire cake. Although in the case of Bruce Bogtrotter an important moral about the dangers of greed and excess is also imparted on the child reader. On a less violent scale, Aunt Gwen in Philippa Pearce's *Tom's Midnight Garden* (1958) overfeeds Tom in an attempt to make him feel at home, to bridge the gap between her role as aunt and impostor mother. Children's literature uses food as part of its disciplinary project. The provision of food becomes part of the ideology that such literature promulgates, and the warnings contained in stories like 'Hansel and Gretel', with the clear example of the bad or impostor mother, teach the child reader to distinguish between good and bad mothers, using food as a signifier of good and evil. Food does not simply act to differentiate between good and bad mothers, but between good and bad families, and as occurs so often in children's literature, the negative examples of poor and unsuitable food, and implicitly families, serves to accentuate the qualities necessary to make the good family. The normative is again defined through the deviant, whether figured in food, fathers, mothers or family.

Food, Family and Cultural Identity

Food signifies a sense of belonging and the need to belong is intrinsic to children's literature and of course to family. But belonging can also entail loyalty to both family and nation and it is noticeable that children's literature is often very conservative about the type of food which it promotes. The children in the 'Famous Five', 'Swallows and Amazons', and 'Narnia' series, the characters in *The Wind in The Willows* and countless others all eat what seems to the modern eye vast amounts but they are not constructed as gluttons and this is because they eat very traditional British food, the type of food that is considered wholesome – that mothers are supposed to put on the table. The children in these texts consume ginger beer, tea, sandwiches, fried breakfasts, potatoes, roast dinners, fish and fruit pies and they avoid foreign food such as Turkish Delight. Even in texts of the late twentieth century, while there exists an attempt to represent a multicultural society, there remains a certain unease about exotic, foreign food. Similarly, processed food is often scorned as, not being home-cooked, it implies a bad family. Food is a strong signifier of the conservative nature of children's literature and it, like the family, remains largely unaltered, constantly promoting a specific ideal.

In eating traditional food, the children demonstrate a double loyalty: first, to their family as they allow the food prepared within the home to penetrate their bodies, and second, to the country as they in effect consume their national culture. The children in the 'Famous Five' series are encouraged to satisfy their appetites:

> The children ate enormously, and mother said that instead of having a tea-picnic at half past four they would have to go to a tea-house somewhere, because they had eaten all the tea sandwiches as well as the lunch ones! (Blyton *Treasure Island* 7)

The food and traditions here are strikingly English: sandwiches in a picnic, afternoon tea at four thirty, and attending a teahouse rather than a café or bar. Eating represents security: the children eat what they know with their own family, and they do not stray into the unknown. In the 'Famous Five' series there is no need to stray to the foreign because French food is depicted as toxic rather than alluring and attractive, as it caused sickness in Julian and acne in Dick (Blyton *Secret Trail*).

The foreign is threatening and unattractive, and the text instils cultural loyalty in its readers by reminding them that home, both in the sense of family and nation, really is best. This fear of the unknown is also evident in Ransome's *We Didn't Mean to go to Sea*:

> Here they stopped, and in a moment a Dutch waiter (who looked quite like an English one) had put two of the small tables side by side, making a big one, and they had sat down, and Daddy had pointed to things on the menu, and the Dutch waiter was hurrying off into the café.
>
> "Can't go far wrong with soup and steak," said Daddy.
>
> "You never know what you get when you try something with a fancy name." (295)

The foreign unknown is defined with regard to the known: the Dutch waiter is ameliorated by the bracketed comment which concentrates on his similarity to an English waiter; he will do for the moment, but is still classed as other. The Walkers are forced to go into a café, there are no tea-rooms here, and in this foreign establishment the father takes control and ensures the children eat what is familiar. Commander Walker's behaviour here contrasts greatly with his epigraph: 'Grab a chance and you won't be sorry for a might-have-been'; with food it would seem that no chances can be taken (Ransome *We Didn't Mean* Title Page). In a post-war period when culture, nationality and identity have been under such threat the children are encouraged to eat traditional food as to eat foreign food would symbolise the embracing of a different culture, thus Commander Walker, like the narrator in the 'Famous Five' series, ensures that the children remain loyal to their family and, by proxy, to the nation.

But conservative attitudes with regard to food are not just confined to texts written during, and in the ten years after, the war. In the recent 'Harry Potter' series Ron refuses to eat *bouillabaisse*, preferring instead to stick to his black pudding (Rowling *Goblet* 221),[13] and in Gillian Cross's *Wolf* (1990) Cassy is less than happy with the eating arrangements at her mother's house. Here, not only does the family eat takeaways but the family members eat them using their fingers. Cassy maintains her cultural allegiance by insisting on eating her Indian food with a knife and fork and by preferring the normality of porridge and traditional food that she has been accustomed to at her grandmother's house. The new or foreign always presents a threat of some sort as they represent a move away from what is constructed to be safe and 'natural'. Equally a move to a new diet may imply that the old diet was not perfect; children's literature depends on the traditional pattern and a certainty that what has gone before, what is known as right and safe.

In Susan Coolidge's *What Katy Did* (1871) the reader is taught through Katy's example not to interfere with the family food as 'after a while Katy grew wiser, she ceased teasing Debby to try new things, and the Carr family went back to plain roast and boiled, much to the advantage of all concerned' (180–1). The family constricts the desire to move towards new things and this is particularly apparent with regard to food, for a change in food symbolises a change in loyalty and tradition. Like Katy, Susan in the 'Swallows and Amazons' series and Anne in 'The Famous Five' series simply reproduce the food traditionally provided within the home, for there is no place for deviation with regard to feeding the family.

To feed the family is to control the family. The family need food to live and the cook must be trusted not to poison the family, to cook wholesome, traditional food and to pass this skill on to the next generation, allowing, indeed, insisting, that the children replicate established food patterns. While the children cook for themselves in Blyton and Ransome's texts they still indirectly receive the food from the hands of their mother. Although not directly at the scene, the mothers still dictate what the children eat both through physically providing the food and through Susan and Anne who function as their doubles. Child and adult worlds in *Swallows and Amazons* are essentially amalgamated despite efforts to separate the two as the children rename their food:

> 'I've got some toffee from the natives as well as some milk,' said Captain John.
> 'Real toffee?' said Roger.
> 'Molasses,' said Titty. 'Toffee is only the native name for it' (Ransome 106)

The food is not simply nourishment but is part of the adult world that by escaping to the island the children are attempting to avoid. Thus the children attempt to distance the adult world by re-naming the toffee and by naming the adults 'natives'. In trying to control their own world, the children operate a system which parallels the adult world. But they still recognise the need for systems of authority, as is indicated by John's position as Captain and Susan's as Mate – an implicit replication of the top male and his mate, or father and mother – and food is part of the system, regulating gender roles and the children's time, as they adhere to familiar mealtime patterns.

While seemingly independent, the children nonetheless remain under parental control, and this too is signified by food. All their nourishment while on the island is provided, directly or indirectly by their mother: she packs supplies for them; she orders, and pays for, the milk, eggs and bread from the local farm; she provides the pocket money the children spend on food; even catching fish is made possible by the equipment provided by the parents. The illusion of autonomy is deconstructed and the children never achieve true independence. While in texts such as *The Lion the Witch and the Wardrobe*, 'Hansel and Gretel' or *Peter Pan*, adult control is invested in bad or impostor mothers or fathers, in the 'Swallows and Amazons' series it is the good mother who retains control, rather as Wendy regains control in *Peter Pan*. The children in *Swallows and Amazons* are not exposed to exotic food, and their re-naming of the food is less an attempt to exoticise it than to maintain the illusion of control. It is in fact, part of the children's enactment of adulthood; it is play, and food is part of the construction of a safe and secure world. Ransome and Blyton's fiction is essentially escapist, and thus food represents security, and the upholding of family and nation, as the children eat traditional English food packed by archetypal mothers.

Food and Family Wellbeing in the Late Twentieth Century

Food cements the family: the sharing of food is conducted on some level in every type of family, and as I have argued, the type of food that is consumed symbolises the wellbeing of the family. Food remains crucial in late twentieth-century children's fiction as it still acts as a signifier of family health, but there exists an increasing recognition that the ideal family meal as depicted in the 'Swallows and Amazons' series or the 'Milly-Molly-Mandy' series has, like the ideal family, become something of an impossible dream. The yearning for this ideal demonstrates the conservativeness of children's fiction and the extent to which society internalises and privileges the mythology surrounding the family meal.

Both the fragmentation of the family and the individuals' move towards a better understanding of each other is symbolised by food in Anne Fine's *Madame Doubtfire* (1987). At the beginning of the narrative family troubles are represented by the bread Daniel has cooked, which 'lay swollen and steaming for several seconds before it collapsed' (Fine *Madame Doubtfire* 5–6). The bread, like the family, has fallen apart, and thus the family, while nourished, cannot share the 'idyllic' family meal as represented by the perfectly cooked food displayed on tables in *Angelina Ballerina* or *Milly-Molly-Mandy Stories*. But, by the conclusion of the text, for Daniel and Lydia food facilitates conversation – as the 'tea and biscuits filled her, her voice warmed up'; and later, Daniel and Miranda renegotiate their differences over a cup of tea, with Miranda promising not to interrupt mealtimes anymore with her phone calls (Fine *Madame Doubtfire* 169–70).

Food and drink symbolise the wellbeing of family and their presence or absence parallels family communication or its lack, and the idyll of the family meal has become naturalised in children's literature. Hence any disruption of mealtimes signifies complications or abnormalities. Families that do not conform to the naturalised image of the nuclear and all-respecting ideal are left to eat collapsed bread; families in the process of re-building relationships might share tea and biscuits, and families that have made it, or were perfect from the beginning, share beautifully cooked meals.

In Jacqueline Wilson's *Double Act* (1995) when the father first brings his new girlfriend, Rose, home for a roast dinner, her intrusion into the family is implicit in the overdone beef and the heavy Yorkshire puddings (25). As with *Madame*

Doubtfire, the text does not offer the traditional closure of 'happy-ever-after', but the family is shown to be progressing as Rose 'tried ever so hard to cook a proper Sunday lunch for everyone, but somehow the beef got burnt'. The good intention combined with failure tells us that Rose will never replace the twins' dead mother, but this family meal signifies that the family is re-united in a fashion (Wilson *Double Act* 156).

In Judy Blume's *Superfudge* the narrator, Peter, explains that 'life was getting better' and justifies this by adding that 'mom and dad were fixing dinner together' as, again, the text emphasises the links between food and wellbeing. In the 'Harry Potter' series, food serves to enhance the continual comparison of good and bad families in children's fiction:

> By seven o'clock the two tables were groaning under dishes of Mrs Weasley's excellent cooking, and the nine Weasleys, Harry and Hermione were settling themselves down to eat beneath a clear, deep-blue sky. To somebody who had been living on meals of increasingly stale cake all summer, this was paradise, and at first, Harry listened rather than talked, as he helped himself to chicken and ham pie, boiled potatoes and salad. (Rowling *Goblet* 57)

The Weasleys represent the perfect family that the families in the domestic texts of the late twentieth century fail to live up to. Mrs Weasley feeds eleven people wholesome British food at seven o'clock exactly, and even the sun shines on them. The ideals are increasingly impossible in reality, but the fact that they remain so prevalent in children's fiction, and that presentation of food gives the experienced reader such detail about the state of individual characters and family, indicates the conservative nature of children's literature: even at the end of the twentieth century, this literature cannot escape the mythologies that surround the food consumed within the family. Having discussed the ambivalence surrounding food, and what type of food children are taught to eat and to avoid, it is important now to turn to when and how they eat it, for it is not only about what and what not to eat but also about where and when food is consumed.

Table Manners: Manners of Table

The categorisation of a family as 'good' or 'bad' is straightforward in children's literature in terms of mealtime practices; it runs throughout all different types of families and across class divides. Mealtime practices in children's fiction suggest that a meal consumed at a table by two parents and their children is synonymous with a good, traditional loving family, whereas a fragmented meal, where individuals eat separately, emphasises a family in decline. Mealtimes should bring the family together, reasserting patterns of control, yet they can simultaneously be a place of disharmony and insecurity. Power can be challenged, family members may be absent, children may refuse to behave or even to eat, and leaving the table can be an act of defiance or rudeness. The family meal is not simply the cosy family get-together that causes a nostalgic feeling of security, but a site of potential conflict, power struggle, and rebellion. The family meal, for all its stereotypical representation in culture may even be a fallacy, for families today, as in the nineteenth century, often eat separately because of non-flexible working hours. But despite all the practical complications, in children's fiction the family meal retains its significance as it reworks a popular family cliché: the family who eat together will stay together.

The family meal, like the family home, is both a public and private affair. It serves as a site in which family problems can be discussed but also as a function at which to impress guests. The dining table is not only somewhere to enjoy each other's company but a place of competition, barter and snobbery and it represents an ideal space in which to flaunt the good manners, heritage and prosperity of the family. The rituals of precedence and presentation are culturally significant as they structure and represent social relations within the family and with outsiders.[14] Mrs Beeton's Household Management listed conventions of presentation for the dinner table and for the food that was to be served, as well as the order in which it should be eaten.[15] Table plans and menus ensured that dinner was controlled, correctly and prescriptively presented and consumed: '. . . the damask table cloth must be spotless, the napkins folded in the latest mode, flowers arranged [. . .] the glasses should be brilliant, the silver well polished' (xxix). The ideal family meal, in the Victorian period, was ritualistic, and the ritualism was part of the control over appetite and implicitly desire that was so important to the ideology of family. While we no longer adhere to the strict conventions laid down by Mrs Beeton, nevertheless in children's literature we still find the core elements of mealtime ritual and the regulation of appetite.

In the nineteenth century Alexander Peterson reiterated the significance of a controlled mealtime and linked this symbolically to the state of the family and nation as he stated that '[I]t is customary to point to the ideal of a united home-loving family as the deepest tradition of English life. The English dinner, with its complete circle – the father at the head, the mother at the foot of the table, and the youngest saying grace' (Quoted in Wohl 10). This archetypal family is clearly successful; it provides sufficient food and maintains traditional customs as the whole family is brought together in controlled and controlling circumstances. But Peterson also demonstrates the importance of the family meal to the symbolic stability of the nation. If the country is to be judged partly on the health and condition of its families, as I argued in Chapter 1, then the family meal is a key part of this image of unity and strength as the prosperous family meal represents a healthy nation. The family meal with all its customs has often been used to reassure the public that the country is in order.

Ivan Day points out that while a complex ceremonial meal to accompany James II's Coronation may seem excessive to a modern reader, to a contemporary Englishman/woman it would have served to reassure, as the adherence to ancient rituals and traditions helped the crown to consolidate its power (Day 'Feasting' 31). And this custom continues, as even in the twentieth century the Royal Family issued a painting of themselves taking tea. Sir James Gunn's painting, 'Conversation Piece at the Royal Lodge Windsor' shows the family taking part in a British cultural tradition – only here it is tea and cake (Day 'Teatime' 107). The whole family sit together round a tidy yet relatively frugal table: they, like the rest of the country after the war, must not be seen as gluttonous but to adhere to food rationing. The country must pull together and achieve unity. In effect, this adheres to Norbert Elias's theory concerning the process of civilisation, for if, as he argues all experiments in living and the family are initiated by the upper classes then other classes will seek to emulate them. With regard to dinner time rituals it seems that this is very much the case and consequently, although very many different types of families exist within children's literature their behaviours become homogenized by their need to adhere to the models established by those who are higher up the social scale. The family at table is a strong cultural signifier representing stability and prosperity and the fact that those in power have used this image to reassure the nation only emphasises its significance.

The overriding image of a happy family round the table has remained static, fixed in the culture, as something that should happen, something that is essential to the well-being of both the family and the nation. This is prevalent in all kinds of different media and here I will touch on a variety of different texts from art and portraiture to Victorian novels and modern day television advertisements as all play their part in naturalising the family meal (Barthes 'Towards a psychsociology' 31). In the same way as certain types of meals or recipes are handed down the generations and thus create tradition, nostalgia and a sense of belonging, modern advertisements for food often draw on cultural imagery as they show a family together at the table eating a Sunday roast. Victorian depictions of mealtimes also play on this ideal. In William Frith's painting 'Many Happy Returns of the Day' (1854), a family is pictured celebrating the little girl's sixth birthday. The father sits at the head of the table content with his well-nourished, well-dressed family, and as Sarah Holdsworth and Joan Crossley observe, the picture demonstrates, 'the importance of ritual and celebration in family life – gathering together and marking occasions of private meaning' (99–100). This same message is conveyed in both Victorian and present day depictions of family meals: a nineteenth-century advertisement for toffee shows the family gathered round the table, and recent advertisements for tables and food frequently show families gathered together around the table.

The dinner table is where the children are taught manners, are civilised and socialised. The Victorian maxim that '[e]very mealtime is a lesson learned' is relevant as the dinner table provided a perfect place to educate children as to the correct methods of behaviour at mealtimes, and to a certain extent the same applies today as children are expected to be able to behave and display politeness at the table. In Charles and Kerr's report in the 1980s they found that most mothers, 'felt that it was important for a child to learn table manners in order to be able to take them out and not be embarrassed by them; in other words so that their behaviour was socially acceptable' (21). The dinner table rituals play a part in civilising the child, and by this adults tend to mean making the children more adult-like. This concept is clearly evident in nineteenth-century advertisements. A series of advertisements for Rowntree products uses an image of three little girls taking tea. In one of them, the language supposedly used by the little girls is typically adult rather than childlike as the phrase at the bottom reads: 'How refreshing this cocoa of Rowntree's is', and by using this type of language it emphasises the adult civilisation of the child.[16] Reminiscent of Kate Greenaway's illustrations, children sit to take 'chocolate' as their mothers would take tea, dressed in bonnets and long skirts and drinking from delicate china.

Mealtimes then are seen as a powerful way in which to regulate behaviour, to tame children into polite young adults. In Heinrich Hoffman's *Struwwelpeter*, a set of German cautionary tales popular in nineteenth-century Britain, Fidgety Philip is unable to 'Be a little gentleman [. . .]. To sit still for once at table' and so plummets to the floor taking the contents of the table with him (22–4). The family meal is laden with nostalgia and harks back to a past age in the above representation, but in reality family meals often fail to live up to this ideal.

The Meal Behind the Ideal

The surplus of books and advice concerning etiquette and household management indicates that the cosy family get-together did not occur as naturally as we are often led to believe. The practicality of preparing food in the nineteenth century for both the working and middle classes reveals distinct obstacles in the idealistic traditional meal prepared at home by the mother. While cooking ranges were invented in the early nineteenth century it was not until the 1860s that they became common in middle-class homes, and prior to this families often had to take their food to be cooked or buy pre-cooked meals from stalls (Tannahill 31–2).[17] In Thomas Webster's painting 'Roast Pig' (1862) the pig is being delivered freshly cooked from the bakery (Mason 72–3), as is the Christmas goose in Charles Dickens' *A Christmas Carol* (1843) (Dickens 93). The image of the nineteenth-century mother preparing home-cooked food is shown to be an illusion for she had neither the time nor facilities to cook meals, and the family often only ate one communal meal per week (Davin 168). In addition, the idealised image of the children waiting to greet their father and to discuss their days over a communal meal seems in reality to be a somewhat rose-tinted fantasy. A series of engravings by Cruikshank 'The Drunkard's Children' (1847–8) which begin with an idealised mealtime scene and end with a picture of drunkenness and violence support the idea that the mythological family meal we nostalgically imagine was, and largely is, a fallacy, at least for the working and lower middle classes (ctd. in Hall 78–80).

At the beginning of the twentieth century, the family meal, despite the fact that wood/coal burning ranges and even gas burning ranges were more common, was still not a permanent feature of homes across the social spectrum. The traditional family meal was, then, a rather far-fetched concept for many of the working classes. But these tensions were not reserved to any particular class; the family meal has always been a site of conflict, as is shown in Vera Brittain's account of family life at the turn of the century:

> Following the long established example of my father's parents, we even had prayers before breakfast, during which performance everybody – from my mother, who perturbedly watched the boiling coffee machine on the table, to the maids who shuffled uneasily in their chairs while the postman banged on the door . . . presented an aspect of inattentive agitation. The ceremony frequently ended in a tempestuous explosion on the part of my father, since Edward was almost always late and could never say the Lord's prayer as fast as the others. (23)

While the rituals dominate, they create tension. Here the father is not in complete control: the prayers are not said in earnest, and a mockery is made of the whole event. The gap between the ideal and the reality remains in the late twentieth century, for as, Charles and Kerr observe, 'conflict at mealtimes rather than peace and harmony seemed to be the norm,' suggesting that, even now, the happy family gathered for dinner is something of a cultural myth (87). The naturalised image plays its part in policing society as ideology insists that the happy family will share good food in a specific way, regardless of the reality in thousands of homes. If this image of the family together at mealtimes is of such importance in general culture then in children's literature, with its ideological and didactic function, the myth is further accentuated in order to instil the ideology into the child.

The Family Meal in Children's Fiction: The Nineteenth-Century Standard

Mary Martha Sherwood's *The History of the Fairchild Family* set a benchmark which determined the way families should behave no matter what class they distinguish themselves as, and, to a certain extent, children's literature ever since has attempted to return to what Sherwood's text constructed as the ideal. Despite many nineteenth-century texts being rich in restrictions and constraints, texts in the twentieth century still utilise the earlier texts' archaic system of signs in order to distinguish between good and bad families. Families in children's literature from the nineteenth to the twenty-first century can be read by their behaviour around the table, as, generally, the same system of beliefs remains intrinsic to our readings. Perhaps the perfect meal is becoming more difficult to achieve in contemporary fiction, but its survival as an ideal suggests the conservativeness of children's fiction and its dependence on compliance with convention and tradition.

The perfect meal as shown in *The History of the Fairchild Family* consists of adult autocracy, frugality and order:

> As soon as the children got up, they used to go into their papa and mamma's room to prayers: after which Henry went with his papa into the garden, whilst Lucy and Emily made their beds and rubbed the furniture: afterwards they all met at breakfast, dressed neatly but very plain. At breakfast the children ate what their mamma gave them, and seldom spoke till they were spoken to. (Sherwood 43)

The breakfast table reunites the family, as ideology dictates it should, but the reunion is based on division; before breakfast the family is divided by gender, during breakfast it is separated on an adult/child basis, as the mother gives the food and the children consume it in silence. The food itself is not described but the plain, neat dress code implies that the food is also plain and wholesome, and that appetites are constrained and implicitly desire is controlled.

The mealtime is also a significant scene of order in Catherine Sedgwick's *Home*. The chapter 'A Family Dinner' is devoted to the mealtime and is placed near the beginning of the story, preceded by chapters on housekeeping and family government; the mealtime is recognised within the structure of the text as the product of good order and is a reflection of good family management. The description of the family mealtime also adheres to conventions of order and routine, for here, although dinner preparations are rushed, it is made clear that this is an exception to normal practice and the rules are still followed:

> The table was set with scrupulous neatness. "Mother sees everything," was their maxim; and sure she was to see it, if the salt was not freshly stamped, the castors in order, and every napkin, glass, spoon, knife and dish put on, as the girls said by plummet and line. These are trifles in detail, but their effect on the comfort and habits of a large family of children can scarcely be magnified. [. . .]
>
> "Here is our dinner," said Mr Barclay, turning his eye that had been riveted on the happy, noisy children to the table [. . .]
>
> "The dinner here, and I have not changed my cap!" said Mrs Barclay.
>
> "And I have not brushed my hair!" – "Nor I," – "Nor I," exclaimed in a breath, half a dozen treble voices.
>
> "It's all my fault, – forgetting to ring the warning bell," said Martha [. . .]
>
> "Never mind, Martha. Better to forget rules for once, than forget your part in the family joy."
>
> "That's good, mother! let us break all rules to-day, – let Wally sit by me."
>
> "O no! mother; by me! by me!" exclaimed other voices.
>
> "No. Take your usual place, Wallace, by Haddy." (Sedgwick 28–9)

The mother keeps a panoptical eye on the setting of the table, emphasising her authoritative position and, while there appears to be disorder, it is carefully controlled as Wallace is not allowed to sit in a different seat. Although the text pre-dates Mrs Beeton's work there is a textbook-like regime to table setting with specific rituals of order and cleanliness that reinforce the importance of the dinner table as a sign of social status and family wellbeing. As in *The History of the Fairchild Family*, the culture of the dinner table demands that the children remain categorised as lesser beings: the mother, father and servant are named after they have spoken, whereas the narrator neglects to distinguish between which children are speaking, describing them as 'half a dozen treble voices', or simply 'other voices'. The dinner table, then, re-asserts adult authority in the Fairchild and Barclay families; it is a place in which to train and civilise the children, a location in which desires and appetites can be constrained in the name of civility. The Barclay children have had their 'monster appetites tamed' as they are transformed from animalistic children to human adult-like individuals (Sedgwick 33). In effect, the Barclay mealtimes train the children. The text implies that all children need to be controlled and that the mealtime with its complex rituals and power structures, has a major role to play in the humanisation and civilisation of the child.

Twentieth-Century Teatimes

The family meal remains central in twentieth-century children's fiction. It is still a place of control and constraint but it is increasingly evident that the ideals established in nineteenth-century children's fiction cannot be maintained. The mealtime still represents a pinnacle of family well-being in children's fiction. In the late 1920s the 'Milly-Molly-Mandy' series depicts the family sitting around the table to share food, and the model of the Fairchild Family is, in part, still valid as the men are named before the women, but the twentieth-century shift to the centrality of the child to the family is clear as Milly-Molly-Mandy is seated at the foot of the table next to her mother and is named first. In Joyce Lankester Brisley's *Milly-Molly-Mandy Stories* (1928) the reader is presented with an ordered symmetry at the dinner table: the table takes a central position; the cat eats on the floor at one end and the dog at the other; the extended family sit opposite each other; and finally the dresser with the plates in tidy rows creates a sense of order and control (23). The table cloth is, like the rest of the room, clean and neat, and the food is only just visible, for the focus is on the characters and behaviour rituals rather than the actual food.

Similarly, in Katherine Holabird and Helen Craig's *Angelina Ballerina* (1983), while the family are not depicted sharing a meal, the pictures use similar symbols to those in the *Milly-Molly-Mandy Stories*: the dresser is in neat order and the table has a cloth on it with a simple meal of bread and tea which is also the only food visible in the *Milly-Molly-Mandy Stories* illustration. The dresser and tablecloth, as I have stated earlier, signify adult order and constantly re-appear in children's literature illustrations. In Jill Murphy's *Five Minutes Peace* (1986), despite the mother being divided from the children by a page and by text, the absence of the father, and the children eating surrounded by mess, a sense of order is still present in the depiction of the dresser in the corner of the illustration (np). The Victorian dresser remains, regardless of the family situation: in combination with the tablecloth and the frugal food it emphasises a sense of continuity from Victorian to contemporary texts. Mealtime conventions and dining room furnishings are a constant in children's fiction, and the mealtime is always regimented and constructed in culturally important signifiers.

The Incomplete Family Meal

However strongly the idyllic family meal is presented, there are always other, not so perfect, mealtimes in children's literature. The idyllic depictions set a standard against which all other representations of mealtimes are measured and there are constant comparisons both in literature and society of the ideal meal and the reality. In Anthony Browne's illustrated version of 'Hansel and Gretel' the experienced reader can foresee the stepmother's wickedness in her actions at dinnertime: she does not join the family at the dinner table, but she sits on an armchair; she admits the outside world to the sanctity of the dinner time scene as she watches television, an activity rarely permitted in good families during mealtimes; and she has failed to place any food on the table and thus cannot fulfil the maternal role expected of her. The location of the mealtime illustration early in the text sets the tone for the stepmother's behaviour in the remainder of the text; she is demonised from the start because she does not conform to the maternal domestic norm as defined by generations of children's texts.

It is in their deviation from the domestic norm that the Wormwood family in Roald Dahl's *Matilda* (1988) is vilified, in much the same way as the stepmother in *Hansel and Gretel*:

> They were all in the living-room eating their suppers on their knees in front of the telly. The suppers were TV dinners in floppy aluminium containers with separate compartments for the stewed meat, the boiled potatoes and the peas. Mrs Wormwood sat munching her meal with eyes glued to the American soap-opera on the screen [. . .] 'Mummy,' Matilda said, 'would you mind if I ate my supper in the dining-room so I could read my book?'
>
> The father glanced up sharply. '*I* would mind!' he snapped. 'Supper is a family gathering and no one leaves the table till it's over!'
>
> 'But we're not at the table,' Matilda said. 'We never are. We're always eating off our knees and watching the telly.'
>
> 'What's wrong with watching the telly, may I ask?' the father said. His voice had suddenly become soft and dangerous. (26–8)

Like the stepmother in Browne's *Hansel and Gretel*, Mrs Wormwood has not cooked, watches television and is separated from the rest of the family. In Quentin Blake's illustration that accompanies the text, she is pictured on a separate page and looks at the television while the father and children look at each other. The sanctity of the family meal is disrupted by the intrusive nature of the television, and the absence of those signifiers of dinnertime order, the table, dresser, even crockery, indicates that the meal does not match traditional standards. The passage is rich in irony, for the father's strict rule that no one should leave the 'table' in order to maintain the 'family gathering' mocks both him as a character and the ideal of sitting together to eat: his use of the cliché demonstrates its cultural strength even as the gap between his words and his actions deconstructs it. To eat at the table would fulfil one convention for Matilda but it would also force her to break the grouping together of the family circle.

The family meal, it seems, has degenerated, leaving the father clinging on to tradition in order to maintain paternal authority. By the end of the passage the idea of an amicable and orderly family gathering seems far removed as the father's voice becomes 'dangerous' and the accompanying illustration shows him grasping his knife in a threatening manner. This dinnertime deviates from the civilised ideal of the previous texts and as with Browne's *Hansel and Gretel*, its placement early in the narrative emphasises the significance of the mealtime as a domestic signifier of family cohesion. The Wormwoods' inability to conform to culinary convention identifies them as a bad family and promotes, by negative example, the right way for good families to behave. Furthermore, *Matilda* also presents the ideal in the shape of Miss Honey who provides a traditional and frugal meal for Matilda following the conventions of good families in children's fiction. Miss Honey and Matilda sit together to have a tea which consists of cups of tea and bread and margarine. Miss Honey plays the proper maternal role as she sacrifices her food for Matilda, and the two share the mealtime experience in a quasi-conventional manner as the boxes in the living room double as a table and chairs. There is no television, no processed food, and the two converse during the meal, conforming to the culturally constructed ideal of the mealtime in children's fiction (Dahl *Matilda* 189–94).

Events in the narrative can be predicted simply by an analysis of the dinnertime scenes in *Matilda* and *Hansel and Gretel*, and countless other texts, as the mealtime is a key signifier of family wellbeing. As far back as Sedgwick's *Home*, good and bad families are distinguished by the quality of their mealtime experience. The fall of Mr Anthon's family in *Home* is predicted by the chapter that parodies the positive example of the Barclays' 'Family Dinner' and is entitled 'The Reverse of the Picture'. It charts the disorder evident in the Anthon's dining room; the children have no set place at the table. They slam doors, refuse to change for dinner and are generally quarrelsome. The narrator, in part, blames Mr Anthon for the disorder as he does not spend the sufficient time, as dictated by the text and by convention, with his family at mealtimes and is shown as being shocked at the amount of time the Barclays devote to dinner: 'An hour! Bless my heart! We get through at our house in about ten minutes, never exceed fifteen' (Sedgwick 43). The dinner at the Anthons is something to 'get through' and so is condemned by the Barclays. The negative depiction of the meal also serves as an important warning to its readers of the importance of maintaining a correct approach to the tradition of family dining.

A similar scenario can be found in Judy Blume's fiction, as in *Superfudge* Fudge's family correspond to the 'correct' code of conduct at mealtimes and this can be seen when, much to the annoyance of Fudge's friend Daniel, Fudge's mother insists that in their house they 'don't watch TV while . . . eating'(49). The habits of the protagonists' family are promoted when they are faced with a child who is not used to the same customs; equally, Daniel's aggressive and awkward behaviour is contrasted with the generally good behaviour of Fudge and Peter. In accordance with the didactic traditions of children's literature, the children from the family who eat what they are given (unlike Daniel who is a very fussy eater), sitting at the table, without the intrusion of the television, are shown to be more balanced than the boy who is not policed in this tradition.

Families in children's literature are judged by their treatment of food: the Barclays, the Fairchilds and Fudge's family are depicted in a positive light and any family that refuses to conform to the rituals of the mealtime is described as being either unsuitable or in some kind of emotional difficulty. Mr Evans in Nina Bawden's *Carrie's War* (1973) ends his life a lonely man as he has never truly embraced the family or the family meal, preferring instead to eat alone 'in the parlour with Miss Evans waiting on him' (30), which contrasts with Hepzibah, who always keeps a warm food-filled kitchen, and non-coincidentally, keeps in touch with Albert and eventually reunites with Carrie.

In *Five on a Treasure Island* George's parents' financial and emotional troubles are made clear by a certain discomfort around the table as the children sit silently under Uncle Quentin's fierce gaze and wonder if they are allowed to speak, and later, they are relieved when Uncle Quentin does not appear at the dinner table (Blyton 30–1). In Michelle Magorian's *Back Home*, Rusty is relieved when her grandmother does not eat breakfast with them, but the turmoil caused by the war and its separation of families is represented in the awkward mealtimes that take place on Rusty's return to England, mealtimes which consist either of arguments or of restrictive and stilted conversations that only involve the grandmother and father (29, 180, 280). Even as far back as Charlotte M. Yonge's *The Daisy Chain* (1856), the meal is used as a signifier for family unity as the father's grief at the death of his wife is symbolised by his avoidance of the family meal: 'He was thought to be desirous of avoiding the family dinners that used to be so delightful' and similarly, his position at the head of the family is questioned as in the absence of his deceased wife he no longer carves the meat or sits at the head of the table (91, 267). The family survive, but their emotional difficulties are articulated in the disintegration of the dinnertime ritual.

The Edible Solutions

As the business lunch has the potential to produce deals, and engagements are debated at banquets in Jane Austen, the family table in children's literature is the ideal place to resolve family problems. In *Superfudge* Peter is persuaded not to run away from home but to stay for dinner instead, after which all problems are resolved with the help of a vanilla pudding (Blume 9–13). In *The Story of the Treasure Seekers* the children solve all their financial problems after a meal with their rich uncle; in *Harry Potter and the Prisoner of Azkaban* Ron suggests that comforting Hagrid and finding solutions to his problems is best begun with a cup of tea, and in Jacqueline Wilson's books contented endings are frequently paralleled by conventional family meals. Indeed, even in books which concentrate on family break ups, there is the longing for a traditional family meal. In *Double Act*, Garnett becomes accustomed to her stepmother and reveals this in describing a family meal in which her father eats everything Rose has cooked, no matter how it tasted, the mutual consumption of food making them 'a family too' (Wilson 157). Similarly, in *The Bed and Breakfast Star*, despite being homeless, the family still manage a meal, albeit in MacDonalds, and the text concludes with the family enjoying a proper breakfast around a table with a cloth and napkins.

The family meal is desired at every turn. Conventions dictate how people should conduct their meals; there is no room in children's literature for anything other than a traditional family meal. Children's literature is again, here with reference to food, confined and constructed by convention: it is unable, even in its most radical examples, to break entirely away from the ideology of the ideal family as it insists on the virtues of one sort of family to the detriment of all those families who happen to subvert the norm. As such as Daniel argues,

> Children's literature consumes aspects of culture, but does not reflect life, that is, it is not true to life. It regurgitates culture and serves it up to children in a heavily mediated form. (212)

The depiction of family and its relationship with food has little to do with a reality or truth. The ideal, be it obtainable or not, remains intrinsic to children's literature, as both children and adults internalise the ideology of the ideal family, immersed into the mythology of family that permits the policing of society.

Conclusion

There are few better places to immerse children in an ideology of family than in children's literature. On the surface Mary Martha Sherwood's *The History of the Fairchild Family* (1818) and contemporary texts by Jacqueline Wilson and Anne Fine might seem worlds apart: the style of writing has changed, no longer are texts punctuated with religious dogma; children are not usually whipped for disobeying their parents and nannies and governesses are, generally, a thing of the past. But what remains strikingly similar is the all-important disciplinary subtext of family ideology: children should be brought up in loving respectful families, preferably by two parental figures, and an experienced reader will be able to recognise a 'good' family by the idealised home in which it lives, by its shared spaces, and by the food it consumes. At the beginning of the twenty-first century, when families and their structures have changed considerably in society we might expect the traditional signifiers of the good family to have become redundant. But as this book has shown, these tropes retain their importance, and those families that do not fulfil the ideal are invariably constructed as 'other' to the desirable norm.

It could be argued that children and children's literature deserve better than this. The family has changed and consequently there should be no stigma about the family that does not share its meals together, or consumes processed food, or the family that lives in a cramped untidy flat in the middle of the city. The child character in children's literature should, perhaps, live in the 'real world' rather than be cocooned in womb-like seclusion, and more importantly he/she should not be encouraged, like Tracy Beaker, in her foster-home, to fantasise about a home with roses around the door, home-baked bread and a loving parent. For many writers, there is a responsibility for those involved in the production of children's literature not simply to recognise the diversity of family in the Western world but to embrace it. Instead of offering a more pleasing conservative middle-class alternative twenty-first century children's literature needs to accept that the family has changed and therefore does not need to return to nineteenth-century conventions.

The future of children's literature and its representation of the family are at a crucial point. In the first decade of the twenty-first century it is teetering on a fence, on one side of which there is the safety of nostalgia and tradition as children's literature encourages the normative family, while on the other hand there is the increasing acceptance that the family has changed, which offers the opportunity of deconstructing ideologies and myths which have traditionally constructed the family.

Nowhere is this better demonstrated than in the two best-selling children's literature series of recent times: J.K. Rowling's 'Harry Potter' (1997–2007) sequence and Philip Pullman's 'His Dark Materials' (1995–2000) trilogy. Rowling's texts have adhered to the conservative conventions of children's literature: Harry, the Cinderella-type orphan figure is left with the 'bad' family as exemplified by the Dursleys, but escapes to Hogwarts school, which acts as an alternative family, and to the 'good' family epitomised by the Weasleys.

Harry's mother made the ultimate sacrifice in dying to save her son; the Mirror of Erised, which shows the onlooker's greatest desire, presented Harry with an image of all his family together and smiling; Harry in times of uncertainty feels that what he really wants is 'someone like a *parent*' (Rowling *Goblet* 25), and Hagrid re-emphasises the significance of family when he states "Makes a diff'rence havin' a decent family" (Rowling *Order* 497). Thus, the ideology of the family remains in these narratives somewhat stereotypical and regressive.

Pullman seems to offer something quite different. His two main protagonists, Lyra and Will, do not have conventional families. Will's father is an explorer who has vanished, and his mother is unable to care for him because of her mental illness. Consequently, 'home was the place he kept safe for his mother, not the place others kept safe for him' (Pullman *Subtle Knife* 321–2). Lyra's parents are Mrs Coulter and Lord Asriel, both of whom are constructed as evil at different points of the text. Lord Asriel is depicted as violent and self-centred, almost breaking Lyra's arm at the beginning of *Northern Lights* and later murdering Lyra's friend Roger. Lyra, 'wrenched apart with unhappiness' feels that 'she could have killed her father: if she could have torn out his heart, she would have done so there and then' (Pullman *Northern Lights* 397). This representation of father/daughter relationships directly opposes that of tradition. Equally, Mrs Coulter, technically the maternal figure, is one of the 'gobblers' who kidnap children and separate them from their daemons, effectively murdering their souls – again, deconstructing the image of the mother most commonly found in children's literature.

This is far from 'happy families'. The text's violence is stark, as children are abused and murdered, and it is the parents who are unreliable and destructive. But alongside this lies a desire for the safety of the domestic: Will loves his mother and wants to keep her safe, and yet also needs the ghost of his father to tell him that he is proud of his son; Lyra knows that fathers *should* love their daughters, wants to return to her home in Jordan College, and holds dear the memory of waking up in her mother's arms – even though she is oblivious to the truth that her mother had drugged her.

The conclusion of the trilogy adds further ambiguity to the state of family: Mrs Coulter and Lord Asriel, like Harry Potter's mother, make the ultimate sacrifice as they fight the angel to 'make the world safe for Lyra. They could not have done it alone, but together they did it' (Pullman *Amber Spyglass* 507). The parents join together to save their child, and the family ideal is seemingly reinstated. But this idealised concept of family, though it might be desired, is unachievable for Lyra and Will. Both have reached puberty and are in love and yet they must return to their own worlds; they are forced to sacrifice their future as a family.

Where Rowling's 'Harry Potter' series largely conforms to the traditional ideology of family, Pullman's trilogy recognises, but simultaneously scrutinises that ideology, seeming to conclude that although the desire for domesticity still exists, the culturally constructed family we know and love is no longer a viable proposition. But he offers no easy solution. These twenty-first-century texts, then, embody the crossroads at which children's literature finds itself today. Yet, as the presence of and desire for family in Pullman's narratives acknowledge, in children's literature, as this book has demonstrated, the normative ideology of family remains a constant refrain, providing a location from which writers can venture into other possibilities, but back to which they usually return, as children return home to the family after an adventure.

Notes

Introduction

1 The term 'blended family' is often used to describe families with a mixture of step-parents, stepbrothers/sisters and/or half-siblings.

2 For examples see Hunt (ed.), *An Illustrated History*; Hunt, *An Introduction to Children's Literature*; Thacker and Webb; John Rowe Townsend, *Written for Children*. This is a brief list of such texts, as there are several other critical histories which are also useful and that are credited in other sections of the book.

Chapter 1

1 In *The Making of the Modern Child* O'Malley gives a detailed discussion of the middle-class values that were prevalent in late eighteenth-century children's literature thus emphasising that the rise of children's literature came from middle-class origins.

2 For more information on the Queen Caroline affair and its effects on the nation see Catherine Hall, 'The Sweet Delights of Home' (47–50).

3 Camilla and Charles married in 2005 and still their marriage caused controversy with various members of the Church speaking out against it. But their union has also returned their relationship to the conventions of social respectability.

4 These fears are demonstrated by the cautious nature of the legislation as the British Parliament voted in July 2004 to allow children to be smacked but qualified this by adding 'with moderation'. news.bbc.co.uk/1/hi/uk_politics/3865277.stm. Accessed 05/06/2005.

5 For a more detailed account of the Caroline Norton story see Alice Acland's work *Caroline Norton*.

6 It is difficult to specify exact ages at which all children left school as they varied with school boards. In 1893 the school leaving age was raised to 11,

but school boards could insist on compulsory attendance until 13. How effectively attendance was monitored and insisted upon is open to question. For further information on this see Brian Simon, *Education and the Labour Movement 1870–1920.*

7   For more information on the rise in female employment refer to Davidoff *et al.,* 194–7.

8   For examples of women hiding their pregnancies and the shame attached to women who failed to conform to the ideal (such as those who suffered mental illness) see Davidoff *et al.,* 251–8.

9   Up-to-date divorce figures show that divorce rates in Great Britain peaked in 1993 with 180,000 divorces in the year, but that there still were 166,700 divorces in 2003. For more information visit www.statisics.gov.uk/cci/nugget_print.asp?ID=170. Accessed 16/08/2005.

Chapter 2

1   Rousseau argues that 'there is no picture more charming than that of the family, but a single missing figure disfigures all the others' and goes on to criticise mothers too sick to nurse, fathers away on business, and siblings at boarding schools (49).

2   Virago published an edition of *The Daisy Chain* in 1988 but this is now out of print. To my knowledge the only paper edition available in the UK is published by IndyPublish although digital downloads are also advertised. This contrasts with the availability of the 'Little Women' series or the 'Katy' series which are available in most high street bookshops.

3   In *The Pleasures of Children's Literature* Nodelman argues that children's literature demonstrates adults' attempts to colonise children, making children feel guilty if they themselves do not fit the adult model, 82.

4   Bratton also suggests that this typical Romantic conclusion to a realistic text emphasises an unselfconscious awareness of wider problems within society, 60–100.

5   In *Children and their Books* Julia Briggs and Gillian Avery argue that in 'adopting the child's voice [Nesbit could] not only locate her own position as a woman in a male-dominated society, but also escape from the pressure to write like a man.' (248).

6   The narrative itself emphasises what Rose terms the impossibility of children's fiction as power relations can never entertain any equality between adult and child, writer and reader.

Chapter 3

1   According to Peter Hunt, William first appeared in a magazine for adults entitled *Home Magazine* as early as 1919, but it was in 1922 that the

stories were collected together and published with a juvenile audience in mind ('Retreatism and Advance' 217).

2   Kimberley Reynolds makes a similar point as she argues that 'adults living between the wars also required their image of childhood to provide a sense of hope, purpose, cleansing and continuity to alleviate the disruption and futility of war' (*Children's Literature* 35).

3   Kimberley Reynolds argues that both the 'Milly-Molly-Mandy' series and Laura Ingalls Wilder's *The Little House in the Big Woods* (1932) are typical of dominant constructions of the family in the children's literature of this period. ('Sociology, Politics, the Family' 29–30)

4   Ransome was advised by his publishers not to mention the war. (Hunt, 'Retreatism and Advance' 219).

5   Various critics chart this new era. For examples refer to Hollindale and Sutherland, 'Internationalism, Fantasy and Realism', 256; Reynolds, *Children's Literature*, 35; and Rustin and Rustin, 1.

6   Rustin and Rustin make similar observations as they emphasise the order in which the children present themselves, 41.

7   Peter Hunt goes on to argue that this simple unimaginative language, 'sits rather uncomfortably with some of the high allegory that many critics have detected in the book' (*Criticism, Theory and Children's Literature* 108–9).

8   Roald Dahl also vilifies characters who refuse to embrace the domestic. Elements of this are evident in much of his work but the best examples are in *The Witches* (1983).

9   John Rowe Townsend suggests that in the 1960s 'The unwritten social contract between parents and children [. . .] was under pressure from both sides.' ('Parents and Children' 85). Les Ingram suggests that the absence of parents post-1960 illustrates a 'lack of solidarity' (193)

10 Both Paul (62) and Rustin and Rustin (202–5) observe that Carrie attempts to stay loyal to all the characters.

11 Peter Hunt quotes from *The New York Times* and *The Times Educational Supplement*'s appraisals of *Madame Doubtfire* as a comedy about divorce (*Children's Literature* 65).

12 Tucker and Gamble also make the observation that children have to learn to accept the rights of their parents in Fine's work, 66–7.

13 Hunt also comments on the non-happy but comfortable conclusion of Fine's texts, using *Madame Doubtfire* as an example ('Anne Fine' 15).

14 Carolyn Daniel includes an interesting analysis of Jacqueline Wilson's *Illustrated Mum* in which she discusses the mother in terms of the food she provides. Daniel argues that the mother's failure is symbolised by her inability to feed her children properly and consequently Wilson is seen to be a conservative writer who provides no role other than motherhood for her adult female characters, 101–3.

Chapter 4

1   A version of this chapter was first published in *New Voices in Children's Literature* (2004), ed. Sebastien Chapleau. Reproduced by permission of Pied Piper Publishing Ltd, Shenstone, WS14 0JU.

2   The civilising of Max with regard to food is discussed in Chapter 6.

3   Pauline Dewan also recognises this pattern further emphasising that the characters return home with an increased knowledge of the world, 272–3.

4   This kind of house was replicated by several children's toy companies as children in the twentieth century played in 'Wendy Houses'. Now the Wendy House has been renamed to a 'playhouse' in order to encourage boys into domestic play and avoid allegations of sexism.

Chapter 5

1   A version of this chapter was first published in the *New Review of Children's Literature and Librarianship.* 11.1 (2005): 15–31. www.informaworld.com. Reproduced here by permission of Routledge, Taylor and Francis Group.

2   Pearson and Richards argue that 'Houses in western society are also status symbols and the hierarchical social order is encapsulated in their variety [. . .] the match between social classes and house types may not be absolute, but the hierarchical classification of dwelling acts as a totemic system of moral and social taxonomies for the British class structure, both exemplifying and reinforcing it' (9).

Chapter 6

1   For more on food as a sign of culture see Barthes, *Mythologies,* 58–64.

2   Roland Barthes suggests that the recipes handed down from generation to generation help form a national identity and goes on to explain, with regard to France, that there are two strands to this – the rustic rural food and the aristocratic food ('Towards a Psychosociology' 24).

3   While Probyn uses the music to the Delia Smith cookery programme as an example, the links between food and sex can be seen in a variety of top chefs' publications – Nigella Lawson being the best example as she is pictured licking fingers and ice cream cones in deeply phallic imagery.

4   Judith Flanders gives an interesting and detailed account of menus in Victorian middle-class homes and of the different types of foods that the members of the households were given, 224–9.

5   Carolyn Daniel incorporates a very interesting and detailed analysis of the Freudian symbolism of food in *Voracious Children.*

6   Keeling and Pollard argue that the child desires to grow larger than his/her parents as this empowers him/her. Part of the process of empowerment

can also be seen when the child rejects food and thus convention, and as a result becomes 'monstrous', 127.

7 Keeling and Pollard also note Max's banishment and later return to food and the family that it symbolises (134–5).

8 McGillis 80; Daniel 81–2; Nikolajeva, *Mythic to Linear* 11; Katz 192.

9 Carolyn Daniel's chapter 'The Land of Milk and Honey' (87–114) gives a detailed discussion of Melanie Klein's theories concerning breast feeding and relates this to a variety of textual examples including: the White Witch's initial seduction of Edmund and later withdrawal of food; and also Pullman's Lyra's need for maternal comfort and sustenance as Ma Costa pulls her close to her chest.

10 Daniel also links the figure of stepmother and witch in Grimm's 'Hansel and Gretel' in her observation that both use the same phrase "Get up you lazy bones" when they wake the children (119).

11 Nikolajeva makes several similar points in her reading of this passage but also observes that Edmund's inability to control his desires could represent a possible metaphor for drug addiction (*Mythic to Linear* 130).

12 The Puffin edition of *Peter Pan* purports to be Barrie's own text published in 1911. The Oxford World Classics edition 'Peter and Wendy' also purports to follow the 1911 edition. There is a disparity here between the editions as the Oxford World Classics edition glosses over this section simply explaining that the pirates left the poisoned cake 'in one cunning spot after another'. The two editions then agree that the cake goes stale, is used as a missile, and that Captain Hook falls over it. (Barrie, 'Peter and Wendy' 138–9).

13 Daniel also remarks on this passage pointing out that it seems strange that a food made from pig's blood remains preferable to risking the new taste of the foreign, 18.

14 For more information on this refer to Charles and Kerr 4, and Barthes, 'Toward a psychosociology', 21–2.

15 Mrs Beeton, of course, is the most famous example for the nineteenth century but it is also worth considering that such rituals have been stipulated by writers for centuries. Norbert Elias includes an in depth analysis of Erasmus' writings on food rituals and goes on to discuss medieval manners at the table.

16 This advertisement can be found at the History of Advertising Archive Trust (HAT), 1891, Classmark 1911717.

17 Also see Judith Flanders' account of different types of stoves, 67–70.

Bibliography

Primary Sources

Picture Books

Ahlberg, Janet and Allan. *Starting School*. 1988. London: Puffin, 1990.

Brothers Grimm. *Hansel and Gretel*. Illus. Anthony Browne. London and New York: Julia MacRae Books, 1981.

Browne, Anthony. *A Walk in the Park*. 1977. London: Hamish Hamilton, 1980.

——. *Piggybook*. 1986. London: Little Mammoth, 1992.

Cole, Babette. *Bad Habits!* 1998. Harmondsworth: Puffin, 1999.

Dupasquier, Philippe. *Our House on the Hill*. 1987. London: Puffin, 1988.

Edwards, Dorothy. *My Naughty Little Sister Storybook*. 1952–62. Illus. Shirley Hughes. London: Little Mammoth, 1991.

Hoffman, Heinrich. *Struwwelpeter*. 1845. London: Pan, 1972.

Holabird, Katherine. *Angelina Ballerina*. 1983. Illus. Helen Craig. Harmondsworth: Puffin, 1987.

Kerr, Judith. *The Tiger Who Came to Tea*. 1968. London: Picture Lions, 1973.

Murphy, Jill. *Five Minutes Peace*. 1986. London: Walker Books, 1988.

——. *All in One Piece*. 1987. London: Walker Books, 1998.

Ormerod, Jan. *Sunshine*. 1981. Harmondsworth: Puffin, 1985.

——. *Moonlight*. 1982. Harmondsworth: Puffin, 1985.

Rosen, Michael. *We're Going on a Bear Hunt*. 1989. Illus. Helen Oxenbery. London: Walker Books, 1993.

Sendak, Maurice. *Where the Wild Things Are*. 1967. London: Red Fox, 2000.

Non-Picture Books

Alcott, Louisa M. *Little Women*. 1868. London: Puffin, 2001.

Barrie, J.M. *Peter Pan*. 1911. London: Puffin, 1994.

——. 'Peter and Wendy'. *Peter Pan in Kensington Gardens / Peter and Wendy*. Ed. Peter Hollindale. Oxford: Oxford World Classics, 1999. 69–226.

Bawden, Nina. *Carrie's War*. 1973. Harmondsworth: Puffin, 1974.

Blume, Judy. *Forever*. 1975. London: Macmillan, 2001.

——. *Superfudge*. 1980. London: Pan, 1982.

——. *Tiger Eyes*. 1981. London: Pan, 1988.

Blyton, Enid. *Five on Treasure Island*. 1942. London: Hodder and Stoughton, 1997.

——. *Five on a Secret Trail*. 1956. London: Hodder and Stoughton, 1960.

Bond, Michael. *A Bear Called Paddington*. 1958. Hammersmith: Picture Lions, 1997.

Boston, Lucy M. *The Children of Green Knowe*. London: Faber, 1954.

Brisley, Joyce Lankester. *Milly-Molly-Mandy Stories*. 1928. London: George G. Harrap & Co, 1949.

Brittain, Vera. *Testament of Youth*. 1933. London: Virago, 1978.

Burnett, Frances Hodgson. *Little Lord Fauntleroy*. 1886. London: J.M. Dent and Sons, 1966.

——. *A Little Princess*. 1905. London: Puffin, 1994.

——. *The Secret Garden*. 1911. London: Puffin, 1994.

Carroll, Lewis. *Alice's Adventures in Wonderland*. 1865. London: Puffin, 1994.

Coolidge, Susan. *What Katy Did*. 1872. Harmondsworth: Puffin, 1995.

Crompton, Richmal. *Just William*. 1922. London: Macmillan, 1995.

Cross, Gillian. *Wolf*. 1990. Oxford: Oxford University Press, 1999.

Dahl, Roald. *James and the Giant Peach*. 1961. Harmondsworth: Puffin, 1985.

——. *Charlie and the Chocolate Factory*. 1964. Harmondsworth: Puffin, 1985.

——. *Fantastic Mr Fox*. 1970. Harmondsworth: Puffin, 1974.

——. *George's Marvellous Medicine*. 1981. London: Puffin, 2007.

——. *The BFG*. 1982. Harmondsworth: Puffin, 2001.

——. *The Witches*. 1983. Harmondsworth: Puffin, 1985.

——. *Matilda*. London: Jonathan Cape, 1988.

Dickens, Charles. 'A Christmas Carol'. *The Christmas Books, Volume 1: 'A Christmas Carol'/'The Chimes'*. Ed. Michael Slater. London: Penguin, 1985.

Fairfax-Lucy, Brian and Philippa Pearce. *The Children of the House*. London: Longman's Young Books, 1968.

Fine, Anne. *The Granny Project*. 1983. London: Egmont, 2002.

——. *Madame Doubtfire*. 1987. London: Puffin, 1995.

——. *Goggle-Eyes*. 1989. London: Puffin, 1990.

Fitzhugh, Louise. *Nobody's Family is Going to Change*. 1976. London: Victor Gollancz, 1977.

Garnett, Eve. *The Family From One End Street*. 1937. London: Puffin, 2004.

Grahame, Kenneth. *The Wind in The Willows*. 1908. London: Methuen, 1973.

Habberton, John. *Helen's Babies*. 1876. London: Hutchinson and Co, nd.

Hegan, Alice Caldwell. *Mrs Wiggs of the Cabbage Patch*. 1901. New York: Century Co, 1902.

Kingsley, Charles. *The Water Babies: A Fairy Tale for a Land-Baby*. 1863. London: Constable, 1915.

Lewis, C.S. 'The Lion, the Witch and the Wardrobe'. *The Chronicles of Narnia*. 1950. Illus. Pauline Baynes. London: Harper Collins, 2000. 72–134.

Lindsay, Norman. *The Magic Pudding*. 1918. London: Angus and Robertson, 1990.

Lloyd, Marjorie. *Fell Farm Campers*. 1960. Harmondsworth: Puffin, 1965.

Magorian, Michelle. *Back Home*. 1985. London: Puffin, 1987.

Milne, A.A. 'The House at Pooh Corner'. *The Complete Winnie the Pooh*. 1928. London: Dean, 1997. 157–316.

Montgomery, L.M. *Anne of Green Gables*. 1908. London: Puffin, 1977.

Nesbit, Edith. *The Story of the Treasure Seekers*. 1899. London: Puffin, 1994.

——. *The Railway Children*. 1905. London: Puffin, 1994.

Norton, Mary. 'The Borrowers'. *The Complete Borrowers*. 1952. Harmondsworth: Puffin, 1997. 7–115.

——. 'The Borrowers Afield'. *The Complete Borrowers*. 1955. Harmondsworth: Puffin, 1997. 117–253.

Pearce, Philippa. *Tom's Midnight Garden*. 1958. London: Puffin, 1976.

Porter, Eleanor H. *Pollyanna*. 1913. London: Puffin, 1994.

Pullman, Philip. *Northern Lights*. 1995. London: Scholastic, 1998.

——. *The Subtle* Knife. 1997. London: Scholastic, 1998.

——. *The Amber Spyglass*. 2000. London: Scholastic, 2001.

Ransome, Arthur. *Swallows and Amazons*. 1930. London: Red Fox, 1993.

——. *We Didn't Mean to go to Sea*. 1942. London, Red Fox, 1993.

Rowling, J.K. *Harry Potter and the Philosopher's* Stone. London, Bloomsbury, 1997.

——. *Harry Potter and the Chamber of Secrets*. London: Bloomsbury, 1998.

——. *Harry Potter and the Prisoner of Azkaban*. London: Bloomsbury, 1999.

——. *Harry Potter and the Goblet of Fire*. London: Bloomsbury, 2000.

——. *Harry Potter and the Order of the Phoenix*. London: Bloomsbury, 2003.

Sedgwick, Catherine M. *Home*. Boston and Cambridge: James Munroe and Company, 1835.

Sherwood, Mrs [Mary Martha]. *The History of the Fairchild Family or The Child's Manual*. 1818. London: James Nisbet & Co, 1889.

Sidney, Margaret. *Five Little Peppers and How They Grew*. 1881. Boston: Lothrop, Lee and Shepard Co, 1909.

Sinclair, Catherine. *Holiday House: A Book for the Young.* 1839. London: Ward, Lock and Co, nd.
Snicket, Lemony. *A Series of Unfortunate Events: The Bad Beginning.* 1999. London: Egmont, 2001.
Streatfield, Noel. *Ballet Shoes.* 1936. Harmondsworth: Puffin, 1963.
Tolkien, J.R.R. *The Hobbit, or There and Back Again.* 1937. London: HarperCollins, 1997.
Townsend, John Rowe. *Gumble's Yard.* 1961. Oxford: Oxford University Press, 2001.
Wilder, Laura Ingalls. *Little House in the Big Woods.* 1932. London: Methuen, 1974.
Wilson, Jacqueline. *The Story of Tracy Beaker.* 1991. London: Corgi Yearling, 1992.
——. *The Bed and Breakfast Star.* 1994. London: Corgi Yearling, 1995.
——. *Double Act.* 1995. London: Corgi Yearling, 2002.
——. *The Suitcase Kid.* 1995. London: Corgi, 2006.
Yonge, Charlotte M. *The Daisy Chain, or Aspirations.* 1856. Virginia: IndyPublish, 2002.

Secondary Sources

Acland, Alice. *Caroline Norton.* London: Constable and Company, 1948.
Alston, Ann. 'Your Room or Mine? Spatial Politics in Children's Literature'. *New Review of Children's Literature and Librarianship* 11.1 (2005): 15–31.
——. '"There's No Place Like Home":The Ideologiocal and Mythological Contracution of Home in Children's Literature'. *New Voices in Children's Literature Criticism.* Ed. Sebastien Chapleau. Shenstone: Pied Piper Publishing, 2004. 55–63.
Almond, Barbara. '*The Secret Garden*: A Therapeutic Metaphor'. *The Psychoanalytical Study of the Child* 45 (1990): 477–94.
Ariès, Philippe. *Centuries of Childhood: A Social History of Family Life.* 1960. Harmondsworth: Penguin, 1973.
Avery, Gillian. *Childhood's Pattern: A Study of the Heroes and Heroines of Children's Fiction 1770–1950.* London: Hodder and Stoughton, 1975.
——. 'Home and Family: English and American Ideals in the Nineteenth Century'. *Stories and Society: Children's Literature in its Social Context.* Ed. Dennis Butts. Basingstoke: Macmillan, 1992. 37–49.
——. *Behold the Child: American Children and their Books 1621–1922.* London: The Bodley Head, 1994.
——. 'The Family Story' *International Companion Encyclopaedia of Children's Literature.* Ed. Peter Hunt. London: Routledge, 1996. 338–47.
Bachelard, Gaston. *The Poetics of Space: The Classic Look at How We Experience Intimate Spaces.* Trans. Maria Jolas. Boston: Beacon Press, 1994.
Banerjee, Jacqueline. *Through the Northern Gate: Childhood and Growing Up in British Fiction 1719–1901.* New York: Peter Lang, 1996.
Barker, Keith. 'The Use of Food in Enid Blyton's Fiction'. *Children's Literature in Education* 13.1 (1982): 4–12.
Barthes, Roland. 'Towards a Psychosociology of Contemporary Food Consumption'. *Food and Culture: A Reader.* Eds Carole Counihan and Penny Van Esterik. London: Routledge, 1997. 20–8.
——. *Mythologies.* Trans. Annette Lavers. London: Vintage, 2000.
Beer, Gillian. 'The Making of a Cliché: No Man is an Island'. *Fonctions Du Cliché du Banal à La Violence.* Eds Claudine Raynaud and Peter Vernon. Tours: l'Université de Tours, 1997. 29–41.
Beeton, Mrs. *Every-Day Cookery and Housekeeping Book: Comprising Instructions for Mistress and Servants.* 1865. London, New York and Melbourne: Ward, Lock and Co, 1984.
Belsey, Catherine. 'Denaturalizing the Family: History at the Level of the Signifier'. *European Journal of Cultural Studies* 4:3 (2001): 289–303.
——. *Shakespeare and the Loss of Eden.* Basingstoke: Palgrave, 2001.
Bettleheim, Bruno. *The Uses of Enchantment: the Meaning and Importance of Fairy Tales.* Harmondsworth: Penguin, 1978.
Blair, Tony. 'Speech to the Labour Party Annual Conference', 30 September 1997. 9 July 2007. http://www.prnewswire.co.uk/cgi/news/release?id=47983
Borrowdale, Anne. *Reconstructing Family Values.* Melksham: The Cromwell Press, 1994.
Bratton, J.S. *The Impact of Victorian Children's Fiction.* London and Sydney: Croom Helm, 1984.
Brayfield, Celia. 'The Death of the Family?' *The Times*, 12 October 1998: 19.
Briggs, Julia. 'Transitions, 1890–1914'. *An Illustrated History of Children's Literature.* Ed. Peter Hunt. Oxford: Oxford University Press, 1995. 167–92.

Briggs, Julia and Gillian Avery. *Children and their Books: A Celebration of the work of Iona and Peter Opie*. Oxford: Clarendon Press, 1989.

Briggs, Julia and Dennis Butts. 'The Emergence of Form, 1850–1890' *An Illustrated History of Children's Literature*. Ed. Peter Hunt. Oxford: Oxford University Press, 1995. 130–67.

Brumberg, Joan Jacobs. 'The Appetite as Voice'. *Food and Culture: A Reader*. Eds Carole Counihan and Penny Van Esterik. London: Routledge, 1997. 159–80.

Bryden, Inga and Janet Floyd, eds. *Domestic Space: Reading the Nineteenth-Century Interior*. Manchester and New York: Manchester University Press, 1999.

——. 'Introduction'. *Domestic Space: Reading the Nineteenth-Century Interior*. Eds Inga Bryden and Janet Floyd. Manchester and New York: Manchester University Press, 1999. 1–17.

Bunkers, Suzanne. 'We Are Not the Cleavers: Images of Non-Traditional Families in Children's Literature'. *The Lion and The Unicorn* 16:1 (1992): 115–33.

Butts, Dennis. 'Introduction'. *Stories and Society: Children's Literature in its Social Context*. Ed. Dennis Butts. Basingstoke: Macmillan, 1992. x–xvi.

——, ed. *Stories and Society: Children's Literature in its Social Context*. Basingstoke: Macmillan, 1992.

——. 'How Children's Literature Changed: What Happened in the 1840s?' *The Lion and the Unicorn*, 21:2 (1997): 153–62.

Carpenter, Humphrey and Mari Pritchard. *The Oxford Companion to Children's Literature*. 1984. Oxford: Oxford University Press, 1999.

Chambers, Aidan. *Tell Me: Children, Reading and Talk*. South Woodchester: Thimble Press, 1993.

Chambers, Deborah. *Representing the Family*. London: Sage, 2001.

Chapleau, Sebastien, ed. *New Voices in Children's Literature Criticism*. Shenstone: Pied Piper Publishing, 2004.

Charles, Nickie and Marion Kerr. *Women, Food and Families*. Manchester: Manchester University Press, 1988.

Cherlin, Andrew. 'Changing Family and Household: Contemporary Lessons from Historical Research'. *Annual Review of Sociology*, 9 (1983), 51–6.

Cohen, Paula Marantz. *The Daughter's Dilemma: Family Process and the Nineteenth-Century Domestic Novel*. Ann Arbor: The University of Michigan Press, 1993.

Counihan, Carole M. *The Anthropology of Food and Body: Gender, Meaning and Power*. London and New York: Routledge, 1999.

Counihan, Carole and Penny Van Esterik, eds. *Food and Culture: A Reader*. London: Routledge, 1997.

Crago, Hugo. 'Can Stories Heal?' *Understanding Children's Literature*. Ed. Peter Hunt. London: Routledge, 1999. 163–73.

Daniel, Carolyn. *Voracious Children: Who Eats Whom in Children's Literature*. New York and London: Routledge, 2006.

Davidoff, Leonore and Catherine Hall. *Family Fortunes: Men and Women of the English Middle Classes, 1780–1850*. Hutchinson: London, 1987.

Davidoff, Leonore, Megan Doolittle, Janet Fink, and Katherine Holden. *The Family Story: Blood, Contract and Intimacy, 1830–1960*. London and New York: Longman, 1999.

Davin, Anna. 'Loaves and Fishes: Food in Poor Households in Late Nineteenth-Century London'. *History Workshop Journal* 41 (1996): 167–92.

Davies, Margaret Llewelyn, ed. *Maternity: Letters from Working Women*. 1915. London: Virago, 1978.

Day, Ivan, ed. *Eat, Drink and be Merry: The British at Table 1600–2000*. London: Philip Wilson, 2000.

——. 'Feasting and Celebrating'. *Eat, Drink and be Merry: The British at Table 1600–2000*. Ed. Ivan Day. London: Philip Wilson, 2000. 15–33.

——. 'Teatime'. *Eat, Drink and be Merry: The British at Table 1600–2000*. Ed. Ivan Day. London: Philip Wilson, 2000. 107–30.

De Certeau, M., L. Giard and P. Mayol, eds. *The Practice of Everyday Life, Vol. 2, Living and Cooking*. Trans. T.J. Tomasik. Minneapolis: University of Minnesota Press, 1998.

Dewan, Pauline. *The House as Setting, Symbol, and Structural Motif in Children's Literature*. Lampeter: Edwin Mellen Press, 2004.

Donald, Moira. 'Tranquil Havens? Critiquing the Idea of Home as the Middle-Class Sanctuary'. *Domestic Space: Reading the Nineteenth-Century Interior*. Eds Inga Bryden and Janet Floyd. Manchester and New York: Manchester University Press, 1999. 103–20.

During, Simon. *Foucault and Literature: Towards a Genealogy of Writing*. London and New York: Routledge, 1992.

Eales, Derek. 'Enid Blyton, Judy Blume and Cultural Impossibilities'. *Children's Literature in Education*, 20:2 (1989): 81–9.

Elias, Norbert. *The Civilizing Process: The History of Manners*. 1939. Trans. Edmund Jephcott. Oxford: Basil Blackwell, 1994.

Estes, Angela M. and Kathleen Margaret Lant. 'Dismembering the Text: the Horror of Louisa May Alcott's *Little Women*'. *Children's Literature* 17 (1989): 98–123.

Ezard, John. 'Narnia Books Attacked as Racist and Sexist'. *The Guardian*. 3 June 2002. 8.

Flanders, Judith. *The Victorian House: Domestic Life from Childbirth to Deathbed*. London: HarperCollins, 2003.

Foley, Timothy P., Lionel Pilkington, Sean Ryder and Elizabeth Tilley, eds. *Gender and Colonialism*. Galway: Galway University Press, 1995.

Ford, Gina. *The New Contented Little Baby Book: The Secret to Calm and Confident Parenting*. London: Vermilion, 2002.

Foster, Shirley and Judy Simons. *What Katy Read: Feminist Re-Readings of 'Classic' Stories for Girls*. Basingstoke: Macmillan, 1995.

Foucault, Michel. *The Archaeology of Knowledge*. Trans. A.M. Sheridan Smith. London and New York: Routledge, 1972.

——. *Power/Knowledge: Selected Interviews and Other Writings 1972–1977 by Michel Foucault*. Trans. Colin Gordon Leo Marshall, John Mepham, and Kate Soper. Ed. Colin Gordon. Harlow: Longman, 1980.

——. *Discipline and Punish: The Birth of the Prison*. 1975. Trans. Alan Sheridan. Harmondsworth: Penguin, 1991.

Freud, Sigmund. *On Sexuality*. Trans. James Strachey. Ed. Angela Richards. London: Penguin, 1991.

Gavin, Adrienne E. and Christopher Routledge, eds. *Mystery in Children's Literature: From the Rational to the Supernatural*. Basingstoke and New York: Palgrave, 2001.

Giles, Judy and Tim Middleton, eds. *Writing Englishness 1900–1950: An Introductory Sourcebook on National Identity*. London and New York: Routledge, 1995.

Godek, Sarah. 'Happy Homes: Houses in Post-War Fantasy'. *Modern Children's Literature: An Introduction*. Ed. Kimberley Reynolds. Basingstoke: Palgrave Macmillan, 2005. 89–107.

Grylls, David. *Guardians and Angels: Parents and Children in Nineteenth-Century Literature*. London: Faber, 1978.

Gubrium, Jaber F. and James A. Holstein. *What is Family?* London: Mayfield Publishing Company, 1990.

Hall, Catherine. 'The Sweet Delights of Home'. *A History of Private Life IV: From the Fires of Revolution to the Great War*. Ed. Michelle Perrot. Cambridge and London: The Bellknap Press of Harvard University Press, 1990. 47–93.

Hardyment, Christina. *The Future of the Family*. London: Phoenix, 1998.

——. 'The Nuclear Family is Dead. Long Live the Nuclear Family'. *The Independent*, 31 October 1998. 7.

Heilman, Elizabeth E., ed. *Harry Potter's World: Multidisciplinary Critical Perspectives*. New York and London: RoutledgeFalmer, 2003.

Hettings, Donald R. and Gary D. Schmidt, eds. *British Children's Writers 1914–1960*. Detroit: A Bruccoli Clark Laymen Book, 1996.

Holdsworth, Sarah and Joan Crossely. *Innocence and Experience: Images of Children in British Art from 1600 to the Present*. Manchester: Manchester City Art Galleries, 1992.

Hollindale, Peter. *Signs of Childness in Children's Books*. Stroud: The Thimble Press, 1997.

Hollindale, Peter and Zena Sutherland. 'Internationalism, Fantasy and Realism'. Ed. Peter Hunt. *Children's Literature: An Illustrated History*. Oxford: Oxford University Press, 1995. 252–88.

Hunt, Peter. *Criticism, Theory and Children's Literature*. Oxford: Basil Blackwell, 1991.

——. 'The Decline and Decline of Children's Books'. *Children's Literature and Contemporary Theory*. Ed. Michael Stone. Wollongong: New Literatures Research Centre, 1991. 1–14.

——. '*Winnie the Pooh* and Domestic Fantasy'. *Stories and Society: Children's Literature in its Social Context*. Ed. Dennis Butts. Basingstoke: Macmillan, 1992. 112–24.

——. *Approaching Arthur Ransome*. London: Jonathan Cape, 1992.

——. *The Wind and the Willows: A Fragmented Arcadia*. New York: Twayne, 1994.

——, ed. *An Introduction to Children's Literature*. Oxford: Oxford University Press, 1994.

——. 'Editor's Preface'. *Children's Literature: An Illustrated History*. Ed. Peter Hunt. Oxford: Oxford University Press, 1995. ix–xiv.

——. 'Retreatism and Advance (1914–45)'. *An Illustrated History of Children's Literature*. Ed. Peter Hunt. Oxford: Oxford University Press, 1995. 192–224.

——. 'Enid Blyton'. *British Children's Writers 1914–1960*. Eds. Donald. R. Hettings and Gary D. Schmidt. Detroit: A Bruccoli Clark Laymen Book, 1996. 70.

——.'"Coldtonguehamcoldbeefpickledgherkins. . ." Fantastic Food in the Books of Kenneth Grahame, Jerome K. Jerome, H. E. Bates and Other Bakers of Fantasy England'. *Journal of the Fantastic in Arts*, 7.1 (1996): 5–22.

——. 'Anne Fine and the Revolution in Children's Books'. *The Lion and the Unicorn*, 23:1 (1999): 12–21.

——. *Children's Literature*. Oxford: Blackwell, 2001.

——, ed. *Children's Literature: An Anthology 1801–1902*. Oxford: Blackwell, 2001.

——. 'An Adults' Book, a Children's Book, a Palimpsest: *The Wind in the Willows* and *Three Men in a Boat*'. *The New Review of Children's Literature and Librarianship*, 8.1 (2002): 177–87.

Ingram, Les. 'A Family Story: A Context For Care'. *Give Them Wings: The Experience of Children's Literature*. Eds Maurice Saxby and Gordon Winch. London: Macmillan, 1987. 177–93.

Jenkins, Alice and Juliet John, eds. *Rereading Victorian Fiction*. Basingstoke: Macmillan, 2000.

Johnson, Matthew H. 'Ordering Houses, Creating Narratives'. *Architecture and Order: Approaches to Social Space*. Eds Michael Parker Pearson and Colin Richards. London: Routledge, 1994. 170–17.

Katz, Wendy R. 'Some Uses of Food in Children's Literature'. *Children's Literature in Education*, 11: 4 (1980): 192–9.

Keeling, Kara and Scott Pollard. 'Power, Food, and Eating in Maurice Sendak and Henrik Drescher: *Where the Wild Things Are*, *In the Night Kitchen*, and *The Boy Who Ate Around*'. *Children's Literature in Education*, 30:2 (1999), 127–43.

Kellaway, Kate. 'Dear Ms Comfort. . .' *The Observer*, 2 March 2003. Available at http://books. guardian.co.uk/Print/0,3858,4616237,00.html (accessed 24 June 2003).

Keyser, Elizabeth Lennox. '"The Most Beautiful Things in the World"? Families in *Little Women*'. *Stories and Society: Children's Literature in its Social Context*. Ed Dennis Butts. Basingstoke: Macmillan, 1992. 50–64.

Klein, Melanie. *Love, Guilt and Reparation: and Other Works 1921–1945*. London: Hogarth Press, 1981.

Kornfield, John and Laurie Prothro. 'Comedy, Conflict, and Community: Home and Family in Harry Potter'. *Harry Potter's World: Multidisciplinary Critical Perspectives*. Ed. Elizabeth E. Heilman. New York and London: RoutledgeFalmer, 2003. 187–202.

Kutzer, M. Daphne. 'A Wildness Inside: Domestic Space in the Work of Beatrix Potter' *The Lion and the Unicorn*, 21 (1997): 204–14.

Labbe, Jacqueline M. 'The Godhead Regendered in Victorian Children's Literature'. *Rereading Victorian Fiction*. Eds Alice Jenkins and Juliet John. Basingstoke: Macmillan, 2000. 96–114.

Langford, Paul. *Englishness Identified: Manners and Character 1650–1850*. Oxford: Oxford University Press, 2000.

Lawrence, R.J. *Housing, Dwellings and Homes: Design Theory, Research and Practice*. Chichester: John Wiley and Sons, 1987.

Lesnik-Oberstein, Karen, ed. *Children in Culture: Approaches to Childhood*. Basingstoke: Macmilllan, 1998.

McGee, Diane. *Writing the Meal: Dinner in the Fiction of Early Twentieth-Century Women Writers*. Toronto, Buffalo, London: University of Toronto Press, 2002.

McGillis, Roderick. *The Nimble Reader: Literary Theory and Children's Literature*. New York: Twayne Publishers, 1996.

Mark, Jan. 'Family Story'. *The Cambridge Guide to Children's Books in English*. Ed. Victor Watson. Cambridge: Cambridge University Press, 2001. 250–2.

Markus, Thomas A. and Deborah Cameron. *The Words Between the Spaces: Buildings and Language*. London and New York: Routledge, 2002.

Mason, Laura. 'By Bread Alone?' *Eat, Drink and be Merry: The British at Table 1600–2000*. Ed. Ivan Day. London: Philip Wilson, 2000. 69–78.

Meek, Margaret. 'The Englishness of English Children's Books'. *Children's Literature and National Identity*. Ed. Margaret Meek. Stoke on Trent: Trentham Books, 2001. 89–100.

Mohanram, Radhika. *Black Body: Women, Colonialism and Space*. Minneapolis, London: University of Minnesota Press, 1999.

Morgenstern, John. 'The Rise of Children's Literature Reconsidered'. *Children's Literature Quarterly* 26 (2001): 64–73.

Nelson, Claudia. *Boys will be Girls: The Feminine Ethic and British Children's Fiction 1857–1917*. New Brunswick and London: Rutgers University Press, 1991.

———. 'Introduction: Fictions about Fatherhood'. *Children's Literature Association Quarterly* 18:3 (1993): 98–100.

Nikolajeva, Maria. *From Mythic to Linear: Time in Children's Literature*. Lanham, MD and London: The Children's Literature Association and The Scarecrow Press, 2000.

———. 'Picturebook Characterisation: Word/Image Interaction'. *Art, Narrative and Childhood*. Eds Morag Styles and Eve Bearne. Stoke on Trent and Sterling: Trentham Books, 2003. 37–49.

Nikolajeva, Maria and Janina Orlov, 'A Room of One's Own: The Advantage and Dilemma of Finno-Swedish Children's Literature'. *Text, Culture and National Identity in Children's Literature International Seminar on Children's Literature: Pure and Applied*. Ed. Jean Webb. Helsinki: Nordinfo, 2000. 77–89.

Nodelman, Perry. 'Cultured Arrogance and Realism in Judy Blume's *Superfudge*'. *Children's Literature in Education* 19.4 (1989): 230–41.

———. 'The Other: Orientalism, Colonialism and Children's Literature'. *Children's Literature Association Quarterly* 17.1 (1992): 19–35.

———. *The Pleasures of Children's Literature*. 1992. New York: Longman Publishers USA, 1996.

Nodelman, Perry and Mavis Reimer. *The Pleasures of Children's Literature*. Boston: Allyn and Bacon, 2003.

O'Malley, Andrew. *The Making of the Modern Child: Children's Literature and Childhood in the Late Eighteenth-Century*. New York and London: Routledge, 2003.

Parille, Ken. '"Wake up and be a man": *Little Women*, Laurie, and the Ethic of Submission.' *Children's Literature* 29 (2001): 34–51.

Parsons, Linda T. '"Otherways" into the Garden: Re-Visioning the Feminine into *The Secret Garden*'. *Children's Literature in Education: An International Quarterly* 33.4 (2002): 247–68.

Paul, Lissa. *Reading Otherways*. South Woodchester: The Thimble Press, 1998.

Pearson, Michael Parker and Colin Richards, eds. *Architecture and Order: Approaches to Social Space*. London: Routledge, 1994.

———. 'Ordering the World: Perceptions of Architecture, Space and Time'. *Architecture and Order: Approaches to Social Space*. Eds Michael Parker Pearson and Colin Richards. London: Routledge, 1994. 1–38.

Pollock, Linda A. *Forgotten Children: Parent-Child Relations from 1500–1900*. Cambridge: Cambridge University Press, 1996.

Probyn, Elspeth. *Carnal Appetites: FoodSexIdentities*. London: Routledge, 2000.

Queen Victoria. *Letters of Queen Victoria 1837–1861*. Eds Arthur Christopher Benson and Viscount Esher. London: John Murray, 1907.

Ray, Sheila G. *Children's Fiction: A Handbook for Librarians*. Leicester: Brockhampton Press, 1974.

Raynaud, Claudine and Peter Vernon, eds. *Fonctions Du Cliché du Banal à La Violence*. Tours: l'Université de Tours, 1997.

Reynolds, Kimberley. *Children's Literature in the 1890s and 1990s*. Plymouth: Northcote House, 1994.

———. 'Sociology, Politics, the Family: Children and Families in Anglo-American Children's Fiction 1920–60'. *Modern Children's Literature: An Introduction*. Ed. Kimberley Reynolds. Basingstoke: Palgrave Macmillan, 2005. 23–41.

Roberts, David. 'The Paterfamilias of the Victorian Governing Classes'. *The Victorian Family: Structures and Stresses*. Ed. Anthony S. Wohl. London: Croom Helm, 1978. 59–66.

Rodger, John. *Family Life and Social Control: A Sociological Perspective*. Basingstoke: Macmillan Press, 1996.

Rose, Jacqueline. *The Case of Peter Pan or, The Impossibility of Children's Fiction*. Basingstoke: Palgrave Macmillan, 1984.

Ross, Ellen. *Love and Toil: Motherhood in Outcast London, 1870–1918*. Oxford: Oxford University Press, 1993.

Rothwell, Erika. '"You Catch It If You Try To Do Otherwise": The Limitiations of E. Nesbit's Cross-Written Vision of the Child'. *Children's Literature* 25 (1997): 60–70.

Rousseau, Jean-Jacques. *Émile, or On Education*. 1762. Trans. Allan Bloom. London: Penguin, 1991.

Rudd, David. *Enid Blyton and the Mystery of Children's Literature*. Basingstoke: Macmillan, 2000.

———. 'Digging up the Family Plot: Secrets, Mystery and the Blytonesque'. *Mystery in Children's Literature: From the Rational to the Supernatural*. Eds Adrienne E. Gavin and Christopher Routledge. Basingstoke and New York: Palgrave, 2001. 82–99.

———. 'The Froebellious Child in Catherine Sinclair's *Holiday House*'. *The Lion and the Unicorn* 28.1 (2004): 53–69.

Rustin, Margaret and Michael Rustin. *Narratives of Love and Loss: Studies in Modern Children's Fiction.* London and New York: Verso, 1987.

Sadker, Myra Pollack and David Miller Sadker. *Now Upon a Time: A Contemporary View of Children's Literature.* New York, Hagerstown, San Francisco and London: Harper and Row, 1977.

Saxby, Maurice and Gordon Winch, eds. *Give Them Wings: The Experience of Children's Literature.* London: Macmillan, 1987.

Simon, Brian. *Education and the Labour Movement 1870–1920.* London: Lawrence and Wishart, 1965.

Stephens, John. *Language and Ideology in Children's Fiction.* Harlow: Longman, 1992.

St. George, Andrew. *The Descent of Manners: Etiquette, Rules and The Victorians.* London: Chatto and Windus, 1993.

Stone, Lawrence. *The Family, Sex and Marriage in England 1500–1800.* London: Weidenfeld and Nicolson, 1977.

——. *Road to Divorce: England 1530–1987.* Oxford: Oxford University Press, 1990.

Stott, Jon C. and Christine Doyle Francis. '"Home" and "Not Home" in Children's Stories: Getting There – and Being Worth It'. *Children's Literature in Education* 24.3 (1993): 223–33.

Stretton, Hesba. 'Jessica's First Prayer'. 1867. *Masterworks of Children's Literature Volume 5.2 1837–1900. The Victorian Age.* Ed. Robert Lee Wolff. London and New York: Chelsea House, 1985. 399–425.

Strickland, Charles. *Victorian Domesticity: Families in the Life and Art of Louisa May Alcott.* Alabama: University of Alabama Press, 1985.

Styles, Morag, Eve Bearne and Victor Watson, eds. *Voices Off: Texts, Contexts and Readers.* London: Cassel, 1996.

Taine, Hippolyte. *Notes on England.* Trans. Edward Hyams. London: Caliban, 1995.

Tannahill, Reay. *Food in History.* London: Penguin, 1988.

Taylor, Stephen. 'The Suburban Neurosis' from the *Lancet* (1938) cited in *Writing Englishness 1900–1950: An Introductory Sourcebook on National Identity.* Eds Judy Giles and Tim Middleton. London and New York: Routledge, 1995.

Thacker, Deborah Cogan and Jean Webb. *Introducing Children's Literature: From Romanticism to Postmodernism.* London and New York: Routledge, 2002.

Thornton, Sara. 'The Vanity of Childhood: Constructing, Deconstructing and Destroying the Child in the Novel of the 1840s'. *Children in Culture: Approaches to Childhood.* Ed. Karen Lesnik-Oberstein. Basingstoke: Macmilllan, 1998. 122–50.

Tosh, John. 'Imperial Masculinity and the Flight from Domesticity in Britain 1880–1914'. *Gender and Colonialism.* Eds Timothy P. Foley, Lionel Pilkington, Sean Ryder and Elizabeth Tilley. Galway: Galway University Press, 1995. 72–85.

——. 'Authority and Nurture in Middle Class Fatherhood: The Case of Early and Mid-Victorian England'. *Gender and History* 8.1 (1996): 48–63.

——. *Masculinity and the Middle-Class Home in Victorian England.* New Haven and London: Yale University Press, 1999.

Townsend, John Rowe. 'Parents and Children: The Changing Relationship of the Generations as Reflected in Fiction for Children and Young People'. *Voices Off: Texts, Contexts and Readers.* Eds Morag Styles, Eve Bearne and Victor Watson. London: Cassel, 1996. 78–89.

——. *Written for Children: An Outline of English-Language Children's Literature Sixth American Edition.* London: The Scarecrow Press, 1996.

Tucker, Nicholas. 'Writing off Mum and Dad', *The Sunday Times,* 5 July 1998. Available at http://web.lexisnexis.com/professional/form?_index=pro_en.html&_lang=en&ut=3306576438 (accessed 14 October 2003).

Tucker, Nicholas and Nikki Gamble. *Family Fictions.* London: Continuum, 2001.

Visser, Margaret. *The Rituals of Dinner: The Origins, Evolution, Eccentricities, and Meanings of Table Manners.* New York and London: Penguin, 1992.

Waddey, Lucy. 'Home in Children's Fiction: Three Patterns'. *Children's Literature Association Quarterly* 8:1 (1983): 13–15.

Warner, Marina. *From the Beast to the Blonde: On Fairy Tales and their Tellers.* London: Vintage, 1994.

Watson, Victor. 'Poetry and Pirates – Swallows and Amazons at Sea'. *Signal* 66 (1991): 154–64.

——. *The Cambridge Guide to Children's Books in English.* Cambridge: Cambridge University Press, 2001.

West, Mark I. 'The Dorothys of Oz: A Heroine's Unmaking'. *Stories and Society: Children's Literature in its Social Context.* Ed. Dennis Butts. Basingstoke: Macmillan, 1992. 125–31.

Wohl, Anthony S. *The Victorian Family: Structure and Stresses.* London: Croom Helm, 1978.

Wolf, Virginia L. "From the Myth to the Wake of Home: Literary Houses". *Children's Literature* 18 (1990): 53–67.

Zipes, Jack. *Sticks and Stones: The Troublesome Success of Children's Literature from Slovenly Peter to Harry Potter.* London and New York: Routledge, 2001.

Index